MEDIATING DIVORCE

JOHN M. HAYNES
GRETCHEN L. HAYNES

MEDIATING DIVORCE

CASEBOOK OF STRATEGIES FOR SUCCESSFUL FAMILY NEGOTIATIONS

Jossey-Bass Publishers
San Francisco • London • 1989

MEDIATING DIVORCE
Casebook of Strategies for Successful Family Negotiations
by John M. Haynes and Gretchen L. Haynes

Copyright © 1989 by: Jossey-Bass Inc., Publishers
350 Sansome Street
San Francisco, California 94104
&
Jossey-Bass Limited
28 Banner Street
London EC1Y 8QE

Library of Congress Cataloging-in-Publication Data

Haynes, John M.
Mediating divorce : casebook of strategies for successful family negotiations / John M. Haynes, Gretchen L. Haynes. – 1st ed.
p. cm. – (The Jossey-Bass social and behavioral science series)
Bibliography: p.
Includes index.
ISBN 1-55542-181-4 (alk. paper)
1. Divorce mediation—United States. 2. Divorce mediation—United States—Case studies. I. Haynes, Gretchen L., date. II. Title. III. Series.
HQ834.H394 1989
306.89'0973—dc20 89-45600
CIP

Manufactured in the United States of America

The paper in this book meets the guidelines for permanence and durability of the Committee on Production Guidelines for Book Longevity of the Council on Library Resources.

JACKET DESIGN BY WILLI BAUM

FIRST EDITION

Code 8955

THE JOSSEY-BASS
SOCIAL AND BEHAVIORAL SCIENCE SERIES

TO SANDY KRAVITZ,
MENTOR AND
CREATOR OF OPPORTUNITIES

CONTENTS

PREFACE

Despite the growth in public and private mediation, there has not been concomitant growth in analytical works that demonstrate the actual process of divorce mediation, nor has a clear theory emerged to guide mediators (Sheppard, 1988). This book meets the first need and lays the foundation for meeting the second.

Divorce mediators in practice quickly discover the need to move away from the fundamental knowledge and skills taught in training programs and toward specific strategies that can be applied to a variety of situations. This book fills that gap, allowing the reader to look over the shoulder of John M. Haynes, the "country's most celebrated mediator" (Folberg and Taylor, 1984), and watch the process he has developed over fifteen years of mediation practice and training. The book's case studies and annotated transcripts allow the reader to experience an unfolding dialogue, anticipate the next step, and learn why each particular step was taken. The annotations explain the clients' and the mediator's behavior, underscoring the theoretical basis of the chosen strategies. Thus, the reader not only follows the transcript, with the mediator as guide, but also experiences firsthand the various theoretical underpinnings of sound mediation practice.

Case studies of divorce mediation do exist in the literature, but to date these are retrospective and are of necessity filtered through the memory of the one reporting the cases. By analyzing mediation dialogues, *Mediating Divorce* shows rather than tells what happens. It also explains why things happen in particular ways. We test some basic assumptions about practice, as part of the struggle to create a theory of divorce mediation, and we invite the reader to join in that struggle.

Audience

This book speaks to divorce mediators in court and in private practice, mediators in community dispute-resolution centers, attorneys, therapists, family court judges, and the academic world (for example, law schools that are adding alternative dispute-resolution courses to their curricula, business schools with negotiation classes, and departments of social psychology).

Practicing mediators will appreciate the range of strategies and skills we demonstrate. They will learn why a certain one is used in a particular situation and how they can apply the strategies to their own cases. Lawyers and judges will gain new insight into how mediation works and into the essential differences between mediation and litigation. The skills and strategies demonstrated and explained in this book will enhance their ability to handle custody negotiations within the adversarial system through an understanding of the motivations and behavior of opposing parents.

The academic reader will find the transcripts especially helpful for negotiation courses because they provide real dialogues that demonstrate negotiation theory in practice. The cases richly demonstrate negotiating behavior and can be used to explain and understand these theories. Students and faculty in postgraduate mediation training programs will also find the materials useful for understanding and teaching about clients' dynamics and mediators' responses.

We draw on a variety of disciplines to explain what the

mediator does in the privacy of the consulting room. Social psychology has made a major contribution to our understanding of mediation practice. We also draw from political science and sociology, particularly from the ideas found in the general theory of symbolic interaction. Of course, the basic systems theory of family therapy is evident in John M. Haynes's work, particularly as reflected in the influence of Luigi Boscolo and his colleagues. Part of the actual negotiation strategies comes from Haynes's experience as a labor-management negotiator.

Overview of the Chapters

The first two chapters provide an overview of mediation as Haynes practices it. Chapter One delineates the eight basic assumptions that inform Haynes's work. These have been tested in numerous training programs he has delivered to over five thousand professionals, and they underlie the work of many practicing mediators. Here, they are spelled out so that the reader can become more aware of his or her own assumptions and see how they affect moment-to-moment interaction in a session.

In Chapter Two we identify generic mediator strategies used in most situations. These strategies include ways the mediator gains control of the process of defining the problem, timing, and summarizing. We also discuss in this chapter the process of hypothesis development, testing, and utilization as a means of increasing mediator efficiency, as well as the use of various kinds of questions.

Chapter Three identifies the specific negotiating behavior of clients and how it affects the mediation process. Here, we analyze the various kinds of negotiating behavior commonly found in mediation, explain them, and then relate them to the specific cases in this book. Mediators' specific responses are also discussed in this chapter.

The next six chapters (Chapters Four through Nine) comprise five case studies with transcripts. They demonstrate the strategies and the assumptions from which the strategies flow, together with clients' negotiating behavior. Each chapter's introduction calls the reader's attention to the interplay between the mediator's assumptions and strategies, on the one hand, and clients' negotiating behavior, on the other. The transcribed dialogue of each session is annotated to explain the mediator's intention and to comment on the outcome of each interaction in these diverse contexts.

Chapter Four looks at a highly competitive professional couple who have been separated for one month. The wife objects to the children's visiting their father while his girl friend is present. The case shows how the marital dynamics are isolated from the negotiations for an interim agreement.

The unit formed by Chapters Five and Six covers two sessions with a recovering alcoholic family. This unit supports the concept of situational mediation by demonstrating a different way of handling a case from the approach described in Chapter Four. It is also a good example of the impact of arena selection on negotiation outcome.

In Chapter Seven, we meet Pat, who has been offered a promotion in another city, and Tom, who opposes her moving because it would interfere with his access to their daughter, Heather. Examining the influence that an underlying issue has on the negotiating behavior of the clients provides useful insights.

An interracial couple redefine their relationship with their three children in Chapter Eight. This session lays the groundwork for the actual negotiations that will take place in a later session and provides a good example of the interplay between therapy and mediation.

The last case study, in Chapter Nine, involves another competitive couple. They have been separated for three years and are locked in a battle over which school their daughter will attend. This case demonstrates how an obvious alternative and the mediator's good timing can help a couple reach an agreement.

Chapter Ten looks at ways for the reader to incorporate the ideas and skills found in this book into mediation practice. We also look at the way a theory of mediation will emerge, and we suggest some directions that future research (including our own) will take.

The five case studies in this book are related to family mediation, but the issues that emerge from the management of negotiation are universal; the applications can be made by all who are engaged in studying negotiating behavior and resolving conflict through negotiation. We offer our insights to date, in the hope that readers will add their own contributions to the emerging and distinctive theory of mediation.

Preparation of the Book

The cases in this book were all videotaped.* Upon reflection, it became clear to us that the tapes could be a powerful training tool, and so Gretchen Haynes, who is an educator, devised a series of training objectives and then analyzed the transcripts to support them. We expanded this approach as the book took shape. We have edited the transcripts slightly to remove repetitions, pauses, and the minor grammatical irregularities that appear in spontaneous conversations. We have been careful, however, not to alter content or the intent of any of the speakers.

With regard to language, we decided to use *I* when referring to the work that John M. Haynes does in the sessions and *she* or *he* when referring to mediators in general. We also chose to speak of the couple as plural and of the individuals as either *she* or *he*, as appropriate.

Acknowledgments

The original tapes of these sessions were produced by Kent Taylor, a mediator with the Edmonton (Alberta, Canada) Custody Mediation Project. Kent also obtained a grant from the Clinical Social Workers of Alberta that enabled us to have the tapes transcribed. Larry Fong, a mediator in private practice in Calgary (Alberta), provided keen insight into the systems aspects

*Copies of these videotapes, together with a training package, are available from Haynes Mediation Associates, 161 E. Main Street, Huntington, N.Y. 11743 [or call (516) 385-2490]. Canadian residents contact Kent Taylor, 407 Lé Marchand Mansion, 11523 100 Avenue, Edmonton, Alberta T5K 0J8.

of this work. Larry suggested a number of ways in which systems theory and theories of strategic family therapy could explain what was happening in the sessions. He is currently preparing advanced training materials for use with the videotapes.

Our colleague John Mince, a mediator in practice with Haynes Mediation Associates, provided invaluable and provocative questioning, which forced us to think more clearly. Many of his ideas appear in this book. Another colleague, Harvey Farberman, has been very helpful in clarifying for us the interface between mediation and symbolic interaction, as well as the potential for elucidating a theory of mediation through the incorporation of symbolic interaction into mediation.

We offer special thanks to Mary Duryea and Robert Benjamin, whose careful reading and thoughtful commentary on an earlier draft helped us organize the final work into a more coherent whole.

Finally, we owe a lifelong debt to Winnie Jolly, director of the Family Studies Center in Huntington, New York, for her willingness to engage in the intellectual struggle of understanding not only what we do and why we do it but also the consequences and implications of what we do for the broad family and social arenas.

Writing this book together has been enormous fun, as well as a great challenge to our marriage and to our respective intellects. Working so closely together has also tested our marriage relationship because our roles have changed. In the past, Gretchen acted as the editor of John's work, and John always had the final say on any issue; as joint authors, we have had to reach consensus on each issue on which we differed. Whenever the search for consensus became difficult, we referred to the text for a solution, and we almost always found a way to arrive at an agreement that was satisfactory to both of us. The result was a strengthening of our relationship and our marriage as we entered a new phase of our lives—as peers in our work, as well as in our thirty-one-year marriage.

Northport, New York
July 1989

John M. Haynes
Gretchen L. Haynes

THE AUTHORS

John M. Haynes is president of Haynes Mediation Associates, a private company that delivers mediation services to families, businesses, and institutions, as well as mediation training to individual professionals, institutions, and companies. He received his Ph.D. degree (1978) from the Union Graduate School in social policy. He was previously associate professor of social welfare at the State University of New York, Stony Brook.

Haynes has trained over five thousand judges, attorneys, and mental health professionals in the art of mediation in the United States, Canada, Europe, Australia, and New Zealand. He was the founding president of the Academy of Family Mediators and received the academy's first Outstanding Contribution to the Profession Award in 1988.

Haynes's first book, *Divorce Mediation: A Practical Guide for Therapists and Counselors* (1981), is widely used by practicing mediators. He has written numerous journal articles on mediation and the management of negotiations. He also serves on the editorial board of *Mediation Quarterly* and on the international advisory board of *Negotiations Journal.*

Haynes was a special assistant to the president of the International Union of Electrical, Radio, and Machine Workers from 1964 to 1972 and was also a speechwriter during this period. He has appeared on major television talk shows, including NBC's "Today Show" with Jane Pauley, the CBS "Morning News" with Diane Sawyer, and ABC's "Nightline" with Sam Donaldson (guest anchor).

He is a member and clerk of the Lloyd Harbor Monthly Meeting of the Religious Society of Friends (Quakers).

Gretchen L. Haynes received her B.A. degree (1955) from Oberlin College in economics and her M.S. degree with distinction (1974) from Hofstra University in education. She has specialized in adult education, both for literacy and at the college level.

As director of education at the Puerto Rican Organization to Motivate, Enlighten, and Serve Addicts (PROMESA), a Hispanic drug-rehabilitation center, and director of the York College Community Learning Center, she developed and delivered training for teachers and supervisors. She also created and developed the Professional Writing Center at the Health Sciences Center of the State University of New York, Stony Brook. Currently, as assistant professor of English and director of the Writing Center at Queensborough Community College, she trains the tutoring staff.

She has assisted John Haynes in mediation training in the United States, Canada, England, Scotland, and Ireland and finds possibilities for many applications of mediation principles to education, particularly in the training of teachers and tutors.

Haynes is the author of "Teaching for Empowerment: A Management Systems Approach," an article that appeared in *Adult Literacy and Basic Education* (Summer, 1981). She is also a Quaker.

She is a member of the American Association of Adult and Continuing Education, the National Council of Teachers of English, and the CUNY Writing Centers Association and has presented numerous workshops at national and regional conferences.

MEDIATING DIVORCE

1

KEY ASSUMPTIONS OF PRODUCTIVE MEDIATION PRACTICE

Mediation, unlike politics, is the art of the impossible. In family mediation, the mediator enters a dispute long after it has solidified and the parties have become entrenched in their respective positions. The parties choose mediation because they are unable to agree. Now, with the aid of the mediator, they will reach an agreement. That is a major transformation, and the art of mediation rests on some basic assumptions that make such a change possible. Those assumptions are keys to the theory and practice of mediation. While individual mediators use variations of the assumptions, productive mediation rests on a core of universal truths about people and conflict.

My experience in training over five thousand professionals in family mediation leads me to believe that assumptions vary widely. Other professionals often draw their assumptions from their professions of origin or from their ideas of the nature of conflict. Some of these assumptions are useful, as are the transferred skills, but mediation is more than an expansion of the practice of law or therapy. Of all the skills and knowledge used in mediation, approximately one-third is taught in most law schools, and about another third is taught in most graduate mental health programs, but another third is unique to both professions (Haynes, 1982). This book will concentrate on identifying that additional third, because working solely with a borrowed set of assumptions transforms mediation into the practice of therapy or law or changes mediation into a hybrid and less than successful practice. While awaiting the emergence of a discrete theory of mediation, each mediator must determine which assumptions he is using.

My experience in mediating over one thousand interpersonal family and business disputes has led me to question my own assumptions, clarify them, and test their usefulness in my practice. These assumptions inform the strategies I use. The outcome is productive mediation, resulting in a high number of agreements. (In the last five years of my practice, 94 percent of all my clients attending an initial session have continued in mediation; of those who continued past the first session, 96 percent reached agreements.) This book, through five case studies, will demonstrate the application of my basic assumptions and the strategies I use based on these assumptions. This chapter explains the assumptions and applies them to practice. I work under eight basic assumptions. First, I will describe each one. Then I will discuss them individually, in depth, as they apply to the cases.

1. *Conflict is healthy, but unresolved conflict is dangerous.* Conflict contains both opportunity and danger. It represents the momentum of change. While change is not necessarily good, change that comes about as a way of resolving conflict is productive.

2. *Conflict over issues is resolvable in mediation; conflict over behavior is resolvable in therapy.* Mediation is an arena in which to resolve disputes over current issues, not over past behavior.

3. *Almost everyone wants to settle.* Conflict is a normal and useful part of everyday life, but prolonged interpersonal conflict is costly and painful for all participants. Frequently, conflict is the result of the parties' not knowing how to resolve an issue, rather than of their not wanting to resolve it.

4. *Successful negotiations are more likely when the par-*

ties to a dispute require an ongoing relationship than when they see no future relationship. When a future relationship is part of the negotiations, the parties must compromise, and joint solutions are more likely as they seek to preserve the relationship while settling the conflict.

5. *The outcome is the responsibility of the parties.* Mediation is an arena in which to settle a dispute on the terms of the parties. The issues the parties bring to mediation are social-psychological problems. If they want to transform their social-psychological problems into legal ones, the parties will seek the assistance of attorneys. In coming to mediation, they have defined their problems as social-psychological issues that they want to resolve.

6. *The mediator is responsible for the process.* Each party needs assurance that the process is neutral and that the other will not benefit unfairly. The only way the parties can be assured of this is for the mediator to be in tight control of the process.

7. *There is "that of God" in everyone.* While it is difficult, when caught in the middle of the parties' maelstrom, to believe that either one has virtue, each person does carry an inner wisdom. The mediator seeks "that of God" in each person, to be able to reconnect him or her to that inner wisdom.

8. *The mediator's behavior is situational.* The conduct of the process is determined by the situation. The mediator tailors his strategies to the situation; they are not applied in "cookbook" fashion.

Assumption 1: Conflict Is Healthy

Conflict is frightening to most people. Most professionals either are scared that conflict between clients will get out of hand and so try to suppress it or believe that it is inherently wrong and so avoid it. Yet conflict is universal to all mediation cases. The question is not whether conflict exists but how it can be made productive.

Deutsch (1973, p. 10) says, "A conflict exists whenever incompatible activities occur." He also points out that conflict can occur even when the parties' goals are compatible. He offers the example of parents who "are in conflict about how to treat their son's mosquito bites." Their goals are concordant, while their behavior is conflictual.

Pruitt (1981, p. 6) provides another definition of conflict: "an episode in which one party tries to influence the other or an element of the common environment and the other resists. By this definition, negotiation can be described as a form of social conflict." This nonjudgmental definition is useful because it legitimates conflict. It also suggests that the mediator is therefore the manager of the negotiation (conflict). Conflict management and negotiation management become the same.

Conflict is a normal part of our lives. According to Swingle (1970, p. ix), "some interpersonal friction is an inevitable product of the negotiations process." Conflict provides us with opportunities to find new ways of relating to others and new ways of solving problems. The normal friction of daily life is eased when people negotiate to find acceptable ways of solving conflicts. The process of solving the conflict strengthens the relationship and makes it possible to deal with and overcome significant external negative events.

When an interpersonal conflict is left unresolved, some people become "married" to the conflict instead of overcoming it and moving forward. The dispute festers between the parties, shaping the rest of their relationship and defining how they deal with other interpersonal problems. Unresolved conflicts are most likely to take couples to therapy. Some unresolved conflicts are the products of different world views; for example, a husband believes that real men socialize "with the boys" and spends most of his free time in bars, but his wife grew up in a family in which her parents did things together. Conflict arising out of these two very different world views will be resolved only in therapy. Sometimes a problem is the product of a conflict within an individual; for example, a person feels strong guilt whenever he enjoys himself, and therefore he denies his family opportunities for fun. Such inner conflict also requires therapy.

Most of us have residual unresolved conflicts within ourselves and in our interpersonal relationships. Couples act to resolve those conflicts when a crisis develops—that is, when the conflict becomes unbearable or moves to a higher and unacceptable level. The couple who had been doing nothing together will be impelled to do something about their conflict if the wife has an affair (and the husband learns about it) or if the husband spends too much of the family's resources at the bar. If they act to resolve the conflict of their marriage, they can also develop a new relationship.

If they cannot resolve the crisis that took them to therapy, one or the other will create a new crisis by seeking a divorce. When the divorce crisis emerges, the social conflict becomes a legal one, and some practical issues require negotiation. Thus, the couple move from unresolved behavioral conflict to issue conflict (for example, how to divide their assets). They also change the arena for settling conflict from therapy to litigation or mediation.

Assumption 2: Mediation Versus Therapy

Raven and Kruglanski (1970, p. 70) point out, "Social conflict is defined as tension between two or more social entities, individuals, groups, or larger organizations, which arises from incompatibility of actual or desired responses." They enlarge this statement with citations from other literature to argue, "Conflict can also arise from incompatibility with respect to means or subgoals. It is not uncommon for persons in work-groups who are directed towards a common goal to have conflicts in coordinating their activities towards these goals."

Another source of conflict arises from the dynamics of the parties—that is, certain behavior differences cause conflicts that are unique to that relationship. In this book, I am using the term *behavior* to describe the dynamic relationship between the parties. Their dynamics govern the way they relate to each other. A spendthrift does not have a behavior problem until he marries a saver. The dynamics of the spendthrift-saver conflict are unique to that relationship. In mediation, we work on the outcome of the behavior conflict (allocation of the family's resources), but we do not try to change the dynamics of the couple's relationship.

In interpersonal dealings, behavior is often more conflictual than the issue under discussion. The mediator must know which type of conflict he is dealing with and whether all conflicts need resolution. An assumption of my practice is that I must help the parties resolve conflicts over issues and values but that their dynamic conflicts do not necessarily need to be resolved and often cannot be resolved in mediation.

Conflict, during interpersonal negotiations, can be classified as disputes over either issues or behavior (dynamics). Issues conflicts are normally disputes over resources, access to resources, or values. Behavior conflicts are usually the results of bad communication or different world views. They can also be the products of an inner conflict of one of the parties, which affects the dynamics of the relationship.

Divorce mediation requires resolution of specific issues (support, asset division, parenting). The behavioral problems that caused the divorce will not be resolved in mediation. The mediator disconnects the issues from the behavior by placing the behavioral dispute in the past and therefore regarding it as unresolvable. Failure to distinguish between issues and behavior can mislead the mediator into trying to resolve the behavioral conflicts instead of dealing with the divorce issues (and thus acting as a therapist).

Conflict over resources is more easily resolved than conflict over values. Ultimately, a resource can be divided mathematically. When resource allocation is the source of the conflict, the mediator can quantify the resource in dispute and find creative ways to divide it. There are 199 different ways to divide one dollar between two people. Conflict over access to resources can be resolved through opening up access to both parties. If a mother has not worked outside the home during the marriage, a support agreement that enables her to return to school and prepare for a career ensures each party's future economic independence and provides the mother with access to future resources.

A conflict over values is much more difficult to resolve. Value conflicts are firmly based in the behavior that has caused the dynamic conflict (such as behavior resulting from different world views). When two fundamentally opposed values are in conflict, resolution usually comes from capitulation of one party to the other. Clients often disguise resource differences as value differences. Thus, in a custody dispute, one parent may cloak a desire to gain more time with the child (a resource goal) with allegations that the other "does not take care of her properly and doesn't put her to bed on time" (a value difference). Value differences can be quantified, to shift them into pseudo-resource differences and enable agreement. In this case, the mediator could separate weekday bedtimes from weekend bedtimes. He could then have the couple negotiate over the different bedtimes according to whether the following day is a school day. The art of reframing issues to make them appear less intransigent is the key to good conflict management. In the case studies in this book, the reader will see examples of my reframing value conflicts into resource conflicts. I quantify them, allowing the parties to negotiate a division of the "resources" and resolve the conflict.

Behavioral conflicts are more diffuse than issue conflicts; since clients' behavior changes, so does the nature of the behavioral conflict. Issue conflicts are more likely to remain constant. The mediator focuses on three basic features of the relationship between the parties.

The first feature is communication. When the parties talk to each other, the receiver often hears a different message from the one the sender believes was sent. These differences lead to conflict, not about the issue, but about what each party mistakenly thinks the other has said about the issue. Management of negotiation in this situation becomes management of the communication patterns.

The second feature is different world views—the basic assumptions that people operate under, and that affect most of their behavior. For example, two people who grew up in families with limited resources may develop very different values. One may hold tenaciously to the pinch-penny values of his family, even though he can now afford a much higher standard of living. Another may become a spendthrift, determined to enjoy the benefits of success, unrestrained by her parents' money values. If these two marry, this difference of world views will control the way they interact and bring them into conflict on these issues.

The third feature is what Wilmot and Wilmot (1978) call

inner conflicts. I use the term *inner conflict* to describe specific dysfunctional behaviors (learned helplessness, unremitting discontent, overanxiousness to please, and so on)—attitudes that govern the behavior that affects resource allocation in the relationship.

Behavioral conflicts need resolution *when they impede the solution of issues conflicts,* but they do not need resolution in and of themselves. Nevertheless, the mediator must contain these conflicts, and he can use a range of strategies while continuing to work on the issues dispute (Haynes, 1988). For example, a mediator may take over the communication process between the parties, to be sure that each receiver hears the message as sent by the sender.

When working with clients whose behavior is a large part of the conflict, the mediator must determine how much behavior conflict to ignore while sticking with the issue conflict. For example, one couple, who were also business partners, sought to divorce while maintaining their business partnership. The mediator had two tasks: to mediate the divorce and to mediate a new partnership agreement. Since the couple agreed to an equal division of their assets and continued shared parenting of their teenaged sons, the problem was to identify and divide all the marital assets, define shared parenting, and divide support for the sons. The new partnership agreement recognized that they were no longer spouses, but the two partners belittled each other's contributions to the marriage and the business. This behavior led to continual bickering and sniping, which frequently blew up into full-scale arguments. While the concrete issues were fairly simple to mediate, the interpersonal dynamics were not easy. My task was to contain the interpersonal fights and prevent them from blocking specific agreement on the substantive issues on which the couple were already in essential agreement. On the one hand, I did not want to suppress the fights and leave each client smoldering over unanswered attacks. On the other, I had to decide when to call a halt to the fighting and refocus the couple's attention on the substantive issues.

The balance the mediator maintains between behavioral and issues conflicts is largely determined by the mediator's tolerance for conflict. The more fear the mediator has of overt conflict, the less tolerance he will have for bickering. The more he recognizes that the issues—not the behavioral conflicts—need resolving, the more tolerance he will have for bickering, and the keener will be his sense of when it is interfering with negotiation and should be cut off.

Many mediators confuse conflict over issues and interpersonal conflict over differences in world view. It is not the responsibility of the mediator to resolve the latter conflicts; reorganizing interpersonal dynamics is the work of a therapist, and negotiating agreement over issues is the work of a mediator. Thus, the mediator can allow a couple to fight and air their feelings for as long as fighting or bickering does not bog down the negotiation process. Too often, mediators clamp down on all conflict, leaving the couple frustrated by the lack of opportunity to air their style differences. The mediator attempts to identify the conflict so he and the parties understand it—and the parties know that the mediator understands it. He must then classify it to be clear when he is dealing with the issue versus the behavior. In this way, the mediator assures himself he is dealing with the real, or core, conflict and not the behavior.

Assumption 3: Almost Everyone Wants to Settle

In observing the parties' behavior while they are fighting, it is often difficult to believe that they really want to settle the conflict. Some therapists report seeing conflict-habituated couples who can relate with each other only through fighting. Nevertheless, many such reports describe behavior conflict, not resource conflicts. Conflict is frequently the result of the parties' not knowing how to resolve a problem, rather than not wanting to resolve it (Haynes, 1985).

Unresolved conflict extracts a heavy toll, which most people simply do not like to live with. Negotiation can take place when the parties to a dispute recognize that they have a dispute and agree on the need to resolve it. They then choose an arena in which to attempt to settle the dispute, and they actively engage in a process designed to settle it (Gulliver, 1979).

When the disputants follow these steps and choose mediation, they have already indicated a desire to settle in the mediation arena. They have come to settle, and so any failure to settle says as much about the process as it does about the parties. If the parties cannot settle the dispute in mediation, this may mean that one party no longer wants to settle in that arena. If both entered mediation to settle, however, and they are unable to find a settlement, their failure is more likely to be the result of the mediator's lack of creativity than of their own lack of desire.

The desire of most parties to settle means that the choice of the arena of dispute resolution does not have to be voluntary to be successful. Mediation, as practiced in the courts, is not a voluntary choice of the participants; the judge orders them to mediation. Pearson (1982) indicates that the success rate of court-mandated mediation is high, even though disputants are forced to use a particular arena in which to settle the dispute.

The action of one party, in filing for a court hearing, forces the other party to deal with the dispute. The court responds by forcing the party who did not want to settle the dispute, or who had a longer time frame for settlement, to deal with it in a time frame more acceptable to the initiating party. For example, the community resident whose dogs bark does not see that as a problem, nor does he recognize that his dogs' barking disturbs his neighbor's peace and quiet. The neighbor can plead, cajole, and threaten the dog owner, all to no avail. The moment the neighbor shifts to the legal arena, however, the state defines the dispute, and the dog owner, under penalty of law, must deal with the issues raised by his neighbor. The dog owner views the court as a hostile environment, since he is the defendant. The neighbor wants the issue resolved. The court, recognizing that the neighbors must have a continuing relationship, refers them to mediation. At that point, the dog owner seeks a solution in mediation, because it is a more attractive arena than the court. Even though the dog owner has been reluctant to recognize the dispute, he must now try to resolve it, either in mediation or in court. Confronted with these choices, his rational goal is to reach an agreement in mediation. A total loss (such as the loss of his dogs) looms as a possibility if the case goes to trial.

Fear of the alternative has important implications for mediation. The parties engage in active negotiation, making offers to settle in mediation rather than move on to litigation. If fear of litigation motivates a party to mediate, then he or she will be more willing to settle in mediation. On one end of the scale is the husband who has an unrealistic fear of litigation. He concedes everything rather than end mediation. The wife who knows of this fear may refuse to make any concessions. Our interest here, however, is in the normative range. Does fear of litigation motivate people to engage in active bargaining? Elsewhere, I suggest that the fear-of-the-alternative factor modifies a negotiator's behavior, making him or her more likely to settle for less (Haynes, 1984).

In the neighborhood example, the dog owner functions under his WATNA (worst alternative to a negotiated agreement), a variation of Fisher and Ury's (1981) BATNA (best alternative to a negotiated agreement). Fisher and Ury argue that in any negotiation, the parties must be aware of the best available alternative to the settlement proposed in the existing arena—that is, they must know whether they can reasonably expect to get a better deal elsewhere. In divorce mediation, the alternative arena is the courtroom.

When a couple are involved in a mediated negotiation, they will continually monitor it against what they may believe to be a better alternative: going before a judge. I have added the WATNA concept to that of BATNA because it recognizes that people are more easily motivated by their worst fears than by their best hopes. While they are in mediation, they must also be able to monitor their developing agreement against the worst alternative that would exist before a judge.

The existence of a WATNA is important in mediation and often governs the parties' desire to reach an agreement. Sometimes one parent threatens to go to court to settle a conflict in the win-lose framework, but the results, even apart from the added cost of the adversarial process, may not be in the best interests of either party. The mediator can only remind each party of the probable consequences and let them decide whether moving to the courtroom would be worse or better than settling in mediation.

With these ideas in mind, the mediator can proceed, in the knowledge that the parties want and therefore can achieve a settlement that meets everyone's needs. The only time mediation is likely to fail is when one or both of the parties has chosen mediation as an arena in which to continue the conflict rather than resolve it or when one party believes she will obtain a substantially better deal in a different arena (for example, before a judge). In all other cases, parties who want to settle a conflict can do it in mediation.

Assumption 4: Ongoing Relationships

Most participants use mediation because they anticipate a future relationship. Divorce, labor-management, community, environmental, school, family, and business mediation all involve situations in which the parties need to resolve a conflict in order to preserve their relationship. When a buyer refuses to pay the seller the balance of a contract, the seller sues, because this is the quickest and surest way of getting the payment; the seller sees no value in a future relationship. Large corporations, historically lawsuit-happy, are now turning to mediation as they realize that suing a competitor or a customer is not in the best interests of the company; rather, a mediated settlement preserves the future business relationship while settling the dispute, whereas the adversarial process can ruin the future relationship. Religious congregations, in doctrinal or policy disputes, are also bringing in mediators to help settle problems and maintain cohesion. Nonprofit organizations, lacking the disciplinary powers of private corporations, also increasingly use mediation to settle intrastaff conflicts.

Mediation is preferable in all these situations, because resolution of conflicts in a mutual, problem-solving way not only settles disputes but also opens the way to better relationships in the future. A winner-take-all dispute-settlement process is good for the winner on the immediate issue, but it is bad for each side's future relationship with the other. Thus, mediation is used in each party's best interests.

The future relationship of the parties is frequently the superordinate goal that provides the impetus for them to settle the dispute. The mediator reminds the parties of the superordinate goal and uses it to establish responsible parameters for the negotiations. The mediator mentions the future relationship when one party takes and maintains a position that, if successful, would damage that relationship. When this happens, the parties are able to measure a temporary tactic or single issue against the larger and more important goal. Thus, the solutions sought are more likely to be mutually beneficial outcomes.

In divorce mediation, most cases involve children. Spouses divorce each other, but they remain parents forever. This unity of role is a key element in the success of mediation. The case studies in this book all demonstrate the importance of the future relationship for the conduct of the parties, the outcome of the negotiations, and the way the mediator enhances the quality of the future relationship.

While the future relationship is key, most cases have one or more additional superordinate goals. For example, in support discussions, the parties share a goal of attaining economic independence from each other. The support discussions are conducted under a mutual understanding that the outcome should promote economic independence. When both parties are working to provide ways for each to be economically independent, they are less likely to want to gain every advantage at the expense of the other.

Assumption 5: The Outcome

Mediation is not arbitration. The parties have not come to hear the mediator tell them what to do. Mediation is an arena in which the parties to the dispute can settle it on their own terms. One outcome of the turbulent 1960s is our continuing demand for greater control over our individual lives. We are less obedient to rules, and such events as Watergate have left us chary of the state as an impartial and omniscient authority. The self-help movement of that period also taught us that we can do more for ourselves than previous generations thought possible to do for themselves. The desire for control is one of the reasons for the popularity of mediation. The freedom to enter into contracts, always the clear prerogative of the rich and powerful, is now available to all.

While divorce mediation is conducted within the shadow of the law (Mnookin and Kornhauser, 1979), it is not bound by legal precedents. Nevertheless, the outcome of mediation cannot be too far outside social norms, or else the parties will be unable to explain it to their friends and families. Mediation outcomes are based on the norms of the parties, their families, and their communities, rather than solely on legal precedents. People have the right to make their own decisions, and mediation guarantees this right.

If disputants go to court, a judge will hear the facts of the case (at least those facts developed for and presented at the trial) and determine the outcome. The outcome will be based on the application of case law to the specific facts of the case. The problem with this system is that fewer than 3 percent of divorce cases actually go to trial, and those 3 percent of cases are not the most typical. The 3 percent of people who must have their cases adjudicated are atypical, and the 97 percent who settle before going to trial are the typical people. If the parties choose the legal system to settle their dispute, the attorneys will refer to the case law involving the atypical 3 percent to determine the outcome. Thus, even though the case may be settled before trial, it will be settled on the basis of the atypical 3 percent. If the only tool one has is a hammer, all problems become nails, and if disputants go to an attorney, the problem is defined as a legal problem. Solutions will be sought within the legal system, a system designed to deal with extremes, not with the regular conflicts of modern life. The legal system treats all participants as adversaries.

The mediator sees the dispute as a social-psychological problem that can be resolved in any way acceptable to the parties. This way of looking at disputes restores the sense of community sensibility, whereby parties to a dispute settle it within the norms of the community. It also permits greater cultural diversity in outcomes, since each outcome reflects the cultural norms of the participants and their communities.

Not being responsible for the outcome is frightening to most professionals, who have a high sense of responsibility to the profession and to the public for the outcome of their work; this sense of responsibility is one of the hallmarks of a profession. Mediators must eschew that concept and take responsibility for the process, leaving the parties total responsibility for the outcome. Mediation returns authority for the outcome to the parties. If the shift were simply from a state representative (the judge) to a process representative (the mediator), then mediation might be an undesirable arena for the disputants. A mediator does not have the sanction of precedence and case law to work with. Therefore, if the mediator acted as a judge and assumed responsibility for the outcome, the parties would have the worst of two arenas rather than the best of both.

In court-ordered mediation, the mediator has power over the clients, which tends to obscure the important fact that the parties must own the outcome. It is their dispute, and the solution should also be theirs. If the disputants cannot find a solution and want one imposed on them, then the imposition should be left to the courts, with all the safeguards that go with the court system and the background and reference to precedence that a judge has.

The mediator is not responsible for the outcome of negotiations except to be able to assure himself and the two parties that the agreement measures up to a standard of fairness that all three agree on. In an earlier book (Haynes, 1981, pp. 127–128), I said that a successful divorce mediation can be said to have taken place when:

"1. there has been a full disclosure of all of the relevant facts,
2. the outcome is essentially equitable and designed to meet the joint needs of the parties and the individual needs of each participant,
3. there are no victims as a result of the agreement,
4. the channels of communication between the parties are open and direct,
5. the parties are empowered to make decisions and given

> the skills in mediation to continue the decision-making process in the future."

One thousand cases later, I remain convinced of the validity of these elegantly simple guidelines.

Assumption 6: The Mediator's Responsibility

Each party to a dispute seems to believe that the other always defines the conflict and controls the outcome. The dog owner feels that the neighbor has control, because she took the case to court and mediation. The neighbor feels that the dog owner has control, because nothing she has done so far has achieved any change.

This is even truer in family disputes, where each family member feels that the other gets to make the decisions. Since the rules of the game in mediation are less rigid than in the justice system, the parties need to know who is in charge. The mediator is in charge of the process. He sets the agenda and determines what facts and data are required, the order in which issues will be dealt with, and the general conduct of the negotiations. When everyone understands the mediator's role as controller of the process, each disputant will believe that the process is indeed neutral. More important, the process will not be seen as favoring the other.

This means that the mediator must always determine the agenda. At times, one party to the dispute arrives at a session agitated and demands immediate consideration of a new issue. For example, the wife may say that she has just discovered that the children do not want to go to their father's next weekend and that she agrees with them. Even though the mediator may agree that the issue is important and should be dealt with, he places it on the agenda for later in the session. Thus, he retains control of the session, while sending a clear message to the husband that the mediator is running the show and that the wife has not gained control of the process.

This all means that the mediator runs the process, freeing the couple to concentrate on the content. It also means that the mediator does not have to worry about who is running the show and can also concentrate on the creative aspects of alternative solutions. The division of responsibility—the mediator's for process, and the parties' for outcome—is efficient as well as fair.

By controlling the process, the mediator helps to balance the power differences between the parties. If, in their relationship, one party has wielded power over the other in various areas of decision making, he or she will also do so in mediation unless the mediator changes the dynamics by controlling the process. If one party has always defined the problem for the couple to resolve, then allowing that spouse to define the problem in mediation will perpetuate the power imbalance. (We have not dealt extensively with power balancing in this book, since it is covered in detail elsewhere; see Haynes, 1988.)

Assumption 7: Inner Wisdom

Everyone has problems. Some problems are greater than others. Most of the time, we resolve our problems without the aid of a third party, but sometimes life problems expand or become intractable, and a solution escapes us. This does not mean that there is no solution; it simply means that at that moment we do not have the resources to find it. Thus, people come to mediation to solve problems that get out of hand. The problems are not necessarily new or unique, but their size and scope cause them to elude unaided resolution.

The problems that bring people to mediation do not need treatment; they need solutions. Each person carries an innate common sense and wisdom. Sometimes circumstances and relationships disconnect us from that inner wisdom, and we behave irrationally in comparison to our normal problem-solving capacity. When that happens, a third party can help to reconnect us with our own wisdom.

Part of this wisdom is "that of God" that each of us carries. This concept is both practical and theological. I believe that nothing is so practical as good theology, but the reader may feel more comfortable in spelling *God* with two *o*'s, so as to say that there is good in everyone. Whichever way it is spelled, that quality is there and waiting to be used. When the mediator searches for goodness, he is not blinded by the temporary behavior clients exhibit during negotiations. He overlooks much negative behavior, preferring to concentrate on finding the goodness in people and working with that, for it is out of the essential goodness of the disputants that a reasonable solution will emerge.

This concept is closely allied with the assumption that the disputants control the outcome of the negotiations. If a mediator does not believe that the parties to the dispute have this innate ability to do what is right within the context of their situation, he will try to impose his own values on the parties. While the mediator's values may be personally useful, they are not the parties' values, and the solution will not be tailored to the parties but rather to the mediator.

Since the parties, and not the mediator, must live with the outcome, an imposed solution has less chance of surviving future changes than a self-created solution does. A self-created solution is more likely to contain not only an immediate solution to the problem at hand but also a formula for determining how to deal with the future and changes in circumstances.

If there is "that of God" in everyone, then the mediator must in all humility seek it. One cannot seek the God in each person if one approaches each situation with biases and preconceived notions about people. Thus, this assumption requires the mediator to enter each session with a clear mind, a tabula rasa. Once that goodness is found, solutions that belong to the couple begin to emerge.

Assumption 8: Situational Behavior

In each of Chapters Four through Nine, you will see the mediator behaving quite differently. There is no one set of "cookbook" strategies that work with every situation; rather, I determine each strategy according to the nature of the issues and the nature of the behavioral conflicts. In some cases, I am controlling, keeping the couple on task and permitting few distractions. At other times, I am more flexible, allowing the couple to deal with the issues in the way that makes them comfortable. With some couples, I am strategic and do not say what I am doing. With others, I carefully explain each of my interventions. Sometimes I am an educator, at other times I am a reality tester, and in a few cases I tell people what to do.

My choice of behavior is further determined by my hypothesis about what is happening. The hypothesis can be about the parties' goals, their behavior, or their strategies. The hypothesis determines how I proceed. As it develops in my mind, according to the information the parties provide me, I ask questions designed to test my hypothesis or enlarge it. When the hypothesis is confirmed, I act on it. When it is proved incorrect, I discard it. When it proves less than useful, as often happens, I modify it. (A detailed discussion of hypothesis development and testing is contained in Chapters Five and Nine.)

Each of the six chapters discusses the mediator's general behavior and explains why particular strategies fit specific situations. In general, this approach is based on the role of the mediator as manager of the process, not controller of the outcome. I eschew strategies that could put me in charge of the outcome, and I adopt interventions that empower the couple to make their own decisions.

These eight assumptions control and determine my role as a mediator. They help me stay out of the "soup" and they inform my strategy selection. They keep me from becoming a judge and they help me maintain humility when working with people who seek too much help. These assumptions alert me when I drift into doing therapy or when I try to practice law. They are the basis of my work.

The next chapter discusses some generic mediation skills and strategies that apply to all the cases in this book.

2

STRATEGIES OF FAMILY MEDIATORS

Each of the case transcripts in Chapters Four through Nine is fully annotated, to describe what is happening and the strategies the mediator uses in specific situations. The way these strategies are used is based on the assumptions discussed in Chapter One. Most of the strategies that are demonstrated in a specific case are generic to all cases, regardless of the assumptions of the individual mediator. In this chapter, we will discuss the generic strategies that appear in the different cases. When these strategies are used successfully, they ensure that the mediator maintains control of the process and that the parties control the outcome. In addition, the strategies culminate in what we term *negotiations* or *process management.*

Defining the Problem

When two people have an intractable dispute that appears unresolvable, the mediator enters to help them settle the dispute by negotiating a mutually acceptable agreement. When the mediator joins the disputing parties, she takes over the management of the negotiations. A significant part of the problem of the disputing parties is their inability to agree on the process of resolving the dispute, as well as on the content of the dispute. Indeed, the two parties often have quite different versions of the nature and history of the dispute.

Each party has a unilateral problem definition, and the parties are in dispute about process and content. Their inability to develop a joint and mutual definition of the problem is in itself a major part of the problem. This means that the mediator's role in the early stages of negotiation is to define the problem to be resolved. Thus, the mediator must attempt to define and control a mutual and neutral problem definition such that, when the problem is solved, its solution will benefit both parties. If the mediator accepts either spouse's definition, she will also "buy into" the solution benefiting that spouse. Therefore, the mediator attempts to create legitimate doubt about the certainty of each party's position, as a step toward taking control of the problem definition to ensure its neutrality. For example, the husband's opening position may be unrealistic—that is, he may want to stop his wife from moving out of town to take a new job, while at the same time he does not want to be the primary parent. That is an unattainable goal in many jurisdictions, and if it is pursued without modification, this position will distort the mediation as that person fights for an unattainable goal. The mediator must help him face reality and, by redefining the problem statement, help him develop a more attainable goal.

Similarly, as long as the mediator accepts and works with two disparate problem definitions, no agreement is possible. The mediator attempts to restate the problem by means of a mutually formulated definition, so that the problem is solvable by means of movement on both sides. The mediator moves to create a mutual problem definition by using strategies to match the clients' behavior. In this case, the mediator normalizes their experiences. When one spouse creates a unique and therefore not easily solved problem, the mediator restates the problem with reference to a normal (and therefore solvable) situation.

Timing

Few people in conflict are ready to move from their initial positions in the early stages of talks. Conflict participants rarely think about the other's position. They come to mediation with their own cases and proposals foremost in their minds. Since they have not heard the other's position in any detail, they have not thought of what movements they will have to make to accommodate the other's needs. Therefore, they often arrive at mediation with unrealistic expectations of what can be achieved. If a compromise solution is offered as soon as the mediator sees it, the couple will reject it, because each party thinks he or she can do better. Later in the process, after the parties share positions and arguments with each other and get a sense of how tough the other is on an issue, alternative ideas begin to look more attractive against the backdrop of what each now knows about the other's position.

A mediator cannot suggest alternatives too early in the session, since each party is wedded to his or her problem definition and solution. If an alternative idea is suggested too early, the parties will reject it. Each one still believes that he or she can convince the mediator of the correctness of his or her position, and therefore that his or her proposal will prevail.

As the process continues, each party's view of his or her own position is affected by the events of the process. Each one hears from the other and learns that the other has an equally tough and clear position and is working hard to convince the mediator that he or she is correct. As this information is absorbed, it becomes clear that winning is not going to be as easy as each one thought.

Each party has also had an opportunity to convince the mediator of the correctness and justness of his or her own position. As the parties realize that the mediator is not easily persuaded and will not become committed to a single vision of the situation, they realize that winning is not going to be possible in this context. At that point, alternatives appear attractive to the parties.

If the mediator—who has seen various alternatives from

the beginning—suggests an idea too early, the parties will reject it, and it will be difficult to resurrect it later. If the mediator uses a hypothesis to check the couple's respective positions, however, she gains a sense of the right time to raise the idea.

By the time the mediator is ready to propose the idea, the parties have a better grasp of the reality of their respective positions and the possibility of winning. At that time, they are usually ready to look at a third idea that does not involve one party's losing and the other's winning. There may be times when the alternative calls for both parties to lose. In that case, the alternative is often more acceptable to both parties than another solution that allows only one party to win.

Displaying the Data

The mediator uses a flip chart to illustrate what is happening and to provide a focus for the couple. The parties become attentive as the mediator diagrams their situation. They see their respective positions identified, clarified, and dignified on the chart, and the mediator gets and keeps the couple's attention focused on the content of the dispute. The mediator avoids an incorrect assumption of either party's position. If she puts up an item incorrectly, one or both spouses will say so.

The diagrams can also get messages across to the couple without the mediator's needing to state them overtly. In Chapter Five, for example, I used the chart to demonstrate that Ron had more to live on than Mary and their daughter did. This summary on the chart helped establish a standard of fairness for the couple. In Chapter Eight, I used the chart to show, in pictures, my view of the family relationships. The diagramming helped the couple see how they were excluding one child and were too involved with another. In each of these cases, I was able to demonstrate an idea through a diagram that displayed the data. The couple saw the idea clearly and grasped an idea that they might not have been able to accept verbally. I was also able to make statements to the couple through the diagrams. This made the couple less defensive about the statements and about the inherent criticism of their behavior contained in the statements.

Monologues

At times, the mediator changes from the pattern of asking questions and uses a monologue to take control of the session. The monologue calms the fighting or tense couple. It gives the mediator time to restore a productive atmosphere to the session. The monologue also imparts information, shares observations (through empathizing, normalizing, and mutualizing), and guides the couple while diverting them from the fight and refocusing them on the task.

The mediator uses the monologue purposefully, to take control of the situation and to accomplish one or more of these aims. If the mediator is to maintain control of the session, she must always end the monologue with a question that brings the couple back to the task. The mediator does not want the couple to replicate her behavior or to respond to an observation that deals with an emotion. Therefore, each monologue closes with a fact-oriented question that redirects the couple back to the task.

Using the Hypothesis

The mediator shifts behavior and strategies according to the hypothesis of what is happening. Once the basic picture is in focus, the mediator can ask questions that lead in a dozen different directions. How does the mediator choose which question to ask? The one the mediator chooses determines the route she will follow in dealing with the couple. The chosen route is based on hypotheses that are developed about the couple, their behavior, and the issues. For example, if the mediator confuses her role with that of a therapist, the questions will explore more of the behavior or the dynamics of the parties. What if she is clear about her role as mediator? How does she choose the next question and each subsequent question?

Some people believe that they ask questions according to the answer that the client gives to the previous question. This still does not tell us why a mediator chooses a particular question to follow up the answer to a previous question. The question is partly shaped by the response of the client to the previous question, but it is also shaped by the mediator's ideas about what is happening.

The mediator is guided by an understanding of what basic information is needed. As she gathers this information, a mental picture is formed of the parties, the issues, and their behavior. The overall composition of the picture is determined by the theory under which the mediator operates.

Let us look first at this idea from the perspectives of the attorney and the therapist, and then let us apply it to the mediator. When interviewing a client, the attorney gathers the same basic data that a mediator does, but the way the attorney uses this information is determined by her theory of the law: Is this a legal problem? In what way is it a legal problem? What is the legal theory that will guide me in helping the client solve the legal problem? The answers to these questions will determine the thrust of later questions, which will help the attorney answer the theoretical questions. The attorney then develops a hypothesis about what the client and the other party want out of the situation. She makes an assessment of their entitlements and proceeds with questioning on the basis of an assessment of those entitlements.

When a therapist conducts an interview, he also gathers the same basic information, but his line of questioning will be determined by a theory of behavior. A therapist who is psychodynamically oriented will ask questions whose answers will reveal more about the psychodynamics of the individuals and the couple. A systems therapist working under the theories of Minuchin (1974) will look at boundaries and the way the family violates them. Thus, the therapist's line of questioning is determined by his theory of human behavior.

The mediator should choose questions according to her understanding of mediation. There is no one clear and current theory of mediation, however. There are theories about conflict and negotiations, but there is still no coherent theory about the management of other people's negotiations. At this stage, mediation is still an art. The assumptions described in Chapter One and the generic ideas in this chapter are the tentative beginnings of a theory of mediation. They are the ideas that help me determine the next question to ask. They guide me in my work with couples and inform my practice.

For example, I have placed emphasis on separating issues from behavior. With this principle in mind, I do not ask questions that tell me about the behavior of the parties. I exclude that information from my process simply by not asking questions about it. Whatever I learn about the dynamics of the parties comes from them voluntarily and from their immediate behavior, not from purposeful questioning on my part. Each of my eight assumptions guides me in asking the early questions, after I have gathered the basic data.

Once the mediator begins to ask questions beyond the data-gathering stage, how does she decide which ones to ask? Assumptions are guides, in the broad sense, but the specific line of questioning is determined by various hypotheses developed about the couple's behavior, bargaining strategies, and issues. The mediator develops hypotheses from the information provided by the couple, as applied to the assumptions.

Once a hypothesis develops in the mediator's mind, she shapes questions that test the hypothesis and selects each new question according to the response to the hypothesis testing. As the mediator tests the working hypothesis, she revises it according to the new data, refines it, and then proposes it in order to gain confirmation. The mediator can also discard the hypothesis if it proves incorrect or not useful.

Selvini-Palazzoli and others (1980) point out that a working hypothesis does not have to be correct, but it must be useful. No hypothesis about a situation involving the parties' issues, behavior, and strategies can be totally correct; the point is whether a hypothesis is useful in shaping the next line of questioning. Does it help keep the mediator focused on the problem?

The mediator begins by collecting basic data. While collecting these data, she develops a hypothesis and then tests that hypothesis. When it appears to be correct, she confirms the hypothesis by asking the couple about it directly. When they indicate that the hypothesis is correct, it guides the mediator's behavior and line of questioning.

At another point, the mediator may develop a hypothesis

about other behavior. This hypothesis may be based on the mediator's theoretical approach to families and on her understanding of the literature. This hypothesis is also tested with the couple. It may be generally correct but still need some modification as more understanding about the couple is developed. This revised hypothesis is used to measure how the couple's behavior will affect the negotiations and to determine the amount of focus to place on it in the talks. There may be a third working hypothesis, which guides the mediator's behavior with respect to the bargaining strategies of both parties and their legitimate goals.

The hypothesis is important. It is not a question of whether one has a hypothesis but of what it is. Every professional operates under a hypothesis. After we gather the basic data, we make a series of assumptions that determine what question to ask next. In everyday life, we call the hypothesis a prejudice or a bias. We use it to monitor everything we see and hear. What makes a hypothesis out of a bias is the professional training of the practitioner and the theoretical framework she uses to reach it.

Clarity about which hypothesis one is using helps one to stay in the mediator's role. When one begins to work under a therapeutic hypothesis, one acts as a therapist. When one struggles with legal theory as it applies to the case, one acts as a lawyer. Awareness of one's hypothesis keeps one on track as a mediator.

Selvini-Palazzoli and others (1980) point out the danger of a hypothesis: The professional can become "married" to it. Sometimes when a mediator tests her hypothesis, it is shown to be less than useful. Instead of discarding or modifying it, the mediator holds on to it and then begins to argue with the clients because they do not accept the hypothesis about them. I know when I do this, because I lean forward and hear myself saying, "No, but you don't understand."

It can be safely stated that a mediator who gets into an argument with the clients is "married" to a hypothesis that is not useful to the professional *as a mediator.* When one purposefully develops and tests a hypothesis, one is less likely to become wedded to it. One is in danger of being "wedded" to a hypothesis when one has not tested it through questions. Mediators are more likely to be "wedded" to biases shaped by life experiences than to hypotheses shaped by theoretical understanding.

Good mediation requires mediators to be aware of assumptions (theories) and the ways in which they shape hypotheses. Good mediation also requires that we test our hypotheses through questioning and revise, modify, or discard them according to the information we receive from clients. When we believe a hypothesis has been confirmed, we can act on it in a way that is acceptable to the clients. (The transcripts and analyses in Chapters Four through Nine show how hypotheses were developed and revised at each stage of a session.)

Dealing with the Mediator's Bias

It is useful to review cases that are giving you problems and to ask yourself four questions. The answers to these questions will quickly reveal your bias.

1. Which partner did you like more? If you preferred one partner over the other, then your bias may have been at work, influencing the outcome of the negotiations. You can then ask yourself to what extent the chemistry of liking one more than the other clouded your neutrality.
2. Which partner was the better parent? If one parent is better, then the other is worse. At this point, you will understand that you have been judging their case, rather than mediating it. A judgment, once made, clouds the mediator's neutrality; it turns the process from mediation to assessment. Once we decide who is the better parent, we redefine the family's problem from a social to a legal one. The purpose of an assessment is to advise the judge on how to decide the case. It does not help the couple resolve their conflict. In doing an assessment, we disenfranchise the parents and substitute a punitive process in which one or both parents will be losers.
3. Which party was more fair? Fairness is subjective, even under ideal situations. Standards of fairness should be set

by the parents, not by the mediator, for it is their agreement, not the mediator's. If the mediator feels that one party is more fair, then the other must be less fair, and it is only a short step to being unfair. The mediator should use Fisher and Ury's (1981) advice and help the parties evaluate the outcome against some previously agreed-upon criterion. Doing that is quite different from evaluating one person against another.

4. Which partner did you agree with more? If you find yourself consistently agreeing with one client more than the other, this usually means that you and the preferred client have similar values or a similar way of looking at issues. Agreeing more with one party simply indicates a consonance of values and beliefs, not the correctness of one party's values versus the other's.

When I am stuck in mediation and unable to help the couple find solutions to their problems, asking myself one or more of these four questions often helps me become unstuck. I find that if I favor one party over the other, then the less favored party recognizes the bias and moves into a defensive position. He or she tries to restore the status quo that existed before I entered the picture, because the status quo was more favorable than the picture my biases present. As I grapple with my biases and develop ways of discarding them or overcoming them, I find that the reluctant spouse reengages in the process, trusting it to help him or her find a solution. The most common cause of stalemate is the mediator's bias.

The problem of the mediator's bias is universal. Awareness of one's bias is a major professional tool, and accepting supervision of one's practice is the most useful way of maintaining that awareness. Sharing cases and problems with another trained mediator often reveals previously missed biases. When relating the case and the particular problem to a supervisor or a peer, the mediator often reveals a bias, either directly or through the use of an inappropriate strategy. As the strategy is discussed and explained, the explanation often reveals the mediator's problem.

My own experience as a supervisor and as a consulting

mediator has been that the answers to problems caused by my own behavior are often revealed to me as I explain the problems. In outlining the situation to a supervisor, one's defenses are weaker, and issues that can be ignored when they run through the mind cannot be overlooked when one is relating problems to another professional.

Mediators in court practice are fortunate in having a structured supervision process. A supervisor or a peer mediator is usually available to discuss difficult cases. The private practitioner is in a more vulnerable position. Because the private practitioner does not have systematic supervision of her caseload, and disposition is a private matter, biases can go uncorrected. Thus, every practicing mediator must arrange for regular and structured supervision on a one-to-one basis or in a peer group. Failure to seek and use supervision is, I believe, unethical behavior.

Summarizing

The mediator continually summarizes the content of the session. I summarize each party's statements to achieve a variety of effects. The summary demonstrates that each partner has been heard and understood by the mediator. If people know they have been heard and understood, they can trust the process. The summary gives the parties an opportunity to correct any of the mediator's misunderstandings and help the mediator grasp the situation.

Earlier, we discussed the use of the hypothesis and how a working hypothesis is continually checked with the parties to determine its usefulness. The summary of statements and understandings helps the mediator check the hypothesis. It also provides the couple an opportunity to make the corrections that will keep the hypothesis useful.

The summary often helps one party understand what the opposing party says. Clients frequently do not listen to each other but use the time while one is speaking to prepare a counterattack or formulate a new one. When the mediator is talking, both parties usually listen. When the mediator summarizes, they sometimes hear what the other has said for the first time.

The summary can remove the kinds of dysfunctional commentary that cause people to tune out or to retaliate against what they hear as bickering. Thus, when a wife makes a reasonable proposal but surrounds it with dysfunctional commentary, her husband hears only the challenge contained in the bickering. Before he has an opportunity to respond, however, the mediator summarizes the content of the wife's statement, omitting the bickering. This gives the husband an opportunity to hear and respond to the negotiating content of his wife's statement. The mediator focuses on the content of the messages, rather than on their context. The content is often a good proposal; the context is usually the marital fight.

The summary also sends messages to the couple about what the mediator thinks is important. Thus, omission of context material is useful, since it indicates to the couple that the mediator is not interested in their past marital disputes. Concise content summaries communicate what the mediator thinks is important: resolution of the issues to be negotiated.

The danger of the summary is that the mediator may omit an important part of a content statement, leading one or both parties to believe that the omitted part of the proposal is unimportant. For instance, the wife may make a conditional proposal: "If you do A and B, I'll concede C." In her thinking, the value of A + B = C. She makes this offer in the middle of a series of negative comments about her husband's behavior. If the mediator summarizes her offer by omitting all the critical remarks and also states, "So if your husband does A, you will do C," the mediator not only omits the bickering but also changes the equation to A = C. While the husband may find this an acceptable proposal, the wife will feel short-changed. Therefore, the mediator must summarize *all* the content, screening out only the marital bickering.

Negotiations Management

The control and management of negotiations begins with the way the mediator opens the session—always with a question about the current events, what is happening this week (not last year). When the session begins in the present, it is a shorter shift to the future. The mediator establishes control of the agenda in the early part of the session as a way of communicating to the clients that she is in control of the process.

When the problem to be solved is appropriately defined by the mediator, and when the mutual and neutral definition is accepted by the parties, the process moves to the point where the mediator orchestrates the negotiations, determining their form, the order of the items to be negotiated, and the amount of concession to be sought from each party. When the mediator determines that reciprocal concessions are the preferred method of negotiating, it is important also to determine who should make the initial movement. (These issues are demonstrated in each of the cases.)

Communications

Question Forms. The mediator accomplishes most of her work through questions. The fewer statements the mediator makes, the fewer errors occur, and the more the parties remain involved in the process and in control of the outcome. Questions give the parties an opportunity to correct false assumptions, and they call for a response. When clients answer a question, they are more likely to own the answer than they would be to own the same idea presented to them by the mediator. Shifts in belief or position come about when one party sees the problem differently as a result of answering a question. Most statements can be turned into questions by voice inflection or by the addition of *Right?* at the end.

Closed questions usually call for a *yes*, a *no*, or another very specific answer: "How old are the children?" *Focused* questions narrow the focus of the response: "What are the current arrangements regarding the children?" This type of question directs attention to a subject. *Open* questions provide clients with latitude for answering: "How do you feel about that?" This question permits a wide range of possible answers. Closed, focused, and open questions constitute one general type of questioning.

The second question type has two forms. *Directed* questions are asked of a specific person. *Undirected* questions can be answered by either party. Who answers the undirected question, and how, provides useful information to the mediator. For example, an undirected question about the birthdays of the children provides the mediator with specific facts as well as indications of parenting roles. Different implications are drawn if the mother responds, the father responds, or they both respond. If the mediator wants to check an impression about the father's parenting involvement, she may direct the question to him, to learn the dates and the father's awareness of them. Thus, the choice of a directed or an undirected question depends on the nature of the information the mediator is seeking.

Undirected questions provide more space for the marital fight to emerge, since it is easy for a dispute to begin over each party's version of the facts. Directed questions leave the mediator in greater control of the process, because she can decide when and whether the other party is given an opportunity to comment or reply to a question that was directed to the other spouse. The mediator also controls whether the client may respond to the other spouse's response.

Open questions also provide space for the marital fight to emerge. They are intentionally vague and give the responder wide latitude, which can be used to launch into a marital fight.

Closed questions leave the mediator in greater control, since the answer given is specific and provides less opportunity for the clients to launch into a marital fight.

Undirected open questions are the most dangerous kind for the mediator to use in the early stages of the session, before he or she knows much about the couple's dynamics. Such questions are rarely used with highly conflicted couples, since the mediator tries to restrict opportunities for the marital fight to emerge.

Purpose of the Questions. The mediator also uses various other forms of questions and comments, which have two purposes: overt communication and covert communication. This discussion of question use is based on the pioneering work of Tomm (1988).

Some questions *create doubt* about the validity of each

party's original position, and this is the first step toward change. *Discriminating/clarifying* questions help the mediator understand each party's position and the facts. A statement by one party often requires further questioning, to ensure the mediator's understanding and to provide space for the other party to offer a contradiction. Hypothesis development and testing require many discriminating and clarifying questions.

An *embedded suggestion* in a question creates a reflexive response. The idea is not necessarily the central thrust of the question but is embedded in the answer the clients make to themselves.

Future-oriented questions help the couple think about their futures, rather than stay in the past. The problem lies in the past; the solution lies in the future. The mediator frequently asks a future-oriented question to get the parties to think about a future without the problem they are trying to resolve. *Past-to-future* questions take a past-focused statement of a client and move it into the future as a way of creating change.

Hypothesis questions help develop, test, or confirm the mediator's hypothesis. *Information-gathering* questions are used primarily at the beginning of the interview but are used each time the mediator changes or modifies the hypothesis and requires new information to test the modification or change.

Process-interruption questions are designed to break the current flow of the process and redirect it. Thus, as the parties begin to escalate a fight, the mediator asks a concrete question about another subject. By answering, the parties are forced to end the fight. *Refocusing* questions bring the parties back to their task when their response to a previous question produces a non sequitur.

General to Specific Questions. In addition to the specific form of a question, its scope also influences clients' behavior. A *generalized* or global question provokes a generalized response. No problem is ever solved through global responses. Indeed, clients frequently stay global in order to avoid dealing with specifics, which could demand justification. Movement usually results when the mediator uses questions that direct clients from the global to the *specific.* The most specific question is a question about quantity, which must be answered with a quantity; it is very difficult to stay in a global, diffuse position while answering such a specific question. I tend to move my questions through stages, from the global to the general to the specific to questions about quantity. Inevitably, by the time I ask the quantity question, some movement has taken place on the part of the respondent, or the respondent's position is clearer to me and to the other party.

Other Communications

In addition to asking the various forms of questions, the mediator communicates directly, to assist the forward movement of the process. *Empathizing* with the clients lets them know that the mediator understands their pain and feelings. There is no need to act on the feelings; the mediator simply notes them, empathizes with them, and moves on. (In Chapter Six, I empathize with Mary's automobile accident, but then I move on to the tasks at hand. She knows that I understand the problems caused by the accident and that I am aware of her feelings. She does not expect me to be able to do anything about the accident and is content not to have the issue dealt with in depth.)

Educating clients about options, realities, and alternatives is an important function. Here, the mediator paints a broader picture for the couple and provides additional tools for them to resolve their conflict.

Mutualizing statements are powerful creators of doubt. Each spouse has his or her own version of the problem, and the problem, as defined, usually seems to require change on the part of the other as its only solution. The mediator mutualizes the parties' concerns, needs, goals, and interests whenever possible, to create doubt about the individual positions and to focus the parties on their overlapping self-interests.

Normalizing the clients' experiences, pain, and problems helps put situations in a clearer perspective for them. Everyone coming to mediation thinks that his or her problem is unique, and idiosyncratic problem definitions are not easily resolved. As long as the parties believe that theirs is a unique situation, they have defined it as difficult or impossible to resolve. Normal problems are solvable and are solved by people every day. Thus, as the mediator normalizes the clients' position, she enhances their belief that they can solve their problem.

Observations can be shared with clients at key moments, when the mediator believes that a client is ready to listen to an observation (sometimes called an insight) and is receptive to the observation. Observations are generally used once the mediator has established a firm working relationship with both parties.

Reciprocal concessions, or tit-for-tat suggestions, are used when the mediator is orchestrating negotiations for parties who are having trouble making offers to each other.

Summaries, as previously discussed, are made frequently, to keep the mediator on track and test understanding of the situation.

Task assignments are part of each session, and the mediator makes them regularly, to keep the process moving during the time between sessions.

The strategies discussed in this chapter are demonstrated in the five case studies (Chapters Four through Nine). The transcripts illustrate the ideas explored in this chapter, and the annotations point out when and why the strategies are used at specific points. These strategies are often modified or determined by the negotiating behavior of the clients. In Chapter Three, we will examine clients' negotiating behavior more closely.

3

UNDERSTANDING THE NEGOTIATING BEHAVIORS OF CLIENTS

A mediation session is a dance in which the steps taken by one participant affect the steps taken by the others. In this chapter, we will focus on the negotiating behavior of clients when they act as negotiators. Most such behavior is universal—that is, it is not peculiar to one type of person; each kind of behavior is found in every type of client. Of course, not every client uses every type of negotiating behavior, but in a typical week a mediator will have to deal with most of the behavior described here. A splendid book on the broader subject of negotiating behavior is Pruitt's *Negotiating Behavior* (1981).

We use the term *negotiating behavior* to mean all the negotiation-related interaction of clients. Some behavior is calculated, and the person using it can predict its outcome. This is *strategic* behavior. Other behavior is accidental, and the person engaging in it has no idea of its probable consequences. This is *uncalculated* behavior. At first glance, it is hard for the mediator to distinguish strategic from uncalculated behavior, yet the outcome of the negotiations may depend on which kind predominates. When a mediator is unaware of clients' negotiating behavior, he will not distinguish between productive and destructive ploys. Moreover, a neophyte partner may not respond to ploys predictably and, using destructive ploys in turn, may escalate a conflict.

The mediator continually monitors the clients' behavior and responds to it—first, according to whether a move is productive and, second, according to whether it is strategic or uncalculating. If the ploy is nonstrategic, the mediator can intervene and educate the client about the consequences of his or her behavior.

When the behavior is positive, even though uncalculated, the mediator may join in and help it along if it seems to be productive. The mediator may also act to deflect or minimize a strategic move if it seems dysfunctional to the process. When negotiating behavior is not accidental and is harmful to the process, the mediator will block the move, to prevent the user from gaining an advantage from this strategy.

This chapter describes types of behavior in the order of their frequency of use. Thus, the kinds of behavior most frequently observed in the case studies are dealt with first. There is no special order of priority, since any combination of negotiating parties will produce a different combination of negotiating behavior. These kinds of behavior affect the role of the mediator as manager of the negotiations. Therefore, every kind of behavior has equal weight, taken over a range of cases, but specific kinds have more meaning in each individual case.

Conflict Expansion

Negotiators often expand a conflict by adding new demands or increasing the cost of a specific demand, as a means of putting pressure on the other party. The conflict may be expanded out of anger or in a coolly calculating way. Sometimes the conflict is expanded when agreement is close. Some parties are afraid of agreement and add new fuel to the fire in order not to reach closure. In this book, we will discuss numerous examples of conflict expansion.

If you think of the area of conflict as a football field, and if you define the field as fifty yards long—and if you see most of that yardage as the other's territory—then you will always settle on the other negotiator's terms. If you enlarge the field to make it one hundred yards long, and if half of that is your territory, then the settlement is more likely to fall closer to the middle. If you increase the size of the field by half, and if one hundred yards are your territory, then any settlement will probably benefit you.

Triangulation

Many clients try to win the mediator over to their side. They are eager to befriend the mediator, in the hope that he will befriend them. Triangulation is an attempt by a negotiator to put the mediator in a position of supporting him or her. Every triangulation strategy is dangerous to the mediator. If the mediator responds in the terms the negotiator is looking for, the mediator will alienate the other negotiator. If the mediator tries to check the triangulator, the mediator is likely to alienate him or her. I usually use a reframing strategy to change the meaning or direction of the triangulation attempt.

Equity Versus Equality

The parties to a dispute can claim an equal outcome (each is entitled to half of the resources) or they can claim an equitable outcome (one party has a claim to more or less than half of the resources). In divorce situations, this distinction is seen in the difference between community property laws, which provide for the assets and liabilities of the marriage to be divided equally, and equitable distribution laws, whereby the same assets and liabilities are distributed unequally, according to a series of criteria.

This distinction is also seen in the difference between joint custody, with equal sharing of parental care, and single custody, with one parent taking the bulk of parental responsibility, to the exclusion of the other. In support discussions, equality divides the family income equally between the parent with the children and the parent without the children, to avoid all but minimum disruption of the children's standard of living. In practice, equity has established a support level that either leaves the absent parent with significantly more income, so that he enjoys an increase in his standard of living while the mother and children suffer a decline in theirs, or leaves the absent parent with insufficient funds.

Obviously, these laws have a significant impact on the behavior of the parties in negotiations. The outcome of cases in community property states is almost always equal distribution of assets and liabilities. Statistics for states with equitable distribution laws (these statistics are hard to determine because of the closed nature of most divorce proceedings) indicate that the typical distribution is 70 percent to the man and 30 percent to the woman. States with a presumption of joint custody have more parents sharing more equally in parental care than do states where a father has to prove that he is capable of being a parent on an equal basis.

In most negotiations involving the family, the men look for economic equity and the women look for equity in dividing custody of the children. Thus, it is not surprising that in mediated negotiations the party who demands equity rather than equality is always the party who wants more than half. The one exception to this rule involves the children of dual-career families: At times, the father will argue for equity (meaning less responsibility for the children), while the mother argues for equality (so that her career will not be more disrupted than the father's).

In some cases, we see that a demand for equity provides one partner with an opportunity to punish the other for leaving. In others, a demand for equity provides a husband with justification for not paying his share of court-ordered support. In each instance, the mediator is careful not to accept either an equality or equity definition of the problem, since this would make the mediator an ally of the person holding that position. Rather, the mediator works to help both parties move toward a more equal position.

Clients in community property states behave differently from clients in equitable distribution states. If the presumption is for equality, then a person making an equity claim must justify it. If the premise is equity, then the debate is over why there should be equality or the extent of the inequality. Thus, there is always a higher possibility for conflict with equitable distribution, because the precise location of an agreement must be negotiated on a variable scale. Obviously, negotiations over equitable distribution take significantly longer and are more expensive than negotiations over equal distribution.

In a state with equitable distribution, the person arguing for equality is at a disadvantage. In community property states, the person arguing for equity (unequal distribution of assets) is at a disadvantage. There are important social policy implications in this concept because, given this idea, the presumption of equality is obviously the fairest set of rules under which to negotiate.

Directional Information

For any negotiation to proceed, one party must develop some idea of where the other party is willing to move. Professional negotiators have developed ways for questioning the other, often using conditional or hypothetical examples to see whether the other side will move in a particular direction. It is easy to see this when a labor representative asks a management negotiator, "If I could convince my members to move on issue A, could you move on position B, to give me something to go back to them with?" This question both gives and seeks directional information. The labor representative's choice of issue tells the management negotiator what is important to the union negotiator and the union members. The management negotiator's response will reveal whether the company shares the perception that A is less important than B to the company, while B is more important than A to the union.

Neophyte negotiators in family situations rarely engage in this kind of thoughtful information exchange. More often than not, directional information is disclosed in the middle of another statement that the mediator hears, but which is often missed by the other party. When the mediator hears what seems to be directional information, and when that information is not picked up by the other party, the mediator must develop ways of raising it. The mediator checks it, so that the other party can understand both that the offering party is willing to move and where that party is willing to move.

In a custody case, for example, a father may say, "I'm not going to take two little kids away from their mother." This tells the mediator that the father's demand for equality of time is not an opening gambit for moving toward equity and a larger share of time with the children; it suggests that he is not seeking to deny the mother her role. The mediator may not be sure that the mother understands this, since she may be defending herself against being displaced as a mother in the way she has been displaced as a wife. The father's statement contains important information that establishes the parameters of the negotiations that concern the children.

Threats

Threats are usually made out of weakness; promises are made out of strength (Haynes, 1988). Threats are most useful when they are believed by the other party. They are also used when the other party is a rescuer. A threat immediately sets the rescuer off into a rescuing mode.

Needs of Third Parties

When my children were growing up and they hit their heads on the table, they would come running to me, complaining that the table hit them. We learn early how to blame either a third party or an inanimate object for something we do not want to be responsible for. In negotiations, this behavior has a special function. If party A comes to the table with full authority, able to reach an agreement, and party B comes with constraints from her constituency, then the agreement will be reached in the area between A's open boundaries and B's closed boundaries. Party B will be unable to make certain concessions, even when those concessions would make sense and could lead to a mutually satisfying agreement. Thus, a labor representative might say, "I would love to be able to concede on this management rights issue in return for movement on the salaries, but we have an agreement with the other unions not to concede in the area of management rights." The management negotiator might say, "We can afford to meet your salary demands, but the manufacturers' association has an agreement not to go above one dollar an hour throughout the industry."

When Sadat and Begin were negotiating the Camp David accords with the help of President Carter, Begin began by saying that he had no authority to cede land that Israel had taken from Egypt. He told Sadat that he could not concede on the issue because the Israeli Knesset would not allow him to do so. Sadat, however, was not constrained by any such instructions.

In this book, we will see third parties used by a number of negotiators to avoid making necessary concessions that otherwise would have to be made. One person's strategy throughout was to say that he would like to pay his share of child support, but that third parties—a boarder who was not paying his rent, the government, the employment situation—prevented him from doing so. If the mediator allows a negotiator to hold on to these third-party excuses, then all the concessions will come from the party who does not use third-party constraints. Thus, the latter party would make too many concessions, and the result would be an unfair agreement. Therefore, the mediator ignores these excuses and focuses on the negotiator's responsibility.

The mediator generally ignores third-party claims. Since they are not given credence, the negotiator is not required to defend them, and the session does not become defined by these artificial constraints. Thus, in some cases, the mediator does not accept or deal with such claims. In other cases, however, the mediator is forced to deal with such claims because the third-party strategy is a large part of one negotiator's behavior. In such a case, the mediator deals with the claims by continually testing reality and pointing out that the person does indeed have options as well as responsibilities.

Concession Protection

When a negotiator makes a concession, he is always concerned that the movement not be used by the other party to gain still more movement—that is, if a negotiator raises an offer from one to two dollars, he does not want the movement to be ignored and the other negotiator to assume that two dollars is the new base from which to resume negotiating. Therefore, a negotiator often hedges a concession, making it possible to withdraw if the movement is not accepted in the way it was offered. Usually, this type of concession protection is helpful, and professional negotiators immediately know how to respond to movement, so as to ensure the mover that the concession is recognized and respected. Neophyte negotiators do not always understand how to protect a concession and sometimes protect it in the wrong way.

In one case, the husband made a concession and then quickly acted to protect it by demanding to know what the reciprocal move would be: "But if I'm going to give up something like that, then I want something in return." When a negotiator demands reciprocity for a concession, the mediator must take him or her seriously and help the other party see the need for a counter concession.

Negative protection occurs when one party carefully hedges a proposal with "maybe." This is a dangerous moment for the mediator. If the other party is allowed to respond to the content of the proposal without dealing with the condition, then the other party may accept the proposal, only to hear "maybe not." When the parties behave in a manner that is detrimental to the negotiations, the mediator intervenes to explain the negative aspects of their behavior. At times, the mediator is an educator who helps both sides improve their negotiating skills.

Negative Characterization of the Other's Position

A favorite strategy in negotiations is a variation on the "straw man" game. One party overstates the other's position and then attacks the exaggeration. This is often an element of the parties' past relationship and can be viewed as a marital fight. In negotiations, it is also a way of denigrating the other's position.

Each time one party makes a negative charge, it becomes more difficult to negotiate a reasonable settlement. If the charge is taken seriously, then the other party must spend all her time defending herself against the attacks, rather than advancing her own case. The only thing the mediator can do is to ignore such charges as often as possible and contain them when they do infect the negotiations.

Various Other Behaviors

Other strategies that we will see in the case studies include the following.

Making a Case in the Other's Alleged Interest. A mother can make the case for a child's being with his father by suggesting that they need to get closer. Her real position may be that the child is difficult to handle, and she would prefer that the father take on the burden.

Predicting the Mediator. When a person's work involves a lot of negotiations, he or she comes to the session with a higher level of expertise than most other clients do. He or she will be able to foresee the outcomes of the mediator's interventions and deflect them whenever he or she disagrees with the possible outcome. For example, when the mediator is trying to weave a shared-interest theme, the person sees what is coming and tries to redirect attention to his or her needs.

Dismissing a Concession as Worthless. Sometimes one party will snort at an offer by the other, exclaiming, "But that does not cost you anything," even though the concession does have value. Another party may reject an action by the other as not special and therefore not warranting reciprocity. A person may belittle a suggestion or an action by the other, sensing that any acknowledgment will have a cost in the subsequent negotiations. In essence, one takes the position that there is no reason to trade for a worthless concession.

Making Verbal Rather than Written Agreements. Often,

one party will offer to do something, provided that the offer is not in writing. Fathers often say that if they are able, in the future, they will do more for their children, but they refuse to put such a commitment into writing. Likewise, mothers often say that fathers can have more access to the children if things work out, but they are unwilling to say so in writing. I usually point out to the parties that the agreement only says what they must do; either is free to do more on any issue. The agreement is what they must do, if they cannot agree to do anything else. Therefore, only what they agree on having to do should be negotiated in mediation.

Toughening Demands to Protect a Position. This is a variation of conflict expansion. Rather than adding a new issue to the conflict, however, this behavior simply makes an existing position tougher. For instance, a mother may not want the children to spend the weekend with their father. If the mediator makes a suggestion on how to share the weekend and it is too early for her to concede, she may toughen her position, saying, "Well, I don't know if I even want them to sleep over at all." This issue must be dealt with through the suggestion that she may be asking too much.

The Mediator's Response

Each kind of negotiating behavior requires a measured response from the mediator. One cannot deal with every strategy every time. If one did, each session would take four hours. Many strategies are best dealt with through benign neglect. There is no need to respond to most strategies. By ignoring them, one does not get caught up in the couple's behavior. A good general rule is to ignore a strategy unless it appears to have a negative effect on the other person or on the process. One party may engage in many of these types of behavior, but most of them are only strategies. There is no need to deal directly with many of them, because the other spouse is often capable of holding his or her own. If the other spouse complains about the behavior, however, the mediator takes a more controlling role and deals with the first party's negotiating behavior.

Manifest and Underlying Conflicts

In addition to the distinctions discussed so far, Deutsch (1973) differentiates between manifest and underlying conflicts. Deutsch believes that an underlying conflict, unless treated separately, may prevent agreement on the manifest conflict.

Manifest conflicts are those presented to the mediator. Underlying conflicts are not presented, but they govern the bargaining behavior of the conflicted person. Obviously, such a conflict cannot be disconnected until it is understood. Many underlying conflicts are really part of dynamic behavioral conflicts (discussed in Chapter One). When an underlying conflict arises out of basic dynamic behavioral conflicts, it is probably best dealt with in therapy, but underlying conflicts over issues, and not behavior, may also exist in mediation.

A party to one conflict may not want to raise an underlying conflict because he believes it may weaken his position on the manifest conflict. He may be embarrassed by the underlying conflict, or he may fear that the other will gain an advantage if she is aware of the underlying conflict. Whatever the reason, the mediator is faced with the same problem: The underlying conflict will prevent agreement on the manifest conflict unless it is identified, legitimated, and dealt with.

An underlying conflict probably exists when, as agreements are reached on the manifest issues, new conflicts are raised to replace the resolved ones. Another indicator is seen when a rational solution that represents the apparent self-interest of the parties is rejected by one party, without that person substituting another rational solution.

When these situations arise in mediation, the mediator should look for an underlying conflict, remembering that a conflict is often a dilemma experienced by one person. It may not prove to be an actual conflict once it is uncovered. When all else fails, the mediator can say to the couple, "I don't understand something. It seems to me that we are resolving problems without getting a general agreement. I wonder if there is an important issue that we are not talking about. Have I missed something?" This gives the parties an opportunity to raise the underlying issue, and a total agreement may become possible.

Inductive and Deductive Thinking

One's style of thinking has a major impact on one's behavior in all areas of life. People generally think either deductively or inductively. Deductive thinkers are more concerned with getting the big picture first and then filling in the details. Inductive thinkers prefer to construct the big picture from the details. A deductive thinker doing a jigsaw puzzle will start with all the straight-edged pieces, construct the outline of the puzzle, and then begin to fill in the various sections. The inductive thinker is more likely to gather the blues and the browns into groups and try to put together whole pieces of the puzzle.

When one negotiator is a deductive and the other an inductive thinker, the mediator has a difficult time, because the parties are talking about the same idea from radically different perspectives. The problem is compounded, because the mediator's own thinking style will align him with one or the other. A mediator who is an inductive thinker will more readily understand what the inductive negotiator is saying and will more quickly translate those statements into ideas for discussion. While this goes on, the deductive thinker will be frustrated: Until she sees the big picture, she will be uncomfortable dealing with the details.

I tend to think deductively; thus, I am always looking for the shape of the big picture before filling it in with the details. Consequently, I need to note the style of each negotiator. When I recognize that inductive thinkers are focusing on details, I adjust my thinking to join them in thinking through the details, so that they can arrive at the big picture in their own way. Deductive-inductive differences can be a major problem if the mediator does not recognize when his style matches with one of the negotiators but opposes the other.

4

MICHAEL AND DEBBIE: NOT WHEN THE OTHER WOMAN'S THERE

Michael and Debbie married fifteen years ago and have two children, Sarah and Daniel. Debbie is a doctor sharing a general group practice with two other women. Michael is an orthodontist in solo practice. They have lived apart for one month. The attorneys referred them to mediation because of their high conflict over Michael's access to the children. They are highly competitive and seek to win over the mediator to their respective positions.

This is the first time the couple has met with the mediator and, given the recent separation, the mediator assumes that the behavioral conflicts will dominate the session. The task of the mediator is to help the couple settle the issue of the access, so that the negotiations between the attorneys for the economic settlement can proceed. Counsel recognized that the economic negotiations could not proceed while the couple remained locked in combat over the children. Failure to settle the issue of the children's access to their father could lead to escalating conflict on all the issues. Therefore, the attorneys chose to bifurcate the issues and refer the parenting part to mediation.

This chapter will illustrate four assumptions and the strategies that flow from them. These assumptions are identified in the annotations and discussed in detail following the transcript of the actual session. I deal with separating issue conflict from dynamic behavioral conflict. The mediator's control of the process, leaving control of the content with the couple, is evident throughout. The mediator identifies and legitimates conflict in the section on "Ventilation," demonstrating how stifling Michael's anger would only prolong the agony. The situational nature of the process is illustrated in the last section. The mediator's strategies found in this chapter include good examples of the uses and outcomes of closed and directed questions, problem definition, controlling the competitive couple, and orchestrating the negotiations.

An interesting management issue emerges in the middle of the session: Who should make the initial movement away from the opening position? The mediator's decision on this subject is annotated and then discussed in detail. The mediator's monologues are featured prominently in this case, and a discussion of the purposes of each and how it affects the process follows the transcript.

Several examples of the clients' negotiating behavior are highlighted, including indicating directional information, equity versus equality, conflict expansion, using threats and triangulation.

Transcript and Annotations

MEDIATOR: Well, the counsel has asked you to come today to see if we can work out an agreement that is appropriate for both of you and in the best interest of Sarah and Daniel. I wonder if you could tell me a little bit about what's happened in the last month.[1] Perhaps if I could ask you to begin, Debbie, in terms of where the children are living currently and what the arrangements are.[2] Then we can see what differences there are between you and see where we go from there.[3, 4]

DEBBIE: Well, the children are with me in the matrimonial home. Michael left a month ago, and I have let him see the children on several occasions.[5] But the children aren't happy seeing their father. They said they don't want to see him. They are very unhappy about the separation.[6] When they come home, they're very upset. They're crying, and it takes me hours to settle them down. I just don't know how they're going to cope with this.

MEDIATOR: So they're currently living in the family home with you, and they're spending time with their dad.[7] Michael, what is your feeling?[8]

MICHAEL: I think that Debra's little . . . ah . . . she doesn't have a grasp on the situation.[9] I've seen these kids now five times over the past month. They are happy to come with me; we have a good time. We've done a lot of things together; they enjoy being with me. They're obviously at strain, because when I was living at home they were seeing me daily, constantly; in fact, I think they were seeing me more than they were seeing their mother. Now they come and see me, they're apprehensive about their visits. I know that, but I don't think that Debra is helping them at all. I'm having a great difficulty in coming back and watching her dissemble. When I bring the kids back home, she starts crying.[10]

The body language (BL) of the couple throughout the session is very revealing. Michael is very closed when I talk to Debbie and tends to open when I talk to him. Debbie looks away from Michael and down on the floor when Michael says something she does not like. Michael frequently turns away from both Debbie and the mediator, gazing at the wall.

1. I open with this information question about the events of the last month to focus on what is current and avoid drifting into the past and the marriage.
2. A focused question, directed at Debbie, is designed to limit the amount of space for a marital fight to develop.
3. This future-oriented question sets the agenda for the session.
4. BL: Michael is not looking at Debbie or the mediator.

His eyes are cast down, and he appears to be in deep thought.

5. "I have let" indicates that Debbie believes she has the power in the situation. If Michael agrees with this assessment, it will provide me with some power-balancing information (Haynes, 1988).
6. Debbie's complaint about Michael is diffuse as she stakes out a tough opening position, defining the problem as the children's unhappiness, which can be solved only by a change in Michael's behavior, as defined by Debbie.
7. This summary of the factual content makes no comment on Debbie's charges, so as not to solidify her position. If the mediator comments or argues with her about this, she will have to defend her position and thereby become more "wedded" to it.
8. "Feeling" is an open question. It is the wrong question form, because it provides Michael with wide latitude in answering.
9. Michael responds to the open question about his feelings by launching a counterattack on Debbie.
10. Michael defines the problem as Debbie's. Therefore, he has the solution—Debbie should change. The task for the mediator is to define the problem in a mutual and neutral way.

MEDIATOR: How old are the children?[11]

MICHAEL: Five and seven.

MEDIATOR: Five and seven, and the older one is . . .

MICHAEL: Daniel.

MEDIATOR: Daniel is seven and Sarah is five. Okay. It's not unusual for them to have this tension and lots of crying when they go back and forward.[12] They have some apprehension because obviously they're still trying to sort out how to behave in relation to each of you when you're living apart, as distinct from when you were living together. So it's perfectly possible for them to have a good time when they're with you, Michael, but also express real concerns and reservations when they're with you, Debbie. That's not an unusual situation. Let me just see now what's the difference between you. What is it that brings you here?[13]

MICHAEL: Well, the difference basically is this: Debra says that I can be a part-time parent and I can see my kids every second weekend from Saturday morning until Sunday night, if I see them alone and so long as she maintains control over it.[14]

MEDIATOR: What does Michael want?[15]

MICHAEL: These are my children. I am one-half of their parents. I want the kids half-time. When we were living together, I was spending most of the time with the children.

MEDIATOR: So you'd like to have the children spend half of the time with you and half the time with Debbie.[16]

MICHAEL: I think so. I don't see that it's inappropriate in our circumstance.

DEBBIE: I don't think he wants to see the children. I think he's using that.[17]

MEDIATOR: What do you want, Debbie?[18] What do you want?[19]

DEBBIE: I want him to come back.[20] My children are devastated. I'm devastated. We had these plans. We had plans for us and for our children, and he's destroyed that. He's giving me no reason. All of a sudden, after fifteen years of marriage, he says that's it, I can't stand it any more. And I think you should know he's seeing someone else, and he's exposing our children to that other person.[21]

11. As Michael continues his complaints, I cut through the "feelings" with a factual (closed) question on a different subject. This process interruption breaks the cycle Michael is about to launch.
12. Michael's answer gives me back control. I use it to normalize the children's reaction and suggest mutuality, be-

cause the tension is an indicator of the children's loyalty to both of them. The monologue educates the couple about child development and creates doubt about the validity of their opening positions.

13. An open, focused question returns the couple to the task.
14. Michael answers by telling me what Debbie wants. In almost all cases, clients have difficulty saying what they want. It is easier for them to complain about the constraints they experience because of what they think the other wants.
15. This refocuses on Michael's needs, asking him to speak for himself by answering an open, future-oriented question.
16. The summary of Michael's proposal reframes it, to help Debbie hear that under his proposal she would also have them half of the time. She probably heard only that he wanted them. By pointing out the "half-full glass," the mediator facilitates the bargaining.
17. Debbie ignores the reframing of Michael's statement.
18. I ask her to state her needs. One advantage of asking the wife to speak for herself is that she cannot complain about the husband while stating her needs.
19. BL: During this reply, Michael is slouched down, with his eyes directed toward the wall.
20. Debbie sends two messages: She wants Michael back, and he is seeing another woman.
21. I develop a hypothesis that the fight is over the other woman and devise questions to test my hypothesis.

MEDIATOR: So you've come to see me in the hope that I can help you work something out so that you can get back together.[22]

DEBBIE: Well, I don't think he understands what he's doing.[23] I think he's depressed, I think he's going through middle-life crisis . . .[24]

MEDIATOR: Help me understand, Debbie, what it is you are looking for me to do.[25]

DEBBIE: I think he has to understand: If he's going to see the children, he has to live properly, he's . . . [26]

MEDIATOR: That's something you want Michael to do. What would you want me to do?[27, 28]

DEBBIE: Well, I'm here because I don't want to go through the court system. If we're going to separate, I don't want a lawyer or judge shoving an agreement down my throat.[29]

MEDIATOR: That's wise. So, what you want me to do is mediate, right?[30]

DEBBIE: Yes.

MEDIATOR: Okay. It's clear that I'm not going to work with you to get back together.[31] If you want to do that, there are other people competent at doing that. That's not my area of expertise. I don't work at putting people back together, and if that's what you want, then clearly I'm the wrong person to work with.

22. I clarify my role, disclaiming responsibility for putting the marriage back together.
23. Debbie ignores the mediator and continues her statement of distress.
24. This is an example of a client's ignoring the mediator's question in her anxiety to tell her story.
25. The "help me" question form takes the responsibility for the digression off the client while focusing her back on the task.
26. Debbie stakes a position for equity.
27. This interruption is designed to focus on Debbie's needs.
28. BL: Michael is paying close attention to Debbie at this point.
29. Debbie's response indicates that she has a grasp on the reality of the separation and the reason for choosing mediation.
30. I compliment Debbie and restate my role in question form, to elicit a specific yes/no response from her.

31. I continue to clarify my role, to be sure that both have heard me and to check that Michael is in the same position regarding the separation.

MICHAEL: John, I would like you to open her eyes.[32] I think that it's time now that she realized I'm not going to be at home anymore. I say *home,* it's where the children are living, it's our home, it's still in joint title.

MEDIATOR: Okay, Michael. Just as I said to Debbie, I'm not here to put it back together again—that is, I'm not here to do that for Debbie.[33] I'm not here to do that for you, to open Debbie's eyes. If you want to explain something, I'll create an environment in which you can be heard and you can get your point across.[34] What I'm going to do is to help you define the problem between the two of you, see what options there are to solve that problem, and help you solve that problem in a way that's mutually acceptable to you, and in the best interests of Sarah and Daniel.[35]

MICHAEL: Well, I respect Debbie. I like her, I love her. I don't want to live with her. I have two wonderful children that I love and cherish and want to have with me as much as I possibly can.[36, 37] My practice is such that I take my appointment book and staple pages together. I don't worry about it. Money isn't an issue. I gave Debra $1,500 when I left. She knows she can count on me for that sort of sum every month, until the matters are resolved.[38] But for me, it's the issue of being able to deal with my children on an honest basis. She . . . she . . . she lies.[39]

MEDIATOR: So you'd like to have them. Right? You'd like to have them half of the time.[40]

MICHAEL: Yes.

MEDIATOR: Debbie, if you were to structure the arrangement for the parenting, how would you structure it?[41]

DEBBIE: Well, I think the children need a home, I think they need one home.[42] They have to know, they're going to school this year, both of them. They have to sleep in one place every night. They have to have their books, they need someone consistent to help them with their homework.[43] If they're staying one week with me and one week with him, it's going to be too disruptive.[44]

MEDIATOR: Don't tell me what you don't want, tell me what you do want.

DEBBIE: Well, I don't want him to expose his friend to those children.[45]

MEDIATOR: Okay, let me try that one again. Don't tell me what you don't want, tell me what you do want.[46]

DEBBIE: I want my family back.

MEDIATOR: Okay. Now we recognize that's not my job.[47] Right? If you want to do work on that, you're going to have to work with someone else. If you want to work with me, it's to structure the parenting while you're apart. You may use that time apart to look at how to get back together again (some people do).[48] But I want you to focus on how I can be helpful, how to structure the parenting if you're living apart.[49]

32. Michael attempts to triangulate by asking the mediator to take his side and convince Debbie for him. If I had fallen into this trap, I would have become his ally and therefore Debbie's adversary.
33. While listening, I decide not to cut Michael off but to use the opportunity to balance my earlier statements to Debbie.
34. This also explains the process to both of them.
35. Gives hope about outcomes and brings the discussion back to the children.
36. BL: Debbie swings her body away from Michael, and her eyes are downcast.
37. This is an indicator of his desire to share in the parenting and represents important information about his perception of his role.
38. This indicates that he is responsible regarding their financial needs.

39. Michael begins to wander again.
40. The restatement of the content of Michael's proposal is designed to redirect the discussion and to emphasize "half."
41. Debbie is asked for the first position statement. Given their respective positions and the fact that hers is unlikely to be supported by the community norms, I decide to look for the first concession from her.
42. Debbie ignores the question. This a common response when a client is not ready to move.
43. BL: Michael slowly tunes out, turning away to face the wall.
44. This redirects Debbie to focus on her needs and to a future orientation.
45. Debbie again raises the issue of the other woman, supporting my hypothesis.
46. My gentle use of humor elicits a smile from Debbie and achieves my goal without putting her down.
47. I join Debbie with the use of "we" and then use "you" in assigning the task of resolving the problem.
48. The mediator provides a face-saver for Debbie.
49. This returns the focus back to the issue of parenting while they are living apart.

(The next series of questions begins with a global query and moves in stages to a specific one, which promotes movement by Debbie.)

DEBBIE: If we have to live apart, then I think that we have to be consistent in what we want for our children.[50]

MEDIATOR: Okay. And that is?[51]

DEBBIE: And that is where they're going to live? How much of the time? What kind of a home they're going to live in?[52] Michael lives in a condominium where there are no children, there's no playground, there's only adults around.

MEDIATOR: Okay. If you were going to organize the week, how would you organize the week?[53]

DEBBIE: My week?[54]

MEDIATOR: With the children.

DEBBIE: Well, I work during the day, I have a nanny, sometimes I'm on call, sometimes I have meetings.[55] I basically keep in touch with the nanny and advise her when I'm going to be home, and as much as I can, I try to follow those plans.

MEDIATOR: How much time, if the children were living with you, would they spend with their dad?[56]

DEBBIE: That's the hard one.

MEDIATOR: Uh huh.

DEBBIE: Because I think they have to have a home. And I don't think he's prepared to give them the proper kind of a home.[57]

MEDIATOR: Okay, let's see if we can separate that out for a moment,[58] assuming that we weren't looking at the kind of home. That's an issue; we will deal with it, because obviously it is an issue between you.[59] But assuming that was not an issue, then how much time would you want Sarah and Daniel to spend with their daddy?[60]

DEBBIE: The children love their father, and I don't want to keep the children away from their father.[61] I suppose if we could sort out other problems, I would want him to see them as much as he could and as much as their schedules would allow.

MICHAEL: When are you going to tell them the facts of life, when they're sixteen?[62] I mean, do you know what she told them when I left? She told them that daddy was setting up a new principal residence for tax purposes.[63] She's misrepresenting me to the children on a constant basis. She tells them that I'm sick, she tells them that I'm depressed, she tells them that poor daddy doesn't know what he's doing, poor daddy has a mean friend, poor daddy has a friend who's taking your daddy away from you.

MEDIATOR: It's very, very hard when you get divorced, isn't it?[64] To deal with all of the emotions and all of the things that happen.

MICHAEL: She's a professional woman, she's a smart lady. I have a lot of respect for her. She moves in those circles, she knows what she's doing.[65]

50. Debbie gives a global response.
51. A general question.
52. Debbie responds with more questions, which are intended to define the issue in her favor. Her response does not concede equal time but seeks to establish an equitable arrangement.
53. A specific, future-oriented question.
54. BL: Debbie leans forward, closer, to understand the mediator.
55. She provides some specifics, but not any "quantity" answers.
56. A "quantity" question, which is most likely to obtain a specific response. I also use "dad" to move Debbie to her parent role.
57. Debbie slips back into defining her "equity" position. This is also her problem definition.
58. I partialize to gain a focus.
59. I promise to cover the second part.
60. Asking Debbie to assume this frees her to look at her children and their father's needs. I keep my language in the parent mode through the use of "daddy."
61. Debbie makes the first significant move, acknowledging Michael's father role. She picks up my language, moving from the spousal to the parenting designation. This movement is the product of the "global" through "quantity" steps that forced change, even though the actual questions were not answered along the way.
62. BL: Michael is not listening, he is thinking of his next attack.
63. I let Michael ventilate, to compensate for the time I spent with Debbie and to engage him in the process.

64. I empathize with Michael and complete the joining to reengage him in the process.
65. Michael acknowledges Debbie as an adult but not as a parent.

MEDIATOR: Let me see now, Michael, you would like the kids to live with you—what, for a week, or two weeks, and then change around?[66] Is that . . .

MICHAEL: I think a week or two weeks, and you know, I've talked to Ruth, the nanny. She's prepared to move.[67] She knows what the situation is. She's got more sense than the kids' mother, I think.

MEDIATOR: So, the children: In your plan of thinking, the nanny would go with the children.[68]

MICHAEL: Sure.

MEDIATOR: Okay. Debbie, you said to me a moment ago that if we could work out some other things, then perhaps you could see your way clear to working out some structure of sharing the parenting in some form or other.[69] What things do you need to work out?[70]

DEBBIE: Well, I don't think the home, if you can call the high-rise condo Michael is living in that, is appropriate for the children.

MICHAEL: I live in a 3,200-square-foot apartment, which has a beautiful view, which has appropriate facilities, which is not an adult-only apartment.

DEBBIE: There are no other children.

MICHAEL: There are other children.

MEDIATOR: So concern number one is the geography, the apartment.[71] Okay, are there any other concerns?

DEBBIE: I don't think he really wants to see his children.[72] I think it's just guilt. He bought a Porsche the other day. It doesn't even have a backseat to transport these children.

MEDIATOR: Let Michael tell me about that part. Tell me about what it is you think needs to get resolved.[73]

66. A "quantity" question designed to begin the negotiation orchestration. I will try to establish some reciprocal concessions based on numbers.
67. Michael provides new information, indicating where his thinking is. This is known as an information exchange. Then he attacks Debbie as a parent. He is not listening to Debbie and has not heard any of her movement.
68. After stating the content of Michael's message, the mediator learns more data regarding the nanny, which suggests an option for the couple.
69. This restatement of Debbie's earlier hints of movement is for Michael to hear. This also clarifies the conflict, Debbie's goals, and possible areas of movement. It facilitates the reciprocal concession process.
70. BL: Each turns away from the other.
71. A summary and identification of one issue. The follow-up question is designed to test my hypothesis.
72. Debbie responds with a global attack. This is her defense against needing to move from "equity." Instead, she seeks movement from Michael's "equality" position.
73. This deflects the marital issue but does not forbid it, thus allowing Michael to respond if it is a "toxic" issue for him.

DEBBIE: Well, I don't see how the children can live one week here and one week there.[74, 75] I think it will be too hard on them. I don't think he's being fair to them. He's the one that broke up this family.

MEDIATOR: So it's the apartment, and your concern as to whether or not the children can handle going back and forth on a regular basis?[76]

DEBBIE: Yes.

MEDIATOR: Are there any other problems?[77]

DEBBIE: I don't think they should be exposed to this woman.[78]

MEDIATOR: Okay. The woman is . . . you're living with somebody, Michael?[79, 80]

MICHAEL: No. I have a relationship with a woman I've come to know over the last period of time. And I can honestly say this isn't the reason that I left. The reason I left is that I was sitting at home and dying, waiting to die in that house.[81] I was sitting at home looking after the kids. Mommy's got a meeting. Mommy's at the hospital. Mommy's not coming home tonight. I don't know where Mommy is.[82] That's what it seemed to me when I was spending my time at home. I'm not going to take two little kids away from their mother.[83] They need their mother, they love their mother. But all of a sudden when I decide that I'm drowning and if I don't get out, that's it. All of a sudden I'm a bad bastard, and I'm getting this number from Debbie that I shouldn't see the children, that I upset the children. I'm beginning to wonder if . . . if . . . the children are so upset when they go back to see their mother, maybe they should stay with me most of the time.[84]

MEDIATOR: I'm hearing Debbie say that.[85] I'm also hearing her say they love their father and they need their father and she would like to work it out so they could be with their father.[86] That's what I'm hearing on two levels and I'm . . . tell me a little bit about . . .

MICHAEL: She's telling me where I have to live, she's telling me who I'm going to see, she's going to tell me what car I'm going to drive. I might as well move back home and die.[87]

MEDIATOR: So those are the issues of conflict between you, and those are the issues that we need to focus on and get some agreement on, right?[88]

74. This is Debbie's secondary concern.
75. BL: Michael's eyes glaze over at this point.
76. A summary defining the two issues. The second issue is defined as Debbie's concern.

77. I continue probing until all the issues are on the table. This helps to test my hypothesis and determine the order of priority of the issues.
78. Debbie restates an untenable demand, confirming my hypothesis.
79. BL: Michael's fingers are twitching nervously.
80. Checking the data with Michael.
81. Michael moves from talking to me to talking directly to Debbie. Therefore, I permit him to continue . . .
82. . . . even though he begins to ventilate.
83. Michael sends a message to Debbie that she will not be displaced. The mediator considers this directional information, indicating where Michael might move in the negotiations.
84. Michael ends by making a threat and moving to a tougher bargaining position.
85. I ignore the threat and positively reframe Debbie's comment, emphasizing similarities and thus validating Michael. This also helps Michael to hear Debbie's view that he is an okay father.
86. "Two levels" tells Michael I am following him, and I understand that Michael feels he is damned if he does and damned if he doesn't.
87. Michael restates the marital fight.
88. This normalizes the conflict and points out that it is an issue for negotiation.

DEBBIE: Because the children don't understand. What am I to tell them?[89]

MEDIATOR: About what?

DEBBIE: This other woman. They see Daddy kissing this other woman. He lets the woman stay the night. I don't think that's right.

MEDIATOR: How do you know that?[90]

DEBBIE: The children have told me.

MEDIATOR: Why did they tell you that?

DEBBIE: They don't understand. They ask me who she is. Their father hasn't explained it to them.

MICHAEL: What do you mean?[91]

MEDIATOR: So you talk to them about the other woman?[92]

DEBBIE: They volunteered it. They don't understand.

MEDIATOR: That surely is not fair to you, to place that burden on you, is it?[93]

DEBBIE: Well, they're young, they don't . . .

MEDIATOR: It might be more useful, when they raise those questions, that you tell them to talk to Daddy and let Daddy sort it out.[94, 95]

DEBBIE: Well, he's obviously not explaining anything to them. He's too guilty about it.

MEDIATOR: Okay, so one concern is that—let me see if I'm right—you'd like them to be clear about the relationship?[96]

DEBBIE: Whatever it is.

MEDIATOR: What would you like?[97]

DEBBIE: Well, I don't think he should be sleeping—letting his girl friend sleep overnight, and sleeping in the same bedroom with her with our children in the house. I don't think it's right.[98]

MEDIATOR: Let me ask you now: A question, if . . . excuse me just one second, but what is her name?[99]

MICHAEL: Jocelyn.

MEDIATOR: Jocelyn.[100] If Jocelyn is not sleeping over, right? would you feel comfortable working out some arrangement for the children?[101]

DEBBIE: I'd feel more comfortable. I'd be more comfortable, as well, if he had a house not too far from ours, so the children could go back and forth on their bicycles. Something more appropriate.[102]

MEDIATOR: So that, in the long run, you'd like to have some close proximity, so that the children can move back and forth quite easily.[103]

MICHAEL: Tell him about what sort of car I should drive. Tell him about where I should take the kids on the afternoons. Tell him about . . . [104]

MEDIATOR: And you, Michael, would like to make your own decisions about these issues?[105]

MICHAEL: Of course. This is ridiculous.

MEDIATOR: Okay. All right.

MICHAEL: I mean, she's menu-driven. I end up with a situation at home where it's the same thing.[106] There's notes on the refrigerator: "Michael, when you come home from work, please do the following six things. I'll be home when I can."[107] Finally, I get out of the arrangement, and it's the same thing, but she sends telegrams.

MEDIATOR: Okay, so you've been living apart for a month. You're both angry with each other, and that's perfectly legitimate, and that's perfectly normal, too.[108]

MICHAEL: If she was angry with me it would be different. I think she just thinks I'm sick.

MEDIATOR: I think I sense a lot of anger on both sides.[109]

89. Debbie again raises her underlying issue of the other woman.
90. This series of questions is designed to enhance Debbie's ability to distinguish between parental and spousal behaviors and recognize her role as a link in the interactional pattern. This is a paradoxical approach, since to keep her current posture, she must also accept the responsibility for putting and keeping the children in the middle of the marriage fight.
91. I keep Michael out of this dialogue.
92. I am using a particularly gentle tone of voice as I pursue this line of questions.

93. The focus is back on Debbie's self-interest.
94. The mediator again provides Debbie with a face-saving way out.
95. This suggests that, even though the children are young, they can understand and deal with the issue with their father. They will have to learn to deal with each parent separately in the future.
96. This summary and reframing is a reality test and helps the wife look at parental and spousal issues and begin to separate the two roles.
97. Focus on positive needs.
98. A first clear, specific demand from Debbie; but is Debbie's agenda to prevent Michael from sleeping with Jocelyn, or just from sleeping with her when the children are with him? If it is the latter, this movement opens the possibility of a reciprocal concession, which raises the need for further hypothesis testing.
99. I decide it is time to bring the other woman into the open.
100. Now I can use her name.
101. Following this slight digression, the mediator continues to orchestrate the negotiations, testing what movement might come from Debbie on the basis of her response at 98.
102. Debbie expands the issues.
103. A reframing into a future goal, not a current impediment, in an effort to decouple the issue from Jocelyn.
104. Debbie's position triggers off the marriage issues for Michael, who responds in kind.
105. This interjection refocuses on the issues and limits Michael's need to respond to Debbie.
106. BL: Debbie has her body turned away from Michael, and her eyes are looking at the floor.
107. Michael returns to the marriage fight and, in the process, indicates important information regarding his parenting role. This is information that I accept, if it is not denied by Debbie.
108. I normalize and . . .
109. . . . mutualize.

MICHAEL: Can't you tell her that what I'm doing is normal, it happens all the time, can't you explain to her where I'm coming from?[110]

DEBBIE: Not in my book.

MEDIATOR: What I was wondering, Michael, much more, was not so much where you're coming from but where you want to go.[111] As I understand it, where you want to go is to have an arrangement where you have good access to your children, share in raising them.[112] That is difficult for both of you to deal with right now, because you've only been living apart for one month.[113] You're both hurting a lot.[114] There's a lot of pain, and it's quite difficult for you at times to separate out the anger you have at each other as spouses and the differences you have with each other as parents. Although, interestingly enough, so far today I've not heard any serious differences emerge between you as father and mother.[115, 116] There's a lot as wife and husband—there you're way apart—but not as mother and father. I'm wondering now where you want to go.[117] Let's see where we fit this one in. My sense is, Debbie, if I'm correct—and check me out, and Michael, you check me out, too—is that if you knew that you didn't have to deal with Jocelyn with the kids when the kids came back, you would be more comfortable at working out some organized way of sharing the parenting.[118] Am I right or am I wrong?

DEBBIE: He's a good father. He's been a good father. I can't deny that. The children love him and he loves the children.[119]

MEDIATOR: And you're a good mother.[120]

DEBBIE: Yes.

(A long silence as the mediator waits for Michael to respond.)

MICHAEL: What am I supposed to do?[121]

DEBBIE: But is it fair to the children to have them one week here, one week there?[122]

MICHAEL: The kids don't mind.

DEBBIE: How would you like to move back and forth?

MICHAEL: The kids are happy. They take their videotapes with them, and they're happy wherever they're staying.

MEDIATOR: Let's make this point.[123] The kids are going back and forth between you in some way, even if it's only one weekend a month. They're still going to move back and forth. The issue is not whether they are going to move back and forth, the question is the schedule around which they're going to move back and forth with you both.[124] So they'll spend time with their dad, and they'll spend time with their mom, and they'll move back and forth.[125] The issue is the amount of time they'll spend at each of the two houses. Right?[126]

good

110. Michael again seeks help, which, if given, would triangulate me onto his side. My tone of voice and summary act as a tranquilizer.
111. BL: I lean forward to capture Michael's close attention as I move him from the past to the future.
112. This reframes the issue to Michael's self-interest and focuses him.
113. I provide no support to Michael in his attempts to triangulate me.
114. Normalize and empathize . . .
115. . . . and provide positive reinforcement while emphasizing their similarities.
116. BL: I use my hands to emphasize what I am saying. When talking about the differences as spouses, I hold my hands up and then bring them down, creating a clear division. When talking about the children, I move my hands through a circle, indicating commonality.
117. This separates their parental and spousal roles, educating them about the differences.
118. Return to the process of reciprocal concessions, alerting Michael to listen to this piece and Debbie's reply.
119. Debbie validates Michael's parenting. He does not respond. She has now made it clear that the issue is not whether but when the children will be with their father.

120. I feel that Debbie's comments about Michael's parenting should be validated and wait for Michael to do this.
121. I maintain a long silence, waiting for Michael, but he is unable to do it.
122. Debbie responds with some guilt of her own.
123. BL: As I begin this monologue, Michael focuses on what I am saying. As the monologue continues, he drifts away.
124. Reality testing, and using my hypothesis that the issue is really the other woman. My language shift from "whether" to "how" is designed to move the couple into their parental roles as I take charge of the problem definition.
125. A suggestion of the maximum joint benefits, without taking a position on equity or equality.
126. The monologue ends with a specific, future-oriented question.

MICHAEL: If these children are visiting me, then what's going to happen to me is that I'm going to become a stranger to them. I'm going to be an interrupter.[127] I'm going to end up with these kids saying to me, "Daddy, if I come and see you, I can't go to Mehitabel's birthday party." It's not . . .

MEDIATOR: Let me ask you a question, Michael.

MICHAEL: . . . it's not fair anymore.

MEDIATOR: Right, and it shouldn't be unfair to either of you, and it certainly should not be unfair to Sarah and Daniel.[128] What do you think you two could organize so that the kids don't get caught in the middle of your arguments as spouses?[129] How can you take them out of moving messages between the two of you, for example, around Jocelyn?[130]

MICHAEL: Well, I think the first step would be for Debra not to refer to her as the beast who has taken your daddy away, or words to that effect.[131]

MEDIATOR: And if Debbie stopped bad-mouthing you and Jocelyn and your relationship with Jocelyn, what could you then do?[132]

MICHAEL: Well, I think that what I would like to do, is I would like to be able to establish a routine with my children.[133] I know that Debra doesn't want the kids around her, and that it's confusing. I've done my best. I mean, it happened on one occasion that Jocelyn and I got tied up with the kids. I'm not putting her in as a new mama, she's not living with me, she hasn't moved in. We don't have plans to move in.

MEDIATOR: In the short run, Michael, could you agree that Jocelyn would not sleep over when the kids are with you?[134]

MICHAEL: What's the short run?[135]

MEDIATOR: Two months.[136] It's two months down the pike, and you will have a little more experience about what it's like to live apart. Give the children a sort of chance to settle in.[137]

MICHAEL: I can live with that. I don't know if Jocelyn can, but I can live with that.[138]

MEDIATOR: Okay, so if you could live with that—Debbie, could you live with that?[139]

MICHAEL: But if I'm going to give up something like that, then I want something in return.[140]

MEDIATOR: Which is?[141]

MICHAEL: I want the kids half-time.[142]

MEDIATOR: All right. Debbie, if, for the next two months, when the children were with Michael, Jocelyn did not sleep over.[143, 144] She might well be around, because obviously she is playing a role in Michael's life, and we all have to come to recognize that at some point.[145] But if she's not sleeping over, at that point, how would you then feel about sharing the parenting?[146]

DEBBIE: Well, I don't know if I even want her around. I think when he sees the children, he can not have her there. He can see her when he doesn't have the children.[147]

MEDIATOR: That may be asking a little too much, mightn't it?[148]

DEBBIE: Well, I don't think it is for two months. He's just trying to set something up here so that the minute it gets working, bang, she's in their life, and they've got a new mother.[149]

127. Michael raises a legitimate underlying fear, which must be acknowledged. He also raises the "needs" rule, which provides that "rewards should be proportional to the strength of needs" (Pruitt, 1981, p. 62). His need is to be recognized as an equal parent. His voice has a whine.
128. The response to Michael's "little boy" complaint discusses the fairness issue and the importance of an outcome that is fair to all parties. A reframing from not fair (– +) to not unfair (+ +) mutualizes it.
129. BL: I again use my hands to visually separate the couple as spouses as I continue to move them from the past to the future.
130. Returns their attention to the task, with a future-oriented focused question at the end of the monologue.
131. Michael indicates the first concession he wants from Debbie. He is now engaging in the reciprocal concession process.
132. A restatement of his position to Debbie in adult language to keep the reciprocal concessions moving. This is an example of the summary's filtering out behavioral aspects and focusing on the content.
133. Michael concedes a point on Debbie's concerns and pledges to act on her fears. This is directional information, indicating his willingness to move toward coordination of the negotiations. Coordination takes place when both parties move into problem solving, rather than winning. At that point, the parties begin to look at what the other needs as well as what they themselves need.
134. I test a general reciprocal concession on the basis of Debbie's statement at 92.
135. Michael asks for specifics. This is an example of how the

parties move into negotiations. Now Michael is not simply rejecting all ideas other than his own; he is beginning to explore alternatives. The two-month suggestion is the mediator's, not theirs. It is long enough to give them a chance to experience the change, but not so long that the change appears permanent. This type of input by the mediator—which is, after all, arbitrary—gives the clients a baseline to work from. If the two-month period is unreasonable for either party, they will renegotiate to expand or contract it. Once negotiating its duration, however, they accept the principle of a hiatus.

136. I give a "quantity" answer . . .

137. . . . and plug the children back into the discussion.

138. Michael kills his concession by returning to the marital dynamics, which tends to undermine the negotiations.

139. A focus on the positive content of Michael's statement, to keep them in a negotiating mode and to see if Debbie is ready to reciprocate. By asking whether she "could live with that," the mediator is not asking Debbie to like it or be happy with it. This language helps lower the expectations of total satisfaction with the outcome. It also allows Debbie to view the move as a concession on her part, which opens the way for more concessions later.

140. Michael quickly limits the concession until he hears exactly what the reciprocity will be.

141. I seek a specific answer from Michael, so that Debbie will know exactly to which idea she is responding.

142. Michael restates his "equality" goal.

143. With this clear, I return to Debbie for the next move.

144. BL: Michael is watching the mediator closely throughout this part.

145. This defines and clarifies the limits of what can be achieved, using "we" language.

146. Here, I am still seeking a general response from Debbie. I am not yet looking for a specific amount of time. Since I am not sure that Debbie is ready to move from her opening position, I seek to establish the principle of movement, rather than a specific move.

147. Debbie returns to a tough position, confirming my hypothesis that the issue is Jocelyn.
148. This educates Debbie and warns her that her position is unrealistic, so as to limit the amount of her retreat.
149. Debbie is also defining the limit of her concession.

MICHAEL: How about if you give up half of your do-gooding enterprises, and you spend some time at home at night, instead of running around proselytizing the entire community to left-wing causes?[150] How about if you give that up and spend some time with your kids when they're with you?[151]

MEDIATOR: You've both lost me.[152] I thought we were talking about whether or not [to Michael] if you agree that Jocelyn would not be sleeping overnight, whether [to Debbie] you could make some movement around the parenting, so the children could share in their dad for a two-month period. We are talking about the next two months.[153, 154]

DEBBIE: Well, I want the children to see their dad, but why does she have to be along?[155]

MEDIATOR: Okay. That may be more than you can impose.[156] If you can get an agreement that she doesn't sleep over, can you then be comfortable about sharing the parenting?[157]

DEBBIE: [to Michael] What are you going to tell the children about who she is?

MICHAEL: I've told them. I've told them that she's my friend. She's told them that she's somebody that Daddy likes, Daddy spends time with her. It's an unfortunate situation that you haven't told them the same thing.

DEBBIE: Well, I didn't know.

MEDIATOR: There's a lot of work to be done by all of us in terms of working out all of the details.[158] We're obviously not going to work it all out today; that is clear.[159] We're going to have to have two or three sessions to work it all out. I was looking at whether we could get an agreement on the short run, which will get you out of the current fix.[160] [to Debbie] You shouldn't have to take all that stuff from the kids when they come in.[161] The time when they're with you should be joyful times. [to Michael] You ought not to have to worry about whether or not you see the kids.[162] You ought to be able to see the kids and have joyful times, too.[163] I'm wondering if we could move for just the next two months, in a sense of trying to get a little space for both of you as we think through all of the issues.

DEBBIE: Well, maybe if he would agree not to hold her hand and kiss her in front of the children—that's just his friend, that's what he's told them. Then, maybe.[164]

MEDIATOR: Well, you can't do that in negotiations, Debbie. You can't say "maybe." You can say, "If you do that, I will."[165]

no maybe's

DEBBIE: All right, if you do that, I will.

MEDIATOR: Okay, so you're saying that if Michael would agree not to be physically affectionate with Jocelyn while the children are there, you'll feel comfortable moving off your position and sharing time for the children with both of you.[166]

DEBBIE: I'm not saying fifty-fifty, but I'd be happier about moving toward Michael spending more time with the children.[167]

150. Michael, frustrated by the lack of movement, returns to the marriage fight.
151. Debbie works part time for Planned Parenthood.
152. The "help me" approach is designed to gain their attention and not assign blame for the digression. This approach also elevates the clients' competence immediately and helps offset the way they are devaluing their own competence as parents.
153. BL: Michael listens intently, with hands over his mouth.
154. A summary of the specifics.
155. Debbie tags on an untenable demand.
156. I educate Debbie about what is "real" because I am afraid that the talks may fall apart if she holds on to her

position. The specific choice of words also indicates to Debbie that she is already imposing on Michael's life and is now risking imposing too much from the mediator's perspective.

157. I then return to the reciprocal concession process.
158. BL: I lean forward and add an urgent emphasis to my voice.
159. This reminds the couple of the small goals I have set for the session . . .
160. . . . and holds out hope for dealing with the issues in the future.
161. I use my hands to differentiate when I am talking to each.
162. These comments reinforce the fairness issue.
163. This language carefully states the similarity of their rights.
164. Debbie tries to protect any possible movement with a "maybe."
165. I educate Debbie on good negotiating behavior.
166. I summarize Debbie's position and note that Michael is not listening.
167. Debbie corrects me, since she has not agreed to a fifty-fifty split yet.

MICHAEL: I don't understand this at all.[168]

MEDIATOR: Okay, what's that, Michael?

MICHAEL: I don't understand this at all. I don't think that Debra will be able to tell you why I shouldn't spend at least half the time with my kids. I think that what Debra is telling me . . . [169]

MEDIATOR: Well, let me ask you, Michael, if you got the children half of the time, could you agree to those conditions?[170]

MICHAEL: Of course, I . . . you know. I don't . . . she's being picky.[171] She's dealing with little things . . . she's trying to control my life. The fact of the matter is I'm prepared to say yes. She wants to write it down, I'll say yes. I'm not coming back. I want to see those kids, I'm prepared to do anything to see those kids in a comfortable environment.

MEDIATOR: That's a very responsible position. Okay, so now, Debbie, you've got quite a bit in terms of what you're looking for. Now could you come back and suggest an amount of time you would feel good about?[172]

DEBBIE: Well, I don't know what he wants. I'm still not happy with a week here and a week there.[173] I would like something more like . . . I would have them during the week, and maybe he would have them on the weekends.

MEDIATOR: Would that be comfortable? That means [to Michael] you would get them all the fun time, and [to Debbie] you would get them all the school time. Do you want that?[174] That's okay; some parents do that.[175]

DEBBIE: Well, they're going to school, Sarah's starting grade one, and I want to make sure she does okay.

MICHAEL: I—you know, I'll be frank, Debbie. If you want to do that, I don't have any problem seeing the kids on the weekends. I don't work weekends.[176] At four-thirty on Friday I leave my office. I'm happy with that, but I'm saying to you that maybe it just isn't my plan. My plan is to have my kids share my home, and maybe I don't feel they would share my home if they were only with me on weekends. I don't know what I'd give up on the weekend, but what you're telling me is that I get to see the kids every weekend, and for the next two months I don't get to see Jocelyn every weekend. Pretty smart, Debbie. It doesn't work like that.

168. Michael responds to the fifty-fifty issue by . . .
169. . . . restating the equity-versus-equality issue.
170. Refocus on seeking reciprocal concessions.
171. Michael sends two messages: He will not return to the marriage, and he is willing to do anything to see his kids.
172. I choose to connote (positive reinforcement) the "do anything" and turn back to Debbie for her concession.
173. She slips back into speaking for Michael in order to avoid answering the question. She then makes a specific proposal regarding the amount of time, according to her "equity" position.

174. A reality test of her proposal shows Debbie her legitimate self-interest.
175. While doing this, I carefully normalize the proposal.
176. Michael picks up on the offer and, thinking out loud, figures out what is in the proposal for him. He picks up on my self-interest statement and finally turns it into a jab at Debbie. In this statement, Michael has also provided some directional information about where he might be willing to settle.

MEDIATOR: Okay, so that wouldn't be acceptable to you, Michael.[177]

MICHAEL: No.

MEDIATOR: Have any other ideas, Debbie?

DEBBIE: No. I think it's important. Those children are going to school, it's important they do well in school, we both want them . . . [178]

MICHAEL: I called the bus service, they'll pick up the kids one week at my place and one week at your place, at no extra cost, Debra. It's the same old thing.

DEBBIE: Well, I can't be sure they'll be getting to bed on time, that they would be getting help with their . . . [179]

MEDIATOR: Do you have to?[180]

DEBBIE: . . . homework.

MEDIATOR: Do you have to be sure?

DEBBIE: Well . . .

MEDIATOR: What role does the nanny play?[181]

DEBBIE: She doesn't help them with their homework, she's an immigrant, she doesn't have . . .

MEDIATOR: She gets them to bed?

DEBBIE: She puts them to bed, but . . .

MICHAEL: When I don't put them to bed, she puts them to bed.

MEDIATOR: Okay. Is there space in your apartment, in the condo, for them?[182]

MICHAEL: I've got 3,200 square feet.

MEDIATOR: Okay.

MICHAEL: I got a condo, and it's close by, and I pay a lot of money on a monthly basis . . .

MEDIATOR: Okay. We're just running out of time for the appointment, so I really need to ask you whether or not you can get some agreement in the next two minutes in terms of what to do for the next few weeks, so as to get you out of the current hole.[183] That gives us some time to look at all of the issues in more detail, in a more leisurely way.

DEBBIE: Well, I would be willing to, again, go along with what I said if he agrees to cool it with his cupcake.[184]

MEDIATOR: That's already been agreed.[185]

DEBBIE: Then he can see the children every weekend, and we'll see how it goes after two months.

MEDIATOR: Michael said that's not acceptable.[186]

MICHAEL: I don't think . . . I don't think it's acceptable.[187]

DEBBIE: But I'm saying if it works, if everything goes well in two months, then . . .

MEDIATOR: Let me ask a question. How would you define weekend?[188]

DEBBIE: From Friday night to Sunday evening.

MEDIATOR: What would happen if you defined it from Friday after school to Monday . . . [189]

MICHAEL: Monday morning.

MEDIATOR: . . . after school?

DEBBIE: Well, that would be fine, because I think I could live with that, because then the children don't really have to do homework on Sunday night.[190]

MEDIATOR: [to Michael] My sense is that you're perfectly capable of helping them do their homework.[191]

MICHAEL: Yeah.

DEBBIE: Oh, I'm not saying he isn't. I want some consistency.[192]

MICHAEL: What do you mean?

DEBBIE: I mean if you help them for one week, how am I going to know where they left off? If we're not talking to each other.

MEDIATOR: Schoolbooks tell you a lot, right? Week by week.[193]

MICHAEL: I'll write a note to you.

MEDIATOR: I don't think you need to be involved about that, Michael. That's just going to create, generate more anger between you.[194] You can follow it, each of you, from the schoolbooks in terms of where they're at. You're very smart, you're a doctor; you're a doctor, you know where the kids are in terms of their education. You can pick that up very easily in terms of where they're at.[195] So that if they came to you from school on Friday and stayed with you through Monday, you'd get them to school on Monday morning, and then they'd be back at your house on Monday after school. Would that meet both needs, on a temporary basis, to give us all space and time to talk about this?[196]

DEBBIE: I'd try.[197]

MICHAEL: I'll live with it.[198]

MEDIATOR: All right. Let's then do that for the next few weeks.[199] Let's review it along the way, and let's get back together next week to talk about some of the other issues that are going on between you, so that we can try to get the children clearly out of the middle of your fight as spouses. Okay?

DEBBIE: Thanks.

MEDIATOR: Goodbye.

177. The mediator legitimates Michael's opposition to Debbie's proposal, since I believe they are in the ball park and close to agreement. I seek an alternative proposal from Debbie, thus limiting Michael's need to respond defensively, since in doing so he would probably escalate the fight.
178. The couple may be afraid of making a deal at this point, but they are also afraid of not making a deal. As cooperation develops, one or the other returns to a more familiar, polarized position.
179. Debbie challenges Michael's parenting again.
180. On the basis of prior information about his role with the children, I challenge Debbie's definition.
181. With this change in the scenario, more data are needed and more reality testing.
182. Double-checking the space data with Michael.
183. I decide to apply a time constraint, to move the couple away from arguing. This also moves them toward closing the deal on a small item.
184. Debbie restates her position, using a derogatory term for Jocelyn.
185. This cuts off Debbie and notes the prior agreement.
186. I speak for Michael, to avoid his having to respond, since he would probably escalate the issue.
187. Given my statement, Michael also responds calmly.
188. I seek clarification of Debbie's position.
189. After restating the question, I add a suggestion that enlarges the weekend.
190. Debbie accepts the increase and adds another attack on Michael's parenting. She is still reluctant to settle without ousting the other woman.
191. This statement is designed to validate Michael as an okay parent, as a way of limiting his need to counterattack.
192. Debbie adjusts her position to get back in line with the mediator.
193. Reality testing.
194. I quickly separate spousal and parental roles in response to Michael's dig.
195. This statement places the couple in a paradoxical posi-

tion. They cannot deny the suggested alternative without denying their own intelligence.

196. A restatement of the terms of a possible agreement.
197. Debbie accepts.
198. Michael accepts.
199. I summarize the agreement and set the agenda for the next session.

Analysis

The Mediator's Assumptions

Four of the assumptions discussed in Chapter One are demonstrated in this case. The separation of issues from dynamic behavioral conflicts leads to the mediator's taking control of the problem definition. Once this is done, the problem is defined as an issue between Debbie and Michael, not as a product of the dynamics. The discussion on ventilation shows how the conflict is legitimated. This is also an example of the assumption that the mediator controls the process and the couple controls the outcome. Process control is further examined in an analysis of the use of questions. The mediator controls the clients' competitiveness, as well as the strategies used to orchestrate the concessions each must make in order to arrive at an agreement. The concession orchestration, together with the mediator's determination of where the initial movement should come from, are part of the overall process, or negotiations management, role of the mediator.

The Mediator's Strategies

Problem Definition. The task for the mediator was to contain the behavioral conflicts and focus on an agreement on the issue of how much and under what circumstances the children would spend time with Michael. The mediator limited his goal to achieving some movement on the access issue. The degree of movement was governed by the couple's readiness to settle and the extent to which they were engulfed by the reasons for the separation. Thus, the mediator also had to separate the feelings about the separation from the task at hand.

A mediator begins by gathering the basic data. Since most data come from the disputants, the mediator faces a quandary: Each party to a dispute has his or her own version of the problem. Each party has a separate version of the events leading up to the current situation, and each has a different definition of the problem. The stories the disputants present have three parts.

The disputants' *versions of the facts* are designed to show the mediator how reasonable they are. Debbie stated, "Michael left a month ago, and I have let him see the children on several occasions. But the children aren't happy about seeing their father." (5)

The disputants' *complaints about the other* are designed to show the mediator how unreasonable the other is. Debbie noted that the children were devastated by the separation and that Michael had destroyed their plans, "giving me no reason." She concluded by reporting that "he's seeing someone else, and he's exposing our children to that other person." (21)

The disputants state that the *problem can be solved only through a change in the other's behavior.* Debbie, who did not want the separation, opened by saying, "They [the children] are very unhappy about the separation. When they come home, they are very upset. They're crying, and it takes me hours to settle them down." (6) Obviously, the only way to solve this problem was for Michael to return home.

Michael responded that the children had spent time with him and enjoyed that time (showing that he is a good father) and that, while the children were apprehensive about the visits, Debbie was not helping matters (Debbie was at fault). He closed with the comment that when he returned the children, Debbie dissembled and started crying. (10) (She could solve the problem by accepting the separation.)

In an arbitration setting, the professional sifts through the evidence and tries to determine the truth. Yet, as we know, in families there is rarely truth, but only perceptions. Thus, the mediator must work to create a shared perception in the form of a problem statement that is both neutral and mutual to both parties and that, once resolved, provides a solution acceptable to both of them.

The mediator acts on the information the clients present, in such a way as to help them see the information in a different light. For example, disputants base most of the problem definitions they present in the early stages of a session on the belief that their situation is abnormal and therefore difficult to resolve. The mediator attempts to normalize the disputants' experiences, because normal problems are solvable.

Following the parents' opening statements, I normalized the children's behavior. (12) Thus, it couldn't be the problem that Debbie had defined. At the same time, I suggested that the children's behavior was a product of their loyalty to both parents, which tended to mutualize the situation. These statements suggested that every separating family has the kind of problem presented by Debbie, and since it is normal, it is solvable.

Each party's problem definition is individual and designed to win the dispute; any action by the mediator to mutualize the problem causes change to take place. Thus, the mediator mutualizes the disputants' concerns, fears, hopes, and goals. As the parties see some commonality, their thinking changes, and they begin the search for a mutual solution to their common problem. Here, I noted their shared pain at the separation and commented that while they were angry with each other as spouses, "I've not heard any serious differences emerge between you as father and mother." (115)

At times when a mediator is gathering facts, he does not learn the particular facts being sought but does learn other information about the parties' bargaining positions. The exchanges from 51 to 56 are interesting in that the wife did not directly answer any of my factual questions. I continued and did not worry about her nonresponses to my data-gathering attempts. She was revealing important information about her position in the bargaining, which I stored away for later use.

Directing Questions. There are numerous examples of closed/directed questions in this chapter. I opened this session by asking Debbie to tell me about the current arrangements. I directed the question to her and closed it down by specifying the focus of the response. (2) Later, when Michael was about to launch an attack on Debbie, I asked him a closed/directed question about the ages of the children.

There are also examples of open/directed questions. For example, I asked Michael, "What is your feeling?" (8) This was a mistake, since it gave Michael the space to launch an attack on Debbie through a "feeling" response. It would have been better to ask him a closed/directed question, to match the one I had asked his wife.

Later, I asked Michael, "What does Michael want?" (15), giving him wide latitude to answer along a specific line of thought. When he completed his reply, I used the same approach with Debbie. (18)

The mediator uses questions as the prime mode of action. The questions are not probing, in the sense of eliciting a yes/no statement based on a preformed strategy of the inquirer. Rather, he asks these questions to provoke answers that the parties can own. The answer to the mediator's question is often more useful to the disputant than any advice the mediator can give.

The questioning provokes shifts in the thinking of the disputants as much as it develops data. I asked Debbie, "If you were to structure the arrangement for the parenting, how would you structure it?" (41) This question basically assumed that the children would have a relationship with their father. Answering it forced the mother to suggest how it could happen, rather than allowing her to defend why it should not happen.

Controlling the Competitive Couple. Michael and Debbie are a highly competitive couple. Each is a successful professional who is accustomed to making decisions and controlling the situation. On the one hand, in their marriage, a prestige hierarchy favored Debbie, the M.D. On the other hand, Michael appeared to have had a larger parenting role than is usual for a father, and it was also larger than Debbie's. The couple could fight at the drop of a hat. I had to decide how to maintain control of the competition as well as of the presenting conflict and the inner conflicts of each parent.

A mediator must understand, before meeting with the couple, that he will control the process. Early in the session, he must decide how to take and maintain control. In this instance, I decided to control the process by sharply limiting the fighting and by focusing on the access issue. The couple had different agendas. Michael wanted me to straighten out his wife and make her accept the separation; Debbie wanted me to straighten out her husband and send him back home. Both of them wanted to ventilate about their marriage. If I had followed either of the couple's agendas, I would have lost my neutrality, and the mediation would have proved unsuccessful.

I needed to select strategies that would enable me to take and maintain control of the process. I frequently interjected questions, to cut off a burgeoning battle. For example, early in the session, Michael gave me his opening statement. As he continued, I sensed that he was beginning to wind up for the marriage fight and to wander from sharing his perception of the facts; he was moving toward an attack on Debbie. (10) I cut in and asked him, "How old are the children?" (11) This is a closed/directed question that requires a straightforward answer. Michael was taken off his attack, and I took back control of the agenda. This type of question is called a *process interruption*—that is, it interrupted Michael's process and required a change in his behavior for long enough to return control to the mediator.

I offered no explanation of this strategy, nor did I seek permission from the couple for such interjections. The relationship and interaction of powerful and competitive couples is often chaotic. They usually welcome a firm structure. I used a direct and at times confrontational approach with Michael and Debbie. They are professionals, and the referring attorneys had informed me of their ability to engage in a high-conflict power struggle. Therefore, I chose this controlling approach to cut off each fight as it broke out and before it could develop. Their old patterns of behavior had not worked for Michael and Debbie. By creating and enforcing new patterns of behavior, I had a chance to transform their unsuccessful problem-solving approach to a new, task-focused interaction.

Ventilation. In this case, there was a lot of hostility and high tension on both sides, which I could not suppress. The mediator must decide when to permit ventilation and when to cut it off. It is the product of conflict, and it can be permitted as long as it is about a person's feelings. It should be cut off when it develops into an attack on the other. Ventilation of feelings does not interfere with mediation; it simply delays it. An attack on the other, however, undermines mediation and therefore needs to be controlled.

Michael was inattentive in the session. He spent a lot of time off somewhere—reliving an old wound, thinking about his hurts, or planning his next smart move against Debbie. I frequently saw Michael's eyes glaze over. When Michael tuned back in, he had not heard what had gone on in his mental absence, and his comments were often inappropriate at that moment. Since I could not make Michael stay focused on the task, I attempted to summarize when Michael reentered. This helped him to catch up on what had happened. I also permitted the initial ventilation, while determining whether it was an expression of feelings or an attack on Debbie.

I permitted Michael to ventilate, without cutting him off, on four occasions. The first time was when I permitted the ventilation but responded critically, to balance my previous criticism of Debbie. (33) Later, I permitted another digression, which came after I had spent a lot of time dealing with Debbie. Although Michael's ventilation added nothing to the session, it did balance the time spent with Debbie. (63) I permitted it a third time and then responded to Michael in a way that let him know I had heard his concerns, to keep him in the process, while continuing to spend more time with Debbie. (82) Toward the end, I permitted Michael to wander and then normalized his feelings to maintain my relationship with him. (107, 108) I kept Michael's ventilation within bounds by preventing it from escalating into overt conflict between the couple. Whenever Michael began to repeat himself, I cut him off in a way that obviated Debbie's need to respond to it.

Determining Initial Movement. On the surface, it seems that I was unbalanced in allowing Michael these frequent ventilations, but another objective governed my response to Michael: managing the negotiations by seeking the first movement. After the initial data had been gathered, it seemed to me that the two positions were essentially as follows: Michael wanted equal access to his children, and Debbie wanted to control when and how Michael saw the children. This was a shift from the position they had taken with the attorneys. There, Debbie had said she would not let Michael see them at all. Still, it was more than she could reasonably expect to get in the legal arena.

The mediator must not be controlled by the legal arena. Rather, he must enable the couple to find solutions to the problems that arise from the decision to separate. The decisions the couple will reach are bounded by the norms of their community—that is, the experiences of their friends and family will affect them. They will not settle on an agreement that is too far removed from their community's norms. In part, community norms are established by local court rulings on similar cases. Those norms will affect the mediator, since his responsibility is to help the couple arrive at an agreement that meets their needs. In this case, the norm in the community was that seeing another woman did not mean that a husband gave up the right to see his children. Thus, Debbie's position was untenable. Michael's desire to share the children on a fifty-fifty basis might not necessarily be practical, but it was certainly a tenable position. Given that he held a tenable position and hers was untenable, the first movement would have to come from her, with subsequent movement from him.

At this stage, I did not have enough data to determine whether Michael's claim for shared parenting on an equal-time basis was practical. Its practicality depended on Michael's prior role as a father and on his work habits and requirements. As the session proceeded, I could see that his proposal was not a strategy on his part; it was essentially a continuation of his past role and relationship with the children. It is not for the mediator to make determinations about the practicality of a given proposal. Rather, he must test reality with the party who is making the proposal. The mediator's principal interest in the proposal concerns whether it is an honest position or a strategy designed to achieve a different goal. In this case, the past parenting roles would reflect the future parenting roles, thus maintaining a level of coherence with which to balance the changes that were taking place as a result of the changing spousal roles.

I concentrated on obtaining the first movement from Debbie, spending more time with her than with Michael. This added to Michael's tendency to "disappear" from the session by giving him additional scope to do so. Since I had not obtained any movement from Debbie's original position, I had no strategy for engaging Michael when he did return to the session, because that might have meant getting a concession from him before Debbie had made any movement. Given this situation, I had no alternative but allowing him to ventilate—as long as it was about his feelings and was not an attack on Debbie.

Debbie's initial movement came at 61, when she finally acknowledged Michael's parenting, his love for the children, and their need for him. Once this statement surfaced, it was hard for her to hold on to her original position of not letting the children spend time with their father.

Michael's initial movement did not come until 138, after I had spent most of the time seeking movement from Debbie. I restated her concession on the parenting, setting the stage for him to reciprocate. It was a long process, but it was important not to push either spouse too hard or too soon for signs of movement.

Orchestrating the Concessions. This couple needed a solution to their problem, quickly. The children were victims of the current crisis, and its continuation would also contaminate the economic negotiations. Therefore, I had to decide the extent to which I would orchestrate the negotiations by suggesting different courses of action. In an ideal setting, the mediator would not make any proposals or suggestions. Without my active intervention, however, Michael and Debbie would have stayed too tied up in their recent separation to be able to come up with a range of ideas for themselves. Therefore, I chose to orchestrate these negotiations and to use a tit-for-tat approach in the negotiations.

Tit-for-tat, or reciprocal, concession bargaining is a useful method of negotiating when the level of mistrust between the parties is high (Pruitt, 1981). In such a situation, the mediator seeks a small concession from one party and then seeks reciprocal action from the other. The concessions are small and slowly build a bridge between the two opening positions, enabling the parties to arrive at a settlement somewhere in between. Thus, the mediator seeks movement from the wife and then turns to the husband for reciprocity. As reciprocity takes place, the level of trust increases. Once the mediator has orchestrated a few reciprocal concessions, the couple begin to take risks with each other and maintain the bargaining process of give-and-take.

The initial response to my attempts to begin tit-for-tat bargaining did not come until 61, when Debbie acknowledged Michael's parenting. Nevertheless, she defended her position carefully and did not follow up this concession with one related to the issue of access. For example, I asked Debbie whether, if Jocelyn did not sleep over when the children were with Michael, she would feel comfortable "about working out some arrangement for the children." (101) I did not ask her to specify the amount of time, but simply to agree on some reciprocal movement. This was also a way of suggesting to Michael what movement he might make that would achieve reciprocity from Debbie. I took this process one step at a time. I simply wanted Debbie to make some small movement, in general terms, because I believed that this was easier for her than making large steps. A small step would also be more believable to Michael, and therefore he would be more likely to reciprocate. Nevertheless, she was stuck and could not go beyond her initial concession. (122)

I finally gave up trying to get the first substantive concession from Debbie (movement on an amount of time). I turned to Michael for the first substantive concession late in the session (134) by asking him whether in the "short run" he would agree that Jocelyn not sleep over when the children were with him. He agreed (138), and I then turned to Debbie for reciprocity. When none was forthcoming, I pursued Debbie until she finally did respond (173) with specific movement.

This series of interactions illustrates how important it is for the mediator to separate process from outcome. At no time did I thrust a proposal on either party; I always left space for either one to reject an idea and supported each one's right to do so. At 177 and 186, I spoke for Michael in rejecting Debbie's proposal, which he had previously rejected. I strategically designed the intervention to obviate the need for Michael to reject the proposal again, since he would probably have done so with some agitation and a counterattack. Instead, Michael repeated my calm words of rejection.

In this case, I also educated the couple on how to negotiate. I was particularly concerned by Debbie's conditional offers ("maybe"). I pointed out that such tentative offers were inappropriate. It was important to do this, since the level of trust I was still building between them could easily have been destroyed if Michael had responded positively and then Debbie had said, "Maybe I won't." When couples engage in dangerous negotiating behavior, the mediator intervenes and explains the problem. If a party is engaging in a dangerous strategy deliberately, then the mediator wants to control that behavior. If the party takes an action through ignorance of its dangers, the mediator explains the consequences of a given strategy. The person can then retract it and use a more practical strategy.

Monologues. I frequently used monologues to keep control of the session. Each time I engaged in a monologue, it had a specific if different purpose. When the marriage fight first emerged, I normalized the couple's situation and educated them about what they were experiencing. (12) I then returned to my agenda. I used another monologue to join Debbie, undermining her position and then allowing her to save face. At the conclusion of the monologue, I returned to the task. (47–49)

Another monologue was designed to test reality and help me formulate a neutral problem statement. I also used this moment to point out the possibility of joint maximum benefit, so that each party would look at the "half-full glass." In doing so, I took control of the problem definition. (124)

When the issues became obscured, I clarified the meaning of fairness for everyone and returned to task. (128) Toward the end of the session, I engaged in a complicated monologue that covered a number of key thoughts but still returned to task at the end. (159–160)

Clients' Negotiating Behavior

Directional Information. During the give-and-take of the parties, the mediator will often hear information indicating the direction in which one or the other is willing to move. Only rarely does the other party pick up on this information. The mediator notes the directional information and uses it later in orchestrating the negotiations. It becomes a guide for determining which way to organize the talks.

Michael indicated early that his parameters were equal time with the children for each parent. Thus, he was not seeking *more* than equal time. Ten minutes later, Debbie also provided some key directional information: "He's a good father. He's been a good father. I can't deny that. The children love him and he loves the children." (119) This information set the other parameters of the negotiations. If Michael was the good father that Debbie now stated he was, then obviously they would not reach an agreement that would deny his parenting role. It meant that Debbie's position of controlled access was not intended to protect the children from their father but to protect herself from Jocelyn. It suggested a direction in which Debbie might be willing to move.

Michael provided some further directional information when he stated, "I know that Debra doesn't want the kids around her [Jocelyn], and that it's confusing." (following 133) This told me that Michael understood Debbie's concerns, and that he might be willing to move to accommodate them. Debbie confirmed this understanding when she stated, "Well, I want the children to see their dad, but why does she have to be along?" (155) These various pieces of directional information helped me determine how to proceed. The ultimate agreement of sharing the week, conditional on Jocelyn's not sleeping over, was designed in part by the directional information Michael and Debbie provided about where they were willing to settle.

Equity Versus Equality. The equity-equality arguments are clearly demonstrated in this case. Michael wants equality of parenting. He makes the case that he has had at least an equal role in the marriage and wants to continue that role after the divorce. Debbie wants an equitable outcome. In her scenario, Michael's access to the children should be controlled by his relationship with the other woman and his proximity to Debbie. Equality arguments are simple to make: "I want my share, not one iota more." The fifty-fifty outcome is very appealing and, if carried across the board on all aspects of the negotiations, should result in an eminently fair agreement. Nevertheless, most parties shift their positions from equity to equality according to the subject.

In this case, it appeared that Michael was willing to share in the parenting equally and to share equally in the costs of raising the children. He stated that he was playing Debbie $1,500 per month in support. Debbie, however, took the equity position—not because it reflected past parenting behavior, but to control Michael's behavior with Jocelyn. Even if Jocelyn had not been a factor, however, Debbie's arguments in favor of equity could still have been a useful strategy, since they could have been based on the "best interests of the children" justification. Thus, Debbie's negotiating strategy would have been equally valid with or without Jocelyn in the picture. To avoid the consequences of Debbie's strategy, I moved to develop an interim arrangement that would give Debbie time to accept the separation and begin to construct a new life for herself, based on an equal sharing of the children in the future.

Conflict Expansion. When I tried to define the problem—that Debbie would feel uncomfortable letting the children sleep over at Michael's if Jocelyn were also sleeping over—Debbie expanded the conflict, suggesting that Michael should have "a house not too far from ours, so the children could go back and forth on their bicycles. Something more appropriate." (102) This was an interesting expansion of the issues; it proposed a situation in which access to the children would in some measure be governed by the children themselves, since, if they lived close enough to bicycle over to Michael's, they could also decide when and when not to go. This expansion, however, was really designed to allow Debbie to avoid having to respond to my previous proposition: that the entire issue was Jocelyn's sleeping over when the children were with Michael.

Using Threats. Michael tried a threat, obviously from a one-down position: "If the children are so upset when they go back to see their mother, maybe they should stay with me most of the time." (84) I ignored this part of his statement and concentrated on the positive content of his comments. This allowed

Debbie to also ignore the threat. Had I identified the threat and attempted to deal with it, the issue might have escalated and developed into a major battle. As the session proceeded and the balance of power became more equal, Michael saw no need for further threats.

Triangulation. The classic triangulation attempt was Michael's. He said, "John, I would like you to open her eyes" (32) and then went on to detail what I should tell Debbie to do. Later, he pleaded with me, "Can't you tell her that what I'm doing is normal, it happens all the time, can't you explain to her where I'm coming from?" (110) Had I tried to explain Michael's behavior to Debbie, I would have become his ally and therefore her adversary. Instead, I reframed the issue with a focus on the future.

Conclusion

It could be argued that Michael lost in this settlement. He did not achieve the fifty-fifty shared parenting he sought, and he did give up his girl friend when the children slept over. It could also be argued that I had a major role in shaping the agreement. These observations are true—in the short run. Note, however, that I sought the agreement only for a couple of months; it was not a permanent agreement. I did not make a moral judgment about Jocelyn's sleeping with Michael; I made a practical one. Debbie was incapable of dealing with her displacement by Jocelyn as wife, and her possible displacement by Jocelyn as mother, while she was still dealing with her loss of Michael. The separation was too recent for her to believe that a permanent agreement could be reached. What this couple needed was a brief respite from the battle, to give them a chance to organize their lives for the next two months. This allowed them to deal with the inner conflicts of the separation.

Mediation is situational. An agreement in a temporary situation is different from a permanent agreement. The couple's readiness to negotiate an agreement is also a factor. It makes no sense for the mediator to try to help a couple reach a permanent agreement when the parties are not ready to make one.

Thus, the outcome of this session was a small movement on each side, which each party could live with for a short time. The agreement provided them with a breathing space in which to collect themselves and sort out the more serious emotional issues. They could get used to sharing the children so that they could return later for the long-term agreement after they had settled the economic issues. At that time, they could define the permanent parenting agreement that was in the mutual interests of Michael, Debbie, Sarah, and Daniel.

5

RON AND MARY: A FAMILY RECOVERING FROM ALCOHOLISM

Ron and Mary sought mediation through a court-sponsored project. I was invited to work with them as a consultant to the mediator. They had lived apart for twenty months, and the presenting issue was child support. The court had ordered Ron to pay $200 per month in child support for their daughter, Lee Anne. He had not paid any support for eight months, and Mary's goal was to get some payments.

Ron was in a court-mandated alcoholism recovery program; he had been convicted of driving while intoxicated. He was not currently drinking and seemed to be taking the first steps on the long road toward recovery. The special issues of working with drug- and alcohol-impaired families are discussed after the transcript. I will also discuss the strategies I used in the session to break old marital patterns that were interfering with the negotiations.

It was difficult to determine why Ron and Mary had chosen mediation. Mary could have returned to court to get the support order enforced, but she was reluctant to do so. She seemed to doubt that she could get the court to enforce the support order. This belief may have reflected her experience during the initial separation hearing, as well as the way Ron's alcoholism-related driving charges had been dealt with in the past. In choosing mediation as the arena in which to get the best deal, the courts were her WATNA. That is, she seemed to believe that she could get a better deal through direct negotiations in mediation than through the courts.

Ron also seemed to fear going back to court. He was probably concerned that his drunk-driving conviction might hurt him there. He also seemed to have chosen mediation because he felt confident of being able to out-negotiate Mary in a one-to-one situation. Thus, the court was also his WATNA. Given their commitment to mediation, the mediator expected to be able to help this couple reach an agreement.

This case illustrates another facet of the mediator's role and demonstrates the situational nature of mediation. My behavior was determined in part by my hypothesis that Ron and Mary were unclear about the divorce. They sent numerous signals that they wanted to get back together. After developing and testing my hypothesis and having it confirmed by the couple, I attempted to help them reach an agreement that would enhance the possibility of their reconciliation. The development of this hypothesis and its subsequent testing and confirmation are annotated; a detailed discussion of the use of this hypothesis follows the transcript.

The effect of the assumption that there is "that of God" in everyone is clearly demonstrated in this case. I stayed essentially nonjudgmental toward Ron and Mary's behavior. Whenever Ron did something that clashed with my value system, I reminded myself to look for the good and work with it, rather than trying to change Ron's values.

This case raises the problem of crossing from process control to content control. In some cases, a mediator is asked by the parties to take control of the content. When the request is clearly stated, it is easy to refuse. Sometimes, however, the mediator must cross over to content control in order to maintain process control. Given the range of issues and behavior exhibited in any one session, it is not surprising that the mediator occasionally owns a piece of the content. I crossed over that line with Ron and Mary. My discussion of the reasons for and implications of exerting content control follows the transcript.

One major strategy that recurred throughout this session was my attempt to break the old marital patterns and help the couple establish productive ways of relating to each other. This strategy was combined with the strategy of linking Ron's work in the alcoholism recovery program to the mediation work, to define a new way of negotiating for both parties. My use of a flip chart to share information, as well as to convey embedded suggestions, is also demonstrated in this case.

Other strategies demonstrated in this chapter concern what a mediator does when the couple appears to be unclear about the divorce. Strategies, which are broad, are implemented through tactics. Tactics are specific interventions within a strategic framework. They include partializing, which is the process of breaking an issue into its component parts, solving each part individually, and then rejoining the component parts to create the total solution. At times, the mediator "joins" a couple by articulating their interests, displaying a special interest in their specific needs, and supporting particular positions of either party.

This couple engaged in interesting negotiating behavior. Some of their behavior was a manifestation of their marital dynamics—for example, Ron's use of a third party to avoid making a commitment. Other behavior included offering to make verbal rather than written agreements and making threats and counterthreats. Most of their negative negotiating behavior was contained through reference to each party's WATNA and BATNA, which ultimately controlled their negotiating behavior.

This case also contains an example of the confusion that can develop in a session when inductive and deductive thinking clash.

The transcript of the actual session follows.

Transcript and Annotations

MEDIATOR: Well, welcome—and glad you were both able to make it. As I mentioned to you a little earlier, I know very little about your situation and where you currently are in terms of the problem. I do know that you have a four-year-old daughter. So I wonder if, perhaps, you could begin by telling me what the current situation is, and then what the problem is that you see for each of you.[1]

MARY: Well, we've been separated for about twenty months, and . . . uh . . . a necessity at that time for safety's sake, and I've been raising our little girl by myself since then.[2]

MEDIATOR: Uh hum; so you've been living apart now for twenty months.[3]

MARY: Yes.

MEDIATOR: Okay. And your daughter's name is?

MARY: Lee Anne.

MEDIATOR: And she's living with you?

MARY: Yes, she is.

MEDIATOR: Okay, Mary. And how much time do you spend with her, Ron?

RON: Oh, at least on a weekly basis, I'd say on the average of ten hours.

MEDIATOR: Uh huh. Okay, so you see her—what, once a week?

RON: Yes.

MEDIATOR: Once a week.

RON: Like, I've got no restrictions or anything like that. It's possible I almost see her every afternoon. So Mary has no restricting orders. There are certain orders that I'm not supposed to drink anything before visiting, but other than that there is not really any restricting orders.[4]

MEDIATOR: Okay. So what is the issue between you?[5]

MARY: Well, it's one of sharing the responsibility. I guess financial matters are of prime importance and are hard to resolve. I find it to be a prime consideration to me.[6]

MEDIATOR: Okay. Are you having any problem around the parenting, at this point, with Lee Anne?[7]

MARY: It's pretty compatible. There's a few differences of opinion, but generally we're pretty understanding of the same feeling.

MEDIATOR: Okay. So it's really a financial question. Is the issue one of support?[8]

MARY: Yes, in my eyes, it's one of the prime matters. Maybe Ron can say if there are other factors with him.

MEDIATOR: [to Ron] How about with you?[9]

1. As in all cases, the opening question asks for the current events, not the past. This is an open, undirected question. I will use many more open questions with this couple, since they are not so overtly conflicted as Michael and Debbie (see Chapter Four), and the open form gives them freedom to find a comfortable way of answering the questions.
2. This comment about safety may indicate abuse, which will need checking. I made a note to check this out during the session. I do not do so immediately, since this would accept Mary's definition of the problem.
3. Each piece of basic data is summarized and played back to the couple, as a way of checking the mediator's understanding.
4. Ron's version of the abuse issue emerges naturally, as alcohol abuse.
5. Because I seek their definition of the issue between them, they are involved in establishing the agenda.
6. This is the first indication that the couple may want to stay together. I develop a tentative hypothesis to this effect.
7. The information gathering is enlarged, to check on whether there are any other major disputes.
8. Mary defines the problem as being over money. This is checked out with both of them. Up to this point, I have

used open questions. Mary always takes the lead in answering. Ron responds only to questions directed to him. This provides some power-balance information: Mary is the spokesperson for the family.

9. The next question is directed to Ron, to lessen Mary's domination of the discussion. As a result, the mediator learns that Ron shares her definition of the problem.

RON: Because right now I could see financial support is really of the greatest importance, because previously I was working. Right now, I am unemployed, and that's pretty hard. It's pretty hard for all . . . myself, to even try to support myself with what I'm receiving, and possibly it should work out in such a way.

MEDIATOR: If we work out a satisfactory arrangement for both of you around the money, would there be any other issues?[10]

MARY: Well, he had a problem with the use of alcohol, and he is on a recovery program from that.[11] I do feel some time is necessary to allow him to carry on with it before I feel I could really have trust that it wouldn't be a relapse. I look at time in that way; it's important to me.

MEDIATOR: Do you mean in terms of Lee Anne?[12]

MARY: In some regards, as a father to her and in our[13] relationship, in any way, I just feel that proving himself of the alcohol is very important to himself and to us.

MEDIATOR: Forgive me for . . . because I don't quite understand: What does Ron have to prove?[14]

MARY: Well, just that he can handle it, a life without it, and can carry on that way, because the use of it was a disruption to our relationship.[15] After our attending this program that he has, and carrying on without alcohol in his life, I would just like to see a little bit more time in that way, to really establish within me that I know it can work, that he can handle life without it.

MEDIATOR: Forgive me. I have to ask a lot of these questions, but I'm trying to understand why that would be important to you. If you . . . you're now separated, right?[16]

10. A double-check on the primacy of the money issue, to make sure that a real issue is not being hidden by both parents. The answer to this will help define the agenda.
11. Mary confirms the alcoholism and then hints at the possibility of reconciliation, tending to confirm the hypothesis that she would like to get back together at some point.
12. A clarifying, specific question . . .
13. . . . and a global response, confirming the hypothesis. Mary also states ownership of the daughter.
14. The tone of my voice adds to the gentle way I correct this type of couple.
15. Mary's use of "our" indicates that she still wants the marriage. Couples who have been apart for twenty months do not normally use "our." This is another hypothesis-confirming statement.
16. Here, I am testing the hypothesis that they really want to get back together. Alerting the couple that they will be asked a lot of data questions involves them in what I am doing and how I am doing it, in contrast to my behavior with Michael and Debbie. This is an example of situational mediation.

MARY: We are separated. It's just that, in visitation rights with him—I don't know, maybe I just still have fears of what the alcohol can do.[17] I look on a shared custody possibility with Lee Anne. But I would like help in sharing the load of responsibility with her, and I just hope that he can handle it.

MEDIATOR: So, Ron, would you like to spend more time with Lee Anne?[18]

RON: Yes, I would.

MEDIATOR: Okay.

RON: I would definitely like to.

MEDIATOR: Yeah, yeah.[19]

RON: 'Cause right now, I don't question it or anything, because I think Mary's pretty fair pertaining to the way I'd like my visiting rights. Like, I go over and spend time with Mary, visiting with Mary and Lee Anne, and I'm not restricted timewise, okay? I'll be here for an hour or two hours, and I think she's very good in that part. Right now, I don't have Lee Anne sleeping over, and maybe to come, if our relationship—according to the outcome of it—that would be something I would like to work towards. Maybe even going on a holiday. Like if Mary don't want to come along or anything, I could take Lee Anne along with me and spend a lot more time with her, seeing her grow up, and try my best.[20] 'Cause another thing is, like, sometime to come—she hasn't seen her grandmother that's living out of the country, and if that were possible, I could take her there.

MEDIATOR: Take her back home and . . . okay. Now I'm sort of getting two messages, so I need to know which one I should be pursuing with you. I'm getting messages that I'm not sure that you want to get divorced. You're separated, and you want to organize the separation, or do you want to get divorced?[21]

MARY: I'm not really sure what the outcome would be. I know at the present time I can't see us as a unit, and the reason being that I don't feel that he is ready to be in a household, one of the heads of the household at the present time.[22, 23]

MEDIATOR: I suppose the question is whether you do, and Ron will talk for himself. I'm going to ask you, because I'm sure you can each speak for the other. We do that after we've been married for a while. We do a lot of talking for each other. I was wondering Mary, for you, which direction you want to go in the future?[24]

MARY: I want security.[25] What I have at present allows for a taste of that, and I don't want to lose it. What I knew in the relationship was very insecure, and I don't want to face that again. So I really feel for my daughter and myself that we need to know what's ahead of us down the line and keep something to hold on to. If we have to live on our own accordingly, okay, I'm prepared to try and make the best. I would look for his assistance in that, though, because she being his daughter, so I would count on his sharing in support of her in that regard.[26] It's not for myself, but it's for her. And also with the responsibility, as he mentioned, about more visitation and[27] overnights, and so on. There have been a couple of instances that have alarmed me. I'm scared that I don't know if he can really handle full-time, like leaving her alone at home and going over to the store or something. It worries me if he really knows the repercussion of a little child not having . . . being a daughter also bothers me.[28]

17. This is the critical side of Mary.
18. Mary's criticism is turned into a positive statement, so that Ron can respond to the content, not the delivery.
19. As Ron talks, he is encouraged to talk more freely. BL: While Ron talks, Mary has a sad, depressed look.
20. Ron indicates that the relationship has not totally ended. The hypothesis is confirmed.
21. It is time to make the hypothesis explicit, in seeking clarification regarding the divorce decision.
22. Mary confirms the hypothesis through use of "unit" and "household" and "at the present time."
23. BL: The couple have identical body positions; both feet on the floor, hands clasped in the lap. Neither has moved since the opening.
24. Mary is encouraged to talk for herself and focus on her own future, through my educating them about behavior. The comments close with a future-oriented question.
25. Mary raises an underlying need for security and . . .
26. . . . raises a demand for equity.
27. Mary also raises a parenting concern, and . . .
28. . . . the possibility that Ron's recovery is far from complete. I make a note to check this out in a way that is not intrusive and does not buy Mary's definition of the problem.

MEDIATOR: Yeah. Okay, let me just ask you a couple of background questions, so that I can be more helpful. How long have you been in the recovery program?[29]

RON: About four months.

MEDIATOR: About four months. Okay. Was it a residential program?

RON: No.

MEDIATOR: So you lived out but went in each day.

RON: It's on a . . . it's a day program.

MEDIATOR: It's a day program. And at this point, now, how often are you going?

RON: Like, it was a four-months . . . uh . . . four-weeks program, sorry, and it was from eight to four. So I completed that, and right now I am in what you call a relapse-prevention program.

MEDIATOR: Okay. Do you go to AA meetings?[30]

RON: No, I don't.

MEDIATOR: You don't.

RON: I haven't.

MEDIATOR: Okay. So all of the work that you're doing around the alcoholism is with the one program?[31]

RON: Yes, it's with the drug and alcohol commission, it's all associated and affiliated with the drug and alcohol commission.

MEDIATOR: All right. And how long do you normally stay in that kind of program? I mean, how long will you be in the relapse-prevention phase?

RON: Well, it is an eight-week program, once a week. So far I did seven weeks.

MEDIATOR: Seven weeks. So you went four weeks on a daily

basis and seven weeks on one . . . okay. What will happen at the end of those eight weeks? I guess that's—what, one week from now?

RON: Well, it's in a way of putting everything to a test.

MEDIATOR: I see. So you get to graduate.

RON: Well, I graduated from one, the day program.

MEDIATOR: Right, and now you're going to graduate[32] from the relapse-prevention program, and then what happens?

RON: There are certain programs. I don't want to really get into too many things at the moment, because I have an exam that I was studying for, and that took a lot of my time.[33] Eventually—I'm seeing a counselor, and after this relapse-prevention program, I was thinking about going in. I spoke to him pertaining to getting into different programs there. Self-esteem, different programs.

MEDIATOR: Uh huh, yeah. I suppose it would be helpful for you, Mary, if Ron is in one of those programs on a long-term basis, so that you know there's somewhere to turn for you. Am I right? I don't want to put words in your mouth.[34]

MARY: Well, it's certainly encouraging.

MEDIATOR: That's what you would want. All right. Put that on hold for a moment, because that's something for you to work on, Ron, with the counselor.[35] Let's turn our attention for a moment to the money issue. Now, [to Mary] you're a teacher?

MARY: I haven't taught in the last couple of years. I'm presently working in the library, and it's just in the last five months that I have been fully employed. I wasn't prior to that.

MEDIATOR: What do you earn now on a yearly basis?[36, 37]

29. This is an attempt to place the preceding information into context by asking Ron questions about his alcoholism.

30. By checking to see if Ron has support in his recovery, the mediator can carry out his work complementarily with the work of other professionals. The mediator should be careful not to interfere with the work of the current treatment program, and so I make a note to check that Ron will have a support system, such as AA, when he completes the day program.
31. An embedded-suggestion question: As Ron answers, he is probably saying to himself that all the work is with one agency, and the answer suggests to him that perhaps he should be doing more.
32. I turn to a future orientation, having gathered the necessary data on Ron's treatment.
33. Ron's lack of a clear plan indicates some problems.
34. This reengages Mary, while sending a message to Ron about what he will probably have to do in order to get back together with her. This also identifies the similarity of their positions.
35. Sensing that Mary may be a rescuer, I place responsibility back with Ron. I have now refined my hypothesis: They want to get back together, but Ron's alcoholism and Mary's rescuing prevent it.
36. Having completed the survey questions, I shift back to the money issue, identified earlier as the key one.
37. BL: The couple still has not moved body or hands.

MARY: Uh . . . it's about fifteen, sixteen thousand, approximately.

MEDIATOR: How much do you take home?

MARY: I clear about one thousand to eleven hundred dollars a month; I'm not quite sure.

MEDIATOR: So, you're living at the moment on a budget of somewhere between ten and eleven hundred a month. Do you get any other support?[38]

MARY: No. There is a court order for him to pay maintenance, but he hasn't for the last seven or eight months.[39]

MEDIATOR: Ron, for you, now—you're currently unemployed, right? So I guess you're drawing unemployment compensation.

RON: Yes, I am.

MEDIATOR: How much does that pay?

RON: Eight hundred dollars a month.

MEDIATOR: Okay. If you get a job—you took this test this morning?

RON: Uh huh.

MEDIATOR: And if you become a technician—how much do air-conditioning technicians earn, approximately?

RON: On a yearly basis?

MEDIATOR: Uh huh.

RON: About thirty, thirty-two thousand a year.

MEDIATOR: Okay, you both know the situation better than I do. If you were earning thirty thousand a year, how much would you take home?

RON: I'd say the take-home would be about twenty-two.

MEDIATOR: About twenty-two.[40] Okay, so if you were fully employed on a full-time basis in air conditioning [to Ron] you might have twenty-two and [to Mary] you might have twelve or thirteen thousand. All right. Now, at this point, you're one person living on eight hundred, and you're two people living on a thousand to eleven hundred, right?

MARY: Uh huh.

MEDIATOR: Okay. What was the original court order for the amount of maintenance?

MARY: It was two hundred dollars per month for Lee Anne.

MEDIATOR: Two hundred a month for Lee Anne. Okay. Just so I can get this fixed in my mind, I'm going to put it up on the board, because I tend to get lost on these figures if I don't keep track, and I find it helpful in that way, too. So, Mary, if we can split the difference somewhere between, and we'll call it one thousand and fifty, okay?[41, 42]

MARY: Yes.

MEDIATOR: And, Ron, you're at the moment at eight hundred?[43]

RON: Yes.

MEDIATOR: Okay. Now, that's right now. That's the present; okay. So do you intend to stay in the library, Mary?

MARY: I hope so. Full-time employment isn't that available right now. I was lucky to get what I did, so I hope I can carry on there.

MEDIATOR: Okay. If we look to the future, then you can continue to expect about one thousand and fifty—and, Ron, yours is open in the future. It can be anywhere up to—we'll put in brackets here—but up to twenty-two thousand.[44] Okay, [to Mary] so now you're raising Lee Anne on yours, and [to Ron] yours is for you? The court order is two hundred a month, so that if you were paying it right now, it would mean that Mary would be getting twelve fifty, and, Ron, you would have six hundred.[45] Okay. So the question we need to talk about in terms of the money is the following: What do we do in the immediate, and then how do we operate once [to Ron] you move into an employment situation.[46] So, just to help me, when would you know about the outcome of the test?

RON: In three to four weeks.

38. As each piece of data is gathered, it is checked with the couple and then further checked through a clarifying question.
39. At this point, I asked myself, "If Mary has a court order, why is she in mediation? Did she try to enforce the court order? If not, why not?" I chose not to pursue this, on the assumption that, given Ron's situation with the alcoholism and the fact that he was currently unemployed,

she was playing her rescuer role. I probably could have checked this out with a simple question: "Why?" Nevertheless, this might have disempowered Mary: She was doubtful of whether she could get the court order enforced, given Ron's unemployment. Therefore, Mary was in mediation to get a better deal.

40. After gathering the data from Ron, I used a summary to bring the discussion back to the current issue.
41. Entering the figures on the board helps maintain a focus on the data—a difficult task for most people. It also helps me catch any errors I might make; if an incorrect figure is entered, the couple will correct me. From now on, the couple will refer to the board, either directly or by looking at it when discussing the money issue.
42. BL: The couple smile, and each party focuses on the mediator.
43. This is establishing a fairness concept simply by displaying the figures in their correct context.
44. When entering figures, the mediator does not put "maybe" data up equally with real data. In this case, given Ron's alcoholism, the twenty-two thousand may be unrealistic. Therefore, I identify it differently from the other data.
45. I restate the equity issue by noting how much each party has and is responsible for. There is, of course, an embedded suggestion in these actions.
46. A separation of the current from the future.

MEDIATOR: In three to four weeks. Okay. At what point will you be eligible for employment?

RON: I am eligible for employment right now. As the situation is, whatever job I can get in heating and air-conditioning outfits, I'd be willing to go. But after I get my certificate, then I would be getting into that thirty-two-thousand-a-year bracket.

MEDIATOR: Okay. So now let me ask you—and this might sound a funny question to you, but I have to ask funny questions sometimes.[47] Why haven't you paid the two hundred dollars?

RON: Because right now I'm running on a monthly deficit.[48]

MEDIATOR: Uh huh.

RON: Because I've got to pay the mortgage, the house mortgage.

MEDIATOR: Uh huh. Who's living in the house?[49]

RON: I am.

MEDIATOR: So you're living in the house that you both lived in before, and [to Mary] you've moved out with Lee Anne. Okay. So you are paying the house mortgage.

RON: And then by the time I pay the utilities and maybe get a sandwich or two per month, I'm running a deficit.[50]

MEDIATOR: What's the mortgage?[51]

RON: Five hundred and fifty dollars.

MEDIATOR: Five hundred and fifty a month. So you basically have two hundred and fifty left to live on.

RON: Yes, on a monthly basis.

MEDIATOR: Mary, what is your rent?

MARY: Three ninety, plus utilities makes it about four fifty.[52]

MEDIATOR: Four fifty. So then from that four fifty, you have about six hundred for food and clothing . . .

MARY: And day care, and so on, another big chunk.

MEDIATOR: Oh, yeah. So, in one sense, you've got a problem in terms of the immediate getting through on the respective budgets? Right?[53]

MARY: Uh huh.

MEDIATOR: You both own that house?

MARY: Yes, we do.

MEDIATOR: Joint? Let me ask you: Why did you choose to do it that way?[54]

MARY: I left for safety's sake, and also the location isn't very suitable. I don't drive, and that was a mistake there, in buying a house in that location, because I can't or couldn't really live there on my own, nor with the . . . like the last . . . I've only been working since March. All last year, I was on benefits, and my unemployment was only five fifty a month. I was supporting Lee Anne and myself on that minimal amount, so I couldn't have handled the mortgage anyway. There was no point in living there at that time. I couldn't have handled it at all. It's just in the last few months that I even had a full-time job. We had been living very meagerly all winter.[55, 56]

MEDIATOR: Yeah. Okay. Well, I guess, with the current housing situation, you can't sell. It's just a question of keeping hold of it.[57]

MARY: It doesn't seem practical to sell it. I would look forward to the day when we did, I think, because . . .

47. The question is designed to bring Ron back to reality. In dealing with this type of couple, it is useful to soften a provocative question.
48. BL: Mary remains impassive.
49. Never take anything for granted; always check the data. In this case, it is important. They have reversed the normal arrangement, whereby the husband moves out.
50. Ron adopts a bargaining position by understating his ability to pay.
51. I do not accept Ron's definition of the problem but continue to gather data.
52. This repeats an earlier strategy of identifying discrepancies of income and responsibilities. This casts doubt on Ron's position.
53. The budget shortfalls are made mutual, validating Ron's earlier point but making it equally true for Mary.

54. Since the husband usually moves out, I want the background data on this unusual arrangement.
55. Mary opens with a criticism of Ron and then softens to take responsibility for her moving. Since the second reason is reality (as are Ron's alcoholism and possible abuse), I note it against my hypotheses that the couple would like to get back together at some time, that money is the major issue for the wife, and that solving the money issue creates a bridge to working on the marriage.
56. Mary displays anger in her facial expression for the first time.
57. Noting the reality of the current real-estate market and realizing that little can be done to sell the house right now is a form of joining.

MEDIATOR: Yeah. Okay. What you might do is think about setting a date or some sort of condition under which that might happen, in terms of economics.[58] Think about what the minimum price would be and if you could get a buyer for that price, and that's when you might do that. Mary, from your perspective now, knowing this data—and, of course, this is not a lot of information to work with—what would you think would be appropriate for you to receive right now in terms of support from Ron?[59]

MARY: Well, I would appreciate a contribution of some sort. Maybe seventy-five dollars a month or something.[60] I just do feel there's been a very little bit, very little contribution to our household in any way. Even ask him to go over and get a quart of milk for me or something, and there seems to be hesitancy. I really do feel that if he really tries, he could give us something, because it hasn't been easy to raise her. A lot of our living last year was on credit. So I'm repaying what we lived on in plastic. That's a factor also. I'm making up for what I didn't have last year.[61] It's just a matter that she and I have been counting our pennies for a good twenty months, and I really feel that we shouldn't do it alone. I do understand that he was having a boarder with him, and if that fellow was contributing to the mortgage or whatever, then that would help his situation.[62]

MEDIATOR: [to Ron] Tell us about the boarder. [to Mary] I'm sorry.[63]

MARY: There are also two vehicles at the house, and he has talked about selling at least one of them, you know, so there's a source of money also.[64]

MEDIATOR: Okay. So let's explore those issues. First, let's hear from Ron. You were going to tell me, I'm sorry, about the boarder.[65]

RON: Yeah, I've got a guy there that—he's not too sure that he would even stay at my place. Right now, he's staying there, and so far it's less than a month that he's been there, and I haven't received anything from him. He has contributed to our groceries. I have not received any dollars towards my income, and he is not too sure if he is going to stay there—'cause right now he's not even staying at my place.[66] He's staying over at another friend's place. So I'm not too sure that I would have him as a boarder on a full-time basis or what. So I have to really get the decision from him what he plans on doing, too.[67]

MEDIATOR: I suppose he has to live somewhere, right?[68]

RON: Yes, he's got to.

MEDIATOR: And I suppose he has to pay somewhere. Right? And I suppose—let me ask you again, forgive me, on some of the details I'm not that aware of. What, normally, would a person like that pay?

RON: About maybe two hundred—two hundred and fifty dollars per month. Or it could be higher.[69]

58. Some practical advice for future attention.
59. I return the focus to the money issue by asking Mary to state her goals.
60. The court order is for two hundred dollars. Mary sets it at seventy-five dollars, confirming part of my hypothesis regarding their dynamics. She opens with a low figure, to match Ron's opening position. In a more balanced couple, the wife would open at a high figure, to counteract the husband's low opening number.

61. BL: Ron is impassive during this monologue.
62. New information emerges. Note that it did not come out in the economic discussion earlier but surfaces now as Mary gains increasing comfort with mediation.
63. I interrupt Mary to question Ron and realize that Mary has more to say, so I stop to listen.
64. This is not an attempt by Mary to expand the conflict as a negotiating strategy; she is rescuing Ron by finding a solution to the basic problem.
65. I continue to be particularly polite, choosing not to pursue the issue of Ron's autos, since my goal is to arrive at a support figure and then make Ron responsible for paying it. Mary's point about the autos is another example of her "rescuing" and "solving" role in the marriage. Thus, the dynamic behavior outweighs the negotiating strategy. In this situation, Mary's strategy is inappropriate.
66. Ron is fuzzy about the money, as he tries to hold to his original bargaining position: that he has no money with which to pay support.
67. Ron makes a slight shift, contingent on a third party. This strategy avoids real movement, since the boarder is beyond Ron's control.
68. A signal to Ron that the mediator does not buy his vagueness about the boarder. A global question. When he replies, I ask a general question and close with a specific question.
69. This series of questions, from global to specific, forces a more specific reply from Ron. The figure he gives is probably the lower level of what the boarder is actually paying.

MEDIATOR: So if you could get two hundred and fifty bucks a month, you could afford to pay a hundred bucks a month, right?[70] You'd be sharing on the food, and then the utilities would go up, but then that would give you some extra, and it would relieve some of the pressure on you, Mary, right?[71]

MARY: Uh huh.

MEDIATOR: Okay. How would you make that decision?[72]

RON: Like, pay?

MEDIATOR: Yeah.

RON: It would be more on a verbal basis, because right now I've got a court order, and I could say I'm grateful towards Mary that she really didn't get the court after me to be paying this money.[73] So I'm pretty grateful there that she really didn't get the courts to say we'll get this money. Right now, the situation is, even if I'm put in court, I can't afford to pay, so maybe I might have to go spend time putting into whatever the sentence might be there.[74]

MEDIATOR: Or they may just deduct it off your unemployment.[75]

RON: Yeah.

MEDIATOR: There are two ways. They don't like to send people to jail, but since they're giving you the money, they can just withhold that part of it and turn it over. You see, my sense is that neither of you really want to do that. The issue is what do you want to do so that you're in control, right?[76] You can sit and wait for someone to tell you what to do, or you can say, "I'm going to make some decisions here" and have control of that situation. I was wondering what you wanted to do so you're in control of the situation.

RON: Well, right now, at least, it's not that I'm sitting around and just trying to enjoy the few dollars I'm getting from unemployment.[77] I've been looking at the paper. I've got a few good applications out, and I'd really like to get back into work. If I get back into work, whatever the salary might be coming from there, and I think things will really fall back into perspective.[78]

MEDIATOR: So, let's sort these into two steps: First, there is the question of how much you get from the boarder.[79] If we can get some agreement around that, we can make the second discussion around what the level of support would be if you have a certain income.

RON: Maybe, John, I should mention this to you. The house is subsidized by the government, and if there is any income pertaining to the house, then the subsidy might be taken off, and that would be an increase of $194.00 there.[80, 81]

MEDIATOR: All right.

RON: So that would—let's say if I declare somehow, that it's known, I have a boarder there . . .

MEDIATOR: Well, that's one of the reasons you don't want to have to go back to court, because obviously[82] you don't want everybody prying into every aspect of your life. But on the other hand, if you're not going to do that, then you've got to have some reasonable agreement between the two of you so that you both share the benefit of that boarder. It seems to me that you either work it out so you both share in it or you don't. Then neither of you share in it.[83] That's really the issue. And so the issue is how do you share it.[84] It would strike me that what we ought to deal with right now is how to share in the income produced by the boarder.

70. On the basis of their bargaining behavior, I unilaterally raise Mary's position to one hundred dollars, to balance the negotiations.
71. I use the extra money to help Ron take charge of getting the money, as part of an effort to raise his self-esteem and limit her need to rescue.
72. Having suggested a figure of one hundred dollars, I ask them how they would do it, leaving the implementation to them.
73. Ron avoids making any concrete commitment.
74. He threatens Mary, knowing that she will rescue him, and thus protects his bargaining position.
75. I intervene before Mary responds, so as to disarm the threat.
76. The issue of control is one Ron is struggling with in the rehabilitation program.
77. Ron opens defensively and . . .
78. . . . moves into a vague future.
79. This division of the issues (a form of partializing) returns

the focus to the boarder income, which is current and available.

80. Ron tries another threat: that he can't afford to pay any support. This is designed to protect his bargaining position.
81. BL: At the conclusion of this statement, he breaks out in a broad victory smile.
82. I counter Ron's threat with the dangers of the alternative arena.
83. This defines the issue as mutual.
84. I return to the issue of the boarder income and define the problem they need to solve.

MARY: Possibly this fellow could purchase the food or pay the utilities, rather than board and room, as such . . . [85]

MEDIATOR: But that doesn't get you money. You want some money.[86]

MARY: What I mean—and then it would allow Ron to share with us. It's just the idea that he's residing there.

MEDIATOR: Okay. [to Ron] You could work out with the guy however you want to work it out, so that it is on or off the books.[87] The issue then is making the commitment to pay the support to Mary and Lee Anne while you're looking for the job, 'cause obviously right now jobs ain't sitting there waiting to be picked off the trees, right? We're all in trouble, and you're no different from anybody else in terms of looking for jobs.[88] If we sit and wait for the jobs, we may wait for a year, and it may not come right there. So, really, we have to focus on that money right now. I'm wondering if, as part of the agreement this afternoon, we could have an agreement that you would be paying Mary one hundred dollars a month and then figure out how to get it from the boarder.[89]

RON: Yeah, because, like, I personally have no quarrels or anything. If I could get a job, I could pay her the two hundred. I'm willing, but the situation is . . . [90]

MEDIATOR: Let's look at that next, Ron, because you're in

the program, you're working hard at that. Jobs are difficult to get, and if we wait until that comes through, we may be waiting for months. By the time that time runs out, you're going to run out of money and [to Mary] you're going to have to take some action, right? So what we really want to do is set it up now around what we're going to do now. I suppose what I really have to ask you is: Are you willing, and can you work out an agreement, so that you could pay, as of now, one hundred dollars a month to Mary for Lee Anne and then get that money from your boarder, in a way that protects your other interests?[91]

RON: Well, maybe I could say that right now, that it could be possible. But let's say the boarder decided he's not going to board at my place. What would be the situation then?[92]

MEDIATOR: So, let's take that in two steps.[93] Let's take step number one. If you can get it from him, then it's one hundred. Right? If he's not your boarder, then you can't get money; you can't get blood out of a stone.[94] If he's not your boarder, then there's no money, but if he's your boarder, and—[to Mary] obviously, you'll know about it, apparently because you know now about the boarder.[95] [to Ron] As long as there's the boarder there, your responsibility is to get money from the boarder, right? Because you're not running a welfare scheme, right? So that the boarder has got to pay you, you have got to then turn over one hundred of that to Lee Anne, to Mary for Lee Anne, right? So that would be step number one.

RON: Okay.

85. Mary problem-solves for Ron to rescue him.
86. A focus on her self-interest is a way to help her desist.
87. This reframing makes the payment Ron's responsibility.
88. This reality statement is empathetic and limits Ron's pie-in-the-sky plans. It is done in a normalizing way: "You're no different."
89. A restatement, making it Ron's problem how to pay it. In doing so, the mediator maintains control of the problem definition.

90. Ron diverts the discussion to his future job, rather than discuss the boarder income.
91. This brings Ron back to the boarder money and his responsibility for figuring out how, and it reminds him of his WATNA while leaving him in control of the implementation.
92. Ron moves slightly and then raises the issue of third-party control, to limit his concession—that is, whether he can pay will be determined by the boarder, not by Ron.
93. A partialization of the issues raised by Ron puts it all into perspective and makes them easier to resolve.
94. While this might appear to be giving Ron a way out, I also have in mind Mary's comments about the autos.
95. This points out to Mary her ability to control this item. The monologue ignores the possibility that the boarder will not materialize and pay.

MEDIATOR: Okay, so step number one is that. Step number two then comes. If you are in an earning capacity, you would obviously be expected then to fully honor the two hundred.[96]

RON: Yes.

MEDIATOR: So that would be step number two. Step number three might be to say to you, "At what point would it be reasonable to think about whether or not one should pay more than two hundred?"[97] I don't want to deal with that today, because I think that is something you might want to deal with a little later; but, clearly, the two hundred was set on a situation that existed a year and a half ago.

RON: Yes, on my income then.

MEDIATOR: If you get a nice job, you may want to share a little bit of that with Lee Anne, right?[98]

RON: But I personally—like, let's say if I get into a job in the field that I would like to get into, and I'm making that money, I definitely would. You know, it's my obligation that I should really take care of a certain part of their financial . . .

MEDIATOR: So let's put that on the shelf for a moment, until we get closer to that reality. Focus now on this part of the agreement–that is, that you will pay to Mary, for Lee Anne, one hundred a month, and you'll get that from your boarder.[99]

RON: Okay.

MEDIATOR: Okay, now, how will you do that? I mean, how will you transfer that money, what's . . . [100]

MARY: He can pay it in checks, if he wants to keep it as a record. That's fine.[101]

MEDIATOR: Okay. Would it be on the first of the month, or the first and the fifteenth?

MARY: Either the first, or if it has to be the first and the fifteenth, but on a regular basis.[102]

MEDIATOR: Perhaps it might make sense to make it on the fifth of the month, because [to Ron] you'd probably collect the rent on the first of the month, right? Then you need a couple of days to get it across.[103] So if you said on the fifth of each month, that money would come across. Does that make sense to both of you?

RON: It does.

MARY: Yes. I just wanted to say that if this boarder isn't going to stay, as such, what about alternatives, like selling one of the cars?[104]

MEDIATOR: Okay. What we might say, in a sense, is that if he doesn't, then [to Ron] that's your problem to figure out how to get the money.[105] [to Mary] See, you ought not to get involved in how Ron gets the money. What you ought to be involved in is that you, as the mother of Lee Anne, get the money for Lee Anne.

MARY: I've heard a lot of promises, and I just like to see some action on it.

MEDIATOR: Okay. Let's turn the coin[106] around the other side. What if there is no action? What are the penalty clauses?

MARY: Well, it has been hard to almost maintain a rooming house the way I have. Like he comes to see Lee Anne and me, but it's always on my provision. I'll have a meal there, or I'll have the ingredients to make a meal. You know, it just seems I'm still supporting him in a lot of ways.

MEDIATOR: You don't charge him for the meals?[107, 108]

96. A future projection to put Ron in a regular job and enable him to pay the two hundred dollars. This future-orientation move is also designed to limit Ron's fantasies.
97. Continuing this strategy puts Ron in a high-paying job, but the mediator freezes it, to strengthen limits.
98. A language shift from spouse to father emphasizes that he is sharing with his daughter, not with his wife.
99. This brings Ron back to the current reality and the real issue.
100. I now begin to tie down the details.
101. Mary rescues Ron from having to make the decision.
102. She maintains the initiative by answering first.
103. I take the decision from Mary, in the hope that it will be more acceptable to Ron, as well as to move to a realistic date. This also places the responsibility back with Ron.
104. Mary picks up the loophole in 94 and reasserts her control through the issue of the autos.
105. A redefinition to a "how" issue, which is the responsibility of Ron.
106. This is an attempt to find some self-interest components to make the plan work. This also limits Mary's rescuing behavior.
107. A gentle confrontation of her rescuing.
108. BL: Ron smiles broadly.

MARY: No. Like, I don't feel I owe him anything, and it's just another bone in the pot to make soup, or whatever. But, still, it's just the idea that I'm not getting the maintenance for my daughter, and yet I'm even allowing him to have a share in what we do have.[109] You can't pull at me from every side, you know, and I don't really like that.

MEDIATOR: It doesn't sound too smart to me.

MARY: No, I don't get it all. When it comes to going with Lee Anne, he needs five dollars for this or something like that. I'm not the banker, or whatever. I really feel that there's got to be some responsibility taken in a financial way.[110]

MEDIATOR: By whom?

MARY: Ron himself. For himself, and as the father of his little girl.

MEDIATOR: But why should he worry if he can come over and get a meal at your house?[111]

MARY: There's one word: N-O. It's very hard to say at times, and I know it's a bad habit of mine, and giving in. I just have to learn to stand up . . . [112]

MEDIATOR: There's nothing wrong with that, is there?

MARY: I know. (laughing)

RON: Well, if that's the way, I'd be nice enough to say I wouldn't have a meal there. But then if the dryer or something needs fixing, then I could charge service rates to compensate for things like that.[113]

MEDIATOR: Yeah, you can work out a financial arrangement like that between the two of you.[114]

RON: Yeah, because right now, the dryer went on the blink, and I went and fixed it. You know, there's little things that you know, seems that . . .

MEDIATOR: It saves your support from going up.

RON: Yes. Everything here seems to be focused on money, to a certain extent. I suppose—but then, okay, providing a meal for somebody and having charges put to that, I think that's . . .

MEDIATOR: Well I'm really joking, because you two know.[115] You've been in the alcoholism program, and you know how, we all know how, in order to get to that situation, you have to have some support from the other members of the family.[116] [to

Mary] You know what role you play in supporting that in the past, and you can see what role you play in a sense of supporting certain things now that you're uncomfortable with. So that, in one sense, you can control that piece. [to Ron] Just as you can control the piece in regard to the boarder and how you get the money.[117] [to Mary] You can control the piece in terms of how comfortable you are, and that you're not spending money, right? I mean, it really is your piece. It's hard.

MARY: It's hard.

MEDIATOR: It sure is. It sure is; it's very hard.

MARY: Like, he's still making use of a lot of my things over there.[118] Things I even had prior to the marriage and everything. It's not as if we have divided the assets.

MEDIATOR: So would you like to do that? Would you like to think about[119] dividing those things? I mean, not this afternoon . . .

109. Mary raises the issue of fairness.
110. She is slowly gaining confidence and moves away from the rescuer mode.
111. I encourage this by helping her see the effects of her rescuing.
112. BL: Mary laughs.
113. Ron launches a counterattack.
114. Ron is disarmed by having his position dignified.
115. An explanation of what is happening for the couple, and . . .
116. . . . identification of her rescuing.
117. Return to the control issue for Ron.
118. Mary raises a new issue.
119. Checking her complaint by asking her what she wants.

MARY: I don't have the accommodation for it right now, like a place to put it and that.[120] But it's the idea he does have the majority of the stuff over there.

MEDIATOR: [to Mary] So you're not so helpless, right?[121]

MARY: No. Well, I've come a long way. I feel that I've done very well in the last year and a half.

MEDIATOR: So now I'm going to push you to do a little better, push you to do a little better, right?[122] Because, obviously, part of it is that you should be able to control your own life, right? [to Ron] And you should be able to control your own life. In marriages, sometimes we get into doing a lot for each other in different ways, and you wind up resenting it, 'cause you feel controlled. You don't like the situation any more than anyone else does, and so we then get angry with each other as spouses, and then it spills over.[123] So it seems to me that it's really time now for you to say, "Okay, I'm going to pick up on this deal.[124] I'm going to pay this hundred bucks a month. I'll worry about where I get it." [to Mary] For you, to stay out of how you get it—[to Ron] whether you sell the car, rent the house, whether you sell Avon door to door: It's all your decision, right?[125] Your decision is just to be there and receive the support, because what we're talking about here is Lee Anne, isn't it? That's who we're talking about, we're talking about her having a good shake at life, right?[126]

MARY: True.

MEDIATOR: And so that's all that you have to worry about, and then [to Mary] you're going to have to focus on how you're going to control your piece of the action. So you don't feel that you have to do everything all the time, because you really want to get on with some independent lives. [to Ron] And as a matter of fact, your best hope of staying out of the relapse situation is indeed [to Mary] if you *don't* take responsibility for it.

MARY: Very much. I understand that I can't rescue forever.[127] I want to maintain a friendship, a positive relationship, but it's still a matter of standing up on our own two feet.

MEDIATOR: Absolutely.

RON: Yeah.[128]

MEDIATOR: And Lee Anne will be the real beneficiary of that, right?[129] Because if she comes out of it, she [to Ron] will get the best of you, [to Mary] she gets the best of you. And you're both feeling more comfortable, you're moving towards a position where [to Ron] you'll be able to take Lee Anne back home and introduce her and share with the family, and where [to Mary] you'll be more comfortable in that parenting, coparenting situation. But you each have a role to play in that regard; each have a role to play. You've got to both take new responsibilities, and you've got to discard some old responsibilities. [to Mary] You have got to take responsibility for you. [to Ron] You have got to take responsibility for you, and you have to discard some of the old stuff that goes on between you. In my sense about this discussion, the end is not whether you can pay; the question is whether you pay on the first or the fifth or on the fifteenth.[130] That, I think, is the issue. The issue is for your self-esteem. If you can do that, that will do as much for you as going on a ten-month self-esteem program, to know that you're kicking in your share, and you're taking care of your kid, and you're not being told how to do it.[131] You're making those decisions. Right?

120. Mary puts it into perspective.
121. This reinforces Mary's changes.
122. This tells them to anticipate movement and begins to define separateness for them.
123. Makes their experience universal.
124. The mediator establishes a nonspecific time deadline.
125. BL: The couple laugh.
126. BL: I circle my hands to catch the child and bring Lee Ann into the room.
127. Mary agrees, and . . .
128. . . . Ron agrees.
129. So I continue and . . .
130. . . . reclaim the problem statement.
131. Here, I pick up on Ron's earlier statement regarding the self-esteem course he wants to take.

RON: Yeah, plus what Mary was saying—like, taking things from the house there, you know, I told her that if ever it's a possibility that we get back together, it's fine.[132] If not, and she wants the house, or whatever in the house, she's welcome to come and have it, I'm not going to query . . .

MEDIATOR: Yes, we can deal with those in later sessions. At this particular junction, I would just really like to tie down the sense that you are going to break out of the past. [to Ron] You're going to take control of your responsibilities, and [to Mary] you're going to take control of your responsibilities and move ahead in that way. Then we can deal later on with a lot of the other items to facilitate that. To help you do that and build on it more, because [to Ron] if you want something good for your self-esteem and your comfort, if you can get between you and say, "I'm paying for my kid"—boom! Right? [to Mary] And you can say, "I'm putting in my share for my kid"—boom! You begin to get free and clear of each other. You don't need to tell how to do it, right, because that's the issue: to free up, free up.

MARY: As far as activities go with the little girl, I would feel a lot better if I know he would be doing what I would call constructive things.[133] Like, sometimes he'll go over to the house and just sleep and something, and I feel awkward about it. I really feel that he would enjoy it, and so would baby. She would benefit.

MEDIATOR: What I'd like to suggest, if I could, is that at some stage, Ron, you and Kent could talk about some parenting stuff.[134, 135] What kinds of things you can do about that, man to man. Okay. [to Mary] Because those are issues, again, for Ron. I know they concern you, because you're both good parents, and you are both concerned about Lee Anne in different ways. But how to do that might be better done on a one-to-one basis. [to Mary] See, then it doesn't become your responsibility; it really is Ron's responsibility. If you could stay out of it, in a sense, and [to Ron] perhaps you have a one-to-one discussion with Kent on different things you can do. A couple of neat little books that you can read on that, because it's not easy, particularly for a four-year-old, to know exactly what to do and how to do it. It sure would be more fun if there were things you could do together that you both enjoyed and got a kick out of. I'm sure you do some of them now. I think Kent could help you, in the long run, work that through. [to Mary] Okay. So the sense is that the more you can let go, the more power you have.

MARY: Yeah. If I let go of the worry and concern, I'll feel better in a lot of ways. Yeah.

MEDIATOR: [to Ron] And the more responsibility you take, the more self-esteem you have, and the more power you have. You really both have a lot of possibilities for personal growth and satisfaction. I think you have a good chance of putting it all back together again.[136] You may not. It may not be right for you, may never be right, but at least you'll do it on a basis that's good for both of you. So, let's see now: What day of the month are you going to get the check?[137]

132. Ron confirms that he would like to get back together.
133. Mary enlarges the conflict as agreement appears near. This could be fear of reaching an agreement, or it could be a desire to settle all the issues, now that the support payments have been agreed to. In either case, it is too late in the session to take up new items.
134. The issue is put on the back burner for a later session, so as not to undermine the agreements reached so far.
135. Kent is the regular mediator to whom I was the consultant.
136. This indicates that I understand their superordinate goal of reconciliation, and I suggest it is possible to achieve.
137. A return to the specific implementation issue.

RON: I'll say maybe—okay, I would prefer to leave it till about the fifteenth, because the first of the month is the mortgage payment. I've got to get the mortgage payment in before they start to get pretty nasty. So I would say it would be more safe to be around the fifteenth.

MEDIATOR: That means—what's today, August twelfth? Thursday?[138]

RON: No, I wouldn't be able to, because I really haven't got anything from the guy yet.[139] I have to speak to the guy, and so forth; so most likely this would be like a September arrangement.

MEDIATOR: That's a whole month, right? Is that fair?[140]

RON: I don't know. Is it?

MEDIATOR: She's your kid. She's not mine.

RON: 'Cause I've got to speak to the guy and see if it's possible, 'cause this way, like, it's no problem. I could even go the other way, too, that at least give her the two hundred dollars and don't pay towards the house.[141] That could be another possibility.

MARY: Then sell the house, then.[142]

MEDIATOR: That reopens it all. [to Ron] At this juncture, you're living in the house, and you're going to have to take care of it, so that the issue is the hundred bucks.[143] Don't put yourself deeper into the hole; you're going to have a hard enough time getting the hundred bucks at this juncture. It's probably another issue between you, but don't go further in the hole. What you've got to come up with is the hundred bucks, not two hundred bucks. In a sense, then, what you might think is . . . let me make a suggestion as a way of hurdling this one.[144] Is that you come up with fifty bucks on the first of September and fifty bucks on the fifteenth of September and then come up with a hundred bucks on the fifteenth thereafter. How you get it is your problem, your responsibility, and you'll do it, you'll do it.[145] You've got a lot of resources. Problems, yeah, but you've also got a lot of resources. You know how to do that, put it together. So you come up with fifty bucks on the first and fifty bucks on the fifteenth, and then running into October, come on to that. Move across on those hurdles. You can do it, I know you can do it. Mary will try and tell you you can't do it, see.[146] She's going to take you off the hook in the next two weeks, because she'll tell you, "You can't do it." You'll buy into that because it's easier to do it that way. I think you can do it, and I think you will do it, because I think you're on the right road to where you want to be, the kind of person you want to be a little bit down the pike. Mary may sabotage that a little bit, and that's all right.[147] [to Mary] You do that because you're a good person, not a bad person. You do that because of the good side of you, but you're going to have to get a handle on that. Because you're going to try to do that, you're going to try and let him off the hook, and [to Ron] it's up to you to make sure that she doesn't let you off the hook. Because that's the old pattern, that's the old crap that got you where you are today. That's not where you want to be.[148] I would suggest that we have a meeting next week with Kent and pick up on what we've been talking about today, to work through some of the other issues. Have a session thinking about the parenting and where you want to go in terms of that, and I think you've got a good future ahead of you. You've got a possibility now, and you can both grasp it—you can both grasp it. [to Ron] You can grasp your future, and [to Mary] you can grasp your future. You'll each have one hand to grasp your own future, and you're going to have another hand to try to take the ring away from the other one, because that's part of the old marriage. It's up to you not to try to take the ring away. To let each of you grasp that ring, to go forward for yourselves. You got it in you, you got it in you.[149] You came here, right? It wasn't easy. Because you want to do it, and you're going to do it. [to Ron] It's up to you to make sure that it isn't undermined.[150] Okay? So on the way out, then, talk to Kent, and set up a schedule for the next meeting. Good.

MARY: Certainly. Thanks.

MEDIATOR: Good. So we'll come to closure on that one.

RON: We surely appreciate it. Thanks a lot.

MEDIATOR: Tell you what—you got it, you got it.

138. This dumb question is designed to get Ron's backsliding into the open, without undermining the previous ten minutes' successes.

139. Ron holds to the third-party defense.
140. I try to hold Ron to his responsibilities.
141. Ron makes another threat.
142. Mary aimlessly retaliates.
143. I deflect the threat and remind Ron of his real self-interest.
144. This "bridging" suggestion is a face-saver for Ron.
145. Ron nods agreement along with my monologue.
146. This paradoxical comment is designed to strengthen their ability not to fall back into old patterns of behavior.
147. BL: Mary shakes her head "no."
148. BL: Mary nods affirmatively.
149. I close on an upbeat note . . .
150. . . . giving Ron the power and the responsibility for making it work.

Analysis

The Mediator's Assumptions

Situational Mediation. The role of the mediator is situational. She deals with different couples differently. When working with Michael and Debbie, I used strategies appropriate to a powerful and competitive couple. I sharply limited their fighting by keeping them focused on the presenting issue of access. I frequently interjected questions, to cut off burgeoning battles. I used process interruption to break their patterns of behavior. I used a direct and, at times, confrontational approach with Michael and Debbie.

Working with Ron and Mary called for a different approach. I believed they were a fragile couple with low self-esteem. Ron was a recovering alcoholic and unemployed. Mary was working at a low-paying job, struggling to make ends meet. Therefore, I changed my behavior from that seen in Chapter Four, to use strategies more appropriate to a fragile couple. I was much more gentle with Ron and Mary. I did not use sharp interjections. I avoided process interruptions. Instead, I carefully explained whatever I was doing, taking responsibility for any misunderstandings in the session. I did not want to lower their self-esteem, and I did not want them to fight about the reasons for any misunderstanding.

For example, at 14 I said, "Forgive me . . . I don't quite understand." This introduced a statement challenging Mary: "What does Ron have to prove?" Although challenging, this statement was not confrontational. She could answer nondefensively, because she was helping me understand, not defending her earlier statement.

When I wanted to alert the couple that I would ask many questions, without necessarily following them up, I again apologized while explaining how I would work with them. I explained the process, so as not to intimidate them. Before confronting Ron about why he had not paid the court-ordered child support, I told him, "I have to ask funny questions sometimes." (47) This took the edge off the question and made it less adversarial.

In this chapter we see a more gentle, patient mediator who is willing to spend more time on the relational issues and who deals carefully with the behavior when it blocks the negotiations. In this session, fewer directed/closed questions were used. While the directed form of question was used, particularly to engage Ron in the process, most of the questions were either focused or open, giving this couple more opportunity to respond beyond their specific answers. They needed this space in order to be comfortable. Unlike Michael and Debbie, Ron and Mary were unlikely to expand their answers unless given permission to do so.

Working with Ron and Mary was a real challenge. Three major themes ran through the first session. The first was the messages they sent to the mediator (and to each other) about getting back together. The second was Ron's alcoholism and Mary's role in his disease. The third was their negotiating behavior, which paralleled their alcoholism-related behavior.

Finding "That of God" in the Clients. It would be easy to dislike Ron for his alcoholism, for his cheating the government on the housing subsidy, and for his reluctance to work for a living as long as he could draw unemployment compensation.

It would also be easy to be sorry for Mary and at times annoyed by her rescuing and punishing behavior.

I was able to stay nonjudgmental on the behavioral issues by seeking and focusing on the couple's goodness. I sought and found a level of responsibility in Ron, from which he began to meet his child-support obligations. I avoided being judgmental about his value system by ignoring our clash of values and building on his essential goodness. Mary was helped to internalize my observations about her rescuing when I pointed out that her tendency to sabotage the deal would come from her good side, not from her bad side. (147)

Crossing from Process to Content Control. During my pursuit of the strategy of empowering Ron to be responsible for his own decisions, I crossed the line from process manager to content manager. As the negotiations proceeded, Mary said she wanted payment of some of the child support, suggesting seventy-five dollars a month. (60) I unilaterally changed this figure to one hundred dollars and proceeded with the negotiations management on that basis. (70) Arbitrarily moving the figure from seventy-five to one hundred dollars was an invasion of content by the mediator.

I carefully observed the impact of this strategy. Had Ron balked at the higher figure, I would have retreated from it quickly. He seemed comfortable with the one hundred dollars, however, so I stayed with it.

Content was almost invaded again when I tried to prevent Mary from rescuing Ron. His strategy was to threaten Mary with a dire consequence, such as losing the house. (80) Mary's normal reaction would be to back off from her demand to save the house or to turn her attention to figuring out how not to lose the house. In either case, she would become distracted from her goal. I intervened to prevent Ron's use of this strategy. (82) I accomplished this not by directly negotiating with him, but by testing reality, to demonstrate that the dire consequence he suggested (losing the house) was not in his best interests, either—a point he could not argue with. Upon hearing that, Mary did not need to respond to his threat by rushing to the rescue.

Thus, intervention in their negotiations was limited, to the extent that Ron was prevented from using his threatening tactics. As I disarmed his threats, I could then pass the ball over to Mary, and she could negotiate in her own best interests. There is a fine line between entering negotiations to prevent a person from using a dysfunctional strategy and engaging in negotiations on behalf of one of the parties. I believe I stayed just on the right side of that line.

The Mediator's Strategies

Breaking Old Marital Patterns. Every couple comes to mediation with a pattern of interaction. Many of these patterns are dysfunctional in the marriage and even more so in the divorce negotiations. Each party feels that what has happened is unfair and blames the other (or, at times, they blame themselves) for the divorce. The solutions that couples attempt to apply to their problems are limited by the terms the partners have developed to explain the divorce. These solutions usually perpetuate the problem.

Ron and Mary demonstrate a classic example of this pattern. Their interaction was a cycle of rescuing, blaming, irresponsibility, and punishment. Mary blamed and rescued. Ron ignored his responsibilities and blamed something beyond his control as preventing him from being responsible. Mary then got angry and punished Ron, fueling his resentment and thereby justifying his continued irresponsibility.

The mediator had to help this couple break this pattern of interaction, to lay the basis for Ron to accept his responsibilities and for Mary to stay clear of the blaming-rescuing-punishing cycle. I accomplished this by asking them to speak for themselves, not for each other. (24) It is more difficult to stay in the past when speaking for oneself, and it is too easy to fall into the past when complaining about or speaking for the other.

I also intervened in the negotiations when the husband used events beyond his control to avoid facing up to his responsibilities. Twice Ron avoided making a commitment to pay child support by saying that his source of funds, the boarder, might not stay. The first time, Ron said, "So I have to really get the decision from him what he plans on doing." (67) I responded, "I suppose he has to live somewhere," adding, "And I suppose he has to pay somewhere." (68) Having established this reality, I then transformed the question from whether the boarder would pay to what a boarder might reasonably be expected to pay.

The second time he tried this strategy, at 92, I partialized the problem. Partializing is a process of breaking a problem or a position into its component parts and dealing with each part separately. Therefore, Ron's position was broken into two parts: how he would pay the support if the boarder stayed, and how he would pay it if the boarder did not stay.

Thus, the problem was redefined as one for the husband to solve. If I had allowed Mary to respond, she surely would have rescued him or become caught up in ways to solve his problem. Ron would have resented this, and the old fights would have emerged. Nevertheless, I had to be careful not to become too involved in problem solving with Ron. If I had, I would have become a surrogate for Mary. I would have been sucked into their dynamics, receiving the same response that Ron normally gave to her.

Ron had another strategy, which worked well for him. Whenever he felt cornered in the negotiations, he threatened Mary with some dire consequence. At one point, he said that they might lose the government subsidy on the house if it were known that he had a boarder. (80) I joined him on this issue. Joining is a strategy that allows the mediator to defuse a threat or challenge a position taken by one client, without engaging in an argument with that person. The mediator accepts the client's position—no matter how outrageous—and helps the client explain it, thus showing how outrageous it is. The mediator may also accept the client's position, acknowledge the validity of the threat, and point out that the threat is equally threatening to the threatener, thus disarming the threat (Haynes, 1988).

In this case, I joined Ron by reminding him of his WATNA: "That's one of the reasons you don't want to have to go back to court, because obviously you don't want everybody prying into every aspect of your life." (82) I redirected the threat from Mary and back toward Ron, demonstrating to Mary that it was not a real threat and eliminating her need to respond to it.

Mary could also get off task easily, by becoming caught up in problem solving for Ron or by punishing him. When Ron balked at paying the support, Mary thought of other ways he could pay her, while at the same time she punished him. For example, she wanted him to sell the cars to pay her. (104) This got Ron off the hook, in the sense that he did not have to think about a permanent arrangement (they would be back in the same boat, however, as soon as the sale proceeds were exhausted). It also punished him by taking something away from him, and it left the decision up to Mary.

I moved to prevent this solution by defining the problem of how the money was raised as Ron's task. (105) Mary's role was redefined as simply making sure that she got the money. The mediator's strategy was to prevent Mary from responding to the threats by dismissing them in a context of reality or by pointing out that they were equally threatening to Ron. At the same time, the problem was placed back into Ron's lap for solution, and he was thus empowered in the relationship.

To get movement on the issue of child support, my task was to control this dysfunctional behavior and place responsibility for solving problems on Ron. I would have preferred to shift it from Mary to both of them, but my assessment was that the old patterns ran so deep that only a shift from Mary to Ron would have any chance of success. Ideally, the couple should engage in joint problem solving; but, if they had shared the responsibility for problem solving at this stage, Ron would quickly have found a way to engage Mary in solving his problems on his terms. Therefore, the solution would be to his benefit.

Ron's negotiating behavior was shaped in part by his alcoholism and by the family dynamics. He created problems and waited for Mary to solve them. As soon as he defined a problem, she tried to solve it. Since he defined problems in such a way that they could only be solved to his benefit, Mary was always hurt by the solutions she developed.

My work in the first session was to help her understand how she did this and suggest how she could avoid rescuing Ron in the future. I did this in an empowering way, helping both spouses take responsibility over their own lives. I added the option of their being in control of their own lives, in preference to the negative aspect of the control they each felt the other exerted.

When Couples Are Unclear About the Divorce. Ron and Mary gave a number of signals that they wanted to get back together. Mary offered various covert and overt messages, such as "I do feel some time is necessary to allow him to carry on with it before I feel I could really have trust that it wouldn't be a relapse." (11) These messages suggested the hypothesis that they could get back together after time had passed. Later, Mary said, "At the present time I can't see us as a unit," (22) suggesting that at some time in the future things might be different. During the first ten minutes of the session, she frequently said "us" and "our," indicating that she was still thinking in "we" terms after twenty months of separation.

Any one of these statements, taken individually, would not be important, but the series of comments, all building on one another, alerted me to her covert desire. Ron's messages were clearer and consistent. At one point, he stated, "If Mary don't want to come along or anything," (20) indicating that he was still thinking about joint (marital) activities with Lee Anne. Later, his comment "I told her that if ever it's a possibility that we get back together, its fine" (132) was a clear indication of his goal.

By uncovering the issue explicitly (21), I was able to check out the hypothesis. If I had been picking up the wrong cues, the couple would have corrected me. This is a good example of the importance of the mediator's checking the hypothesis. The mediator does not act on a single comment. She listens for a series of comments and checks to see whether the view is shared. If only one party talks of reconciliation while the other rejects those suggestions, the mediator points out this difference. In this session, I suggested that the reconciliation issues would be best worked on with a therapist. If both parties agree and support each other's comments about reconciliation, then, once it is clear that the desire is mutual and real (it is repeated) and shared (it is accepted by the other on those occasions), the mediator can shape strategies to match the couple's goal.

Forming and Testing Hypotheses. In the first session, I was guided by two working hypotheses. The first was that Ron and Mary wanted to get back together at some point. This hypothesis was developed as a result of the way the couple answered the initial information-gathering questions. The second hypothesis was based on my professional knowledge of the dynamics of alcoholic families: The nonalcoholic spouse is often a rescuer.

The first indicator of the desire to reconcile came at 6: "It's one of sharing responsibility." I tested this further, to clarify that the money was the only significant issue. (10) Mary's response (11) revealed Ron's alcoholism. She bolstered the hypothesis at 13, "and in our relationship." Her use of joint language, such as "our" (15), unusual in couples who have lived apart for almost two years, was another indicator. I continued to test the hypothesis (16) by an embedded-suggestion question. Ron added his confirmation (20), noting that he would like to take Lee Anne on holiday even "if Mary don't want to come along or anything." This statement led me to make the hypothesis explicit, to give the couple an opportunity to confirm or reject it. (21)

With the hypothesis confirmed (22), I was able to act on it during the session—for example, by suggesting to Ron that if he wanted to get back together with Mary, he would have to be in a recovery program on a long-term basis. (34) Later, this hypothesis (that the couple would like to get back together) was expanded to include the idea that money was the major issue for Mary; solving the money issue would create a bridge to working on the marriage. (55) With this clarity of mission, it was easier for me to avoid crossing the line from mediation to therapy.

At the end of the session, Ron was very explicit about getting back together with Mary (132), which indicated that the work in the session had achieved the goal of structuring an agreement that enhanced the possibility of reconciliation.

The other working hypothesis that increased my efficiency

in this first session came from my professional knowledge of alcoholic families. I believed that Mary was a rescuer or enabler of Ron's alcoholism and acted under that hypothesis. My first use of it came at 34, when I told Ron what he would have to do in order to get back together with Mary.

I used it again later, when Mary set a figure of seventy-five dollars for child support. (60) I believed that she had set the figure this low partly as a response to Ron's opening low position of nothing, and partly out of her enabling behavior. Thus, by raising the figure to one hundred dollars (70), I not only reduced her enabling but also gave Ron a figure that Mary did not control. My professional training tells me that those who are enabled or rescued usually resent the rescuers. I felt that raising the figure would meet with a positive response from Ron, since it was a figure that Mary had not set. In this instance, my use of the hypothesis paid off for the couple.

This concept was followed up at 87, 89, and 91, where Ron was empowered to take responsibility for some decisions. Mary had to be disempowered and not allowed to make decisions for Ron. I repeatedly ignored her point about selling the autos, believing that if the idea were pursued, I would become identified with Mary's enabling. I stayed out of the family's "soup" by ignoring the demand. At the same time, the couple was empowered to allow each other to make decisions over discrete areas of responsibility.

Mary's tendency to make decisions for Ron popped up again (101 and 102) when she responded to a question directed to Ron. In turn, I identified this behavior at 107, by gently confronting her for providing Ron with "free" meals. This intervention paid off, because Mary then moved away from the rescuing mode at 110. I reinforced this movement at 111 by pointing out the effects of her rescuing. Mary responded with a further insight. (112)

I used this work at the close of the session to anchor the changes we had achieved earlier. I explained this behavior to them (115) and identified her rescuing (116), while keeping the control over Ron's behavior his responsibility. (117) Finally, I predicted that Mary might undermine the agreement through her rescuing. (146) She shook her head in a vigorous "no" to my comment, indicating that she was thinking about it and integrating it.

The couple controls the content of the agreement. They also control the decision about whether to stay separated or get back together. The mediator exercises control of the process in a way that honors this decision and enhances rather than inhibits it.

In this case, I actively managed the process to the extent of becoming involved in the content of the agreement, because the couple's behavior made it difficult for them to handle the content. Taking my cue from Ron and Mary, I crossed the line between process and content management in order to protect their future relationship.

Most of the first session was devoted to helping them negotiate a money settlement, while also helping them deal with their behavioral issues. The husband was empowered to make his own decisions and accept responsibility for paying support for his daughter. At the same time, the wife was empowered to ask for what was fair while avoiding her tendency to rescue Ron.

In a personal communication, Helena Cornelius, an Australian colleague at the Conflict Resolution Network in Sydney, has suggested that my work with couples is essentially *option design,* which is future-oriented. She points out there are times when such clients as Ron and Mary need a *clearing,* which she defines as a tidying up of past misunderstandings (what I describe as behavior). Helena Cornelius believes that the clearing stages of the mediation process require a mirroring technique, with instruction from the mediator on how to apply it. Mirroring is a combination of active listening and "I" statements in a structured process of communication. The latter part of the first session with Ron and Mary is a clearing time. Here, I suggested ways for them to deal with their dysfunctional behavior as they applied the financial agreement in the future.

The *clearing* was used to help the couple integrate the financial agreement with their future behavior, to increase the possibility of achieving their goal of reconciliation. The mediator accepts nonjudgmentally the clients' decision to separate or to reconcile. It is always nice to have a couple reconcile. Indeed, many of us would consider reconciliation a greater success than successfully negotiation of a separation agreement. It is equally important to accept the decision to separate, however.

Working with Drug- and Alcohol-Impaired Families. I frequently work with active and recovering alcoholics in my practice. The neutrality of the mediation arena has a special appeal to people caught up in a disease that is still viewed as a weakness by many professionals. The decision of whether to work with them is clear, provided that the ground rules are understood. I will not work with a couple if one of them attends a session under the influence of drugs or alcohol. If either party is impaired for that session, it is cancelled and rescheduled.

A generalized impairment does not rob people of the right to mediate their separation, however. A person who is addicted will not function effectively, even when he or she is not under the influence of the drug. That is true in whatever arena the couple chooses to negotiate a separation agreement. The sensitivity of mediators to such issues is important, and the process can be shaped to protect the addicted person from most self-destructive behavior.

The mediator must be careful when the issue of addiction is first raised. When one spouse alleges that the other has a "problem," the mediator cannot simply accept that definition of the problem and begin working with it. Acting on one spouse's problem definition—"He is an alcoholic"—is likely to offend the spouse who does not think he has a problem. He will reject any attempt to pin the "addict" label on him if he has not accepted his addiction. If the mediator uncritically accepts the wife's definition of the husband's problem, then the husband will reject the label and, along with it, the mediator and mediation.

When the allegation is first made, the mediator notes it, observes the other spouse's response, and waits for the allegation to be raised a second time. The mediator then checks it with the accused spouse, asking, "Is that your opinion?" The mediator cannot begin to act on the issue until both spouses agree that the label is more or less accurate. I will also act when the accused spouse exhibits behavior indicating that he does indeed have the problem his wife has mentioned. I identify the behavior and share it with the couple.

Ron's alcoholism is a family problem. Families often support the disease of alcoholism. Family dynamics play a role in how fast and how far into alcoholism the alcoholic will fall. The dynamics also help determine how long the alcoholic denies the problem. An alcoholic, well insulated by his family, will have a harder time pulling out of alcoholism than will someone whose alcoholism is confronted by his family and peers.

The mediator's process management must protect the recovery of the alcoholic. The way the agreements are reached, as well as the nature of the agreements, should enhance the chances and speed of recovery. The mediator must work in conjunction with whatever the staff in the client's recovery program is doing. I also like to see the recovering person in AA, since the success rate of people who recover with the aid of AA is significant. Ron was asked explicitly about AA. (30) When he said that he was not attending AA meetings, I asked an embedded-suggestion question about whether Ron was doing more than just working in the state alcohol recovery program. (31) I then linked the reconciliation to his recovery. (34)

In retrospect, it would have been helpful to the couple if I had spent a few minutes to see if Ron would agree to seek long-term help on his alcoholism and if Mary would agree to join Alanon to help with her enabling pattern. This way, both could get help. They would be on the same logical level, and Mary could move away from her implied power position of being the "savior." This also suggests the importance of the mediator's having a working knowledge of drug and alcohol dependency if she is to work with families that have these problems.

Displaying Ideas and Data. In this session, I used a flip chart to illustrate what I was doing. The flip chart visually reinforces what the mediator is doing verbally. At one point, while trying to establish a credible standard of fairness, I wrote Mary: \$1,050 X 2; Ron: \$800 X 1. I pointed out that if the court-ordered support were paid, the distribution would be \$1,250 for two people (Mary and Lee Anne) and \$600 for one person (Ron).

During this time, the couple's attention was riveted on the chart. They easily followed the reorganization of their data and the idea I was developing. Working on the chart has another value. In the give-and-take of information and ideas, it is easy for the mediator to misunderstand a specific piece of data. Writing the information on the chart displays it publicly, and if the mediator has made a mistake, one or both parties will correct it immediately.

Publicly sharing data is a power-balancing strategy. If one party withholds data from the other, the mediator shares it with the unaware party through the chart. If one party takes more time to absorb and understand information, putting it on the chart gives that person extra time to mull it over, understand it, and integrate it into his or her thinking.

I remained balanced during this flip-chart activity by not challenging Ron. The ideas of fairness were developed from the couple's information. I pointed out to Ron how the proposal under discussion (payment of the one hundred dollars) was in his best interests. While this was happening, Ron was kept focused on the task, and Mary was kept out of the conversation, so that she would not rescue him from his difficult spot.

Clients' Negotiating Behavior

Using Third Parties. Ron frequently used external third parties to control his behavior and limit his ability to meet his commitments. He argued that he could not pay the court-ordered child support because "I'm running on a monthly deficit. Because I've got to pay the mortgage." (48) Later, when discussing the other income he had that would enable him to pay the support, Ron said of his boarder, "So I have to really get the decision from him what he plans on doing." (67) Thus, payment of the support became contingent on a third party. When the mediator tried to get Ron to pay the support as a first priority and then take responsibility for finding the money, Ron defended himself by saying, "But let's say the boarder decided he's not going to board at my place. What would be the situation then?" (92)

Verbal Versus Written Agreements. Ron used the strategy of offering to agree verbally, but not in enforceable writing, in the first session. (73, 90) The mediator cannot allow the couple to make verbal agreements that one party is unwilling to commit to writing, since such an agreement would be unenforceable.

Using Threats. Ron frequently used threats to provoke Mary into rescuing him from a tight spot. He first suggested that if Mary forced the issue, "Even if I'm put in court, I can't afford to pay, so maybe I might have to go spend time putting into whatever the sentence might be there." (74) Later, he suggested that he would lose the government subsidy if he were forced to take a boarder to raise the money to pay Mary. Each time he used these threats, the mediator responded by pointing out the negative consequences to Ron, thus obviating the need for Mary to respond to them. In this case, the threats were not directed toward the other—that is, the threats, if carried out, would harm Ron, not Mary. Nevertheless, the marital interaction pattern would cause Mary to react to the threat just as if it were directed at her.

Conclusion

Mary is an inductive thinker, focusing on the details before constructing the big picture. In both sessions, I developed a big picture of the spouses' gaining economic independence from each other and changing their dynamics. Essentially, this involved getting Ron to take responsibility for his actions, while helping Mary not to rescue him. The focus was on looking at a macro change in their dynamics. Mary was looking at the micro issues that would show her that such a change was taking place. Thus, for example, she frequently sought to have Ron sell one or both of his cars. Each time she did this, I deflected her from that issue, wanting to gain agreement on the big picture. If I had acknowledged her need for action on the micro issue, the session might have been completed sooner.

I have already described how the mediator does not deal with behavior except when it interferes with the content of negotiations. Nevertheless, it is appropriate and useful to deal with behavior in order to protect an agreement on the issues. In this case, I spent time at the end of the session dealing with behavior, predicting what the couple could do, and giving them the courage not to repeat old patterns. I did all this to protect the content of the agreement they had reached. Thus, the time spent dealing with their behavior did not impede my work on the issues negotiation; it protected the outcomes of the earlier work on the child-support payments.

The session closed with an increasing number of monologues, which pointed out to them how Mary might be tempted to sabotage the agreement—not because she was "bad," but because she was too helpful. I was prepared to focus on their behaviors after I had helped them reach an agreement, since I believed that their behavior could undermine the agreement they had reached.

6

RON AND MARY: SEVERAL MONTHS LATER

I met with Ron and Mary for one hour in August and returned in November to meet with them a second time. The intervening months saw important developments. Mary suffered serious injuries in an auto accident and another period of unemployment. Ron moved in with her when she returned from the hospital, but the cohabitation did not work. It demonstrated to both of them that reconciliation was not feasible. Mary seemed clearer about not getting back together; Ron also accepted the idea. Ron had not found a job and, despite an agreement to look for work in other fields, he had not done so. Ron had paid the one hundred dollars support in two installments of fifty dollars in September and October. He had paid the first fifty dollars for November and was late on the second payment.

In the second session, I accepted their decision not to reconcile. This time, therefore, I managed the process to obtain a settlement on the finances, without trying to protect the future spousal relationship. I focused only on the continuing parenting relationship. In the second session, I paid very little attention to behavior and focused simply on how to get the child-support order enforced.

The intervening events, and Ron's and Mary's reactions to them, caused me to view my role in the second session differently from my role in the first. I received most of the new information before the session began from Kent, their regular mediator, who had met with them twice in the intervening three months. The new information changed my working hypothesis about their goals. Developments during the session also caused a further change in my working hypothesis.

One aspect of situational mediation is the way the mediator's behavior changes as the couple's goals change. As the parties' goals change, their negotiating behavior changes, and the mediator's behavior must change accordingly.

Ron and Mary had arrived for their first session apparently sharing the goal of reconciliation. I worked with them to structure an agreement that enhanced that possibility. Their negotiating behavior was consonant with their shared goal of reconciliation. They shared the same WATNA, that of staying out of the court—Ron, because of his alcoholism; Mary, because of the poor deal she had received the previous time.

The events between the first and second sessions caused a shift in their goal of reconciliation. Mary threw Ron out of the house after he attempted to reconcile with her. It became clear that her bargaining behavior was no longer shaped by the hope of getting back together with Ron.

Ron's bargaining behavior changed dramatically during the second session. At first, he adopted a defensive position against increasing the payments beyond one hundred dollars a month, but he appeared willing to negotiate. The language he used in the first part of the second session, regarding his ability to pay the full two hundred dollars, was similar to the language he had used in the first session. Given his compromise from his opening posture in the first session, I expected him to move above the one-hundred-dollar figure.

Even after Mary's rejection of the reconciliation possibility, Ron still seemed willing to negotiate about the money. After Mary's conflict expansion, however, Ron's position changed. His change appeared to be shaped by two considerations. The first was his negotiating response to Mary's toughening bargaining position. The second was the reinforcement of his new belief that he could get a better deal in court. He now believed that the court not only might forgive him the nonpayments but also would probably lower his current monthly payment of two hundred dollars. My behavior changed accordingly. This demonstrates that an alternative arena may appear more attractive if either party believes that the other arena is his or her best alternative to a negotiated agreement in mediation. I discuss this issue, as well as the shift in Ron's position, after the transcript.

Hypothesis development, testing, and confirmation are further demonstrated in the second session. Parallels with hypothesis development in the first session are discussed in detail and help explain the shift in the mediator's behavior between the first and second sessions. I also reinforce my earlier proposition about the situational nature of mediation.

The second session with Mary and Ron brought a significant shift in Mary's behavior as she assessed her interest in a future relationship with Ron. In the first session (see Chapter Five), she seemed anxious to preserve the spousal and parenting relationship. I worked with the parties to structure an agreement that improved the chances of their getting back together as spouses. Nevertheless, important events took place between the first and second sessions and caused her to reassess her desire to maintain the spousal relationship. This shift is clearly seen in her different negotiating behavior in the second session. Mary's change was matched by Ron's, and I also changed my behavior. I suggested a more appropriate arena in which to settle the dispute, even though I understood that the courts would do nothing to enhance the future relationship.

The assumptions demonstrated in this chapter are that mediation is situational (as seen in the shift in my own behavior after the first session with this couple). This chapter also demonstrates the assumption that maintenance of the ongoing relationship enhances the possibility of success. Mary's switch from the desire to reconcile and maintain a future spousal relationship was accompanied by a lower need to settle in mediation. This also demonstrates the idea that almost everyone wants to settle. Here, the couple decided to settle in another arena.

The mediation strategies found in this chapter include hypothesis development and use. The couple's bargaining behavior involves conflict expansion, the issue of equity versus equality, and changing WATNAs and BATNAs.

Transcript and Annotations

MEDIATOR: Well, it's good to see you both again, Ron and Mary. Let me tell you what Kent has told me since I saw you in August, and here we are in November. We ended our session on two notes. One was that you, Ron, were going to begin paying one hundred dollars a month to Mary and Lee Anne, and at that point you had just completed the certificate program and you were looking for—for what?[1]

RON: I wrote the exam on that day.

MEDIATOR: On that day. Now, that's where we left it, and [to Mary] you had agreed not to rescue, right?[2]

MARY: Yes.

MEDIATOR: All right. Kent tells me that in between, you had an awful auto accident and got hit?[3]

MARY: Two days later I was struck by a car and hospitalized. I'm still undergoing physiotherapy for it, but the prognosis isn't too good for both arms. One arm was crushed, they had to do surgery, and the other one doesn't have much strength in it. So I'm not sure what's going to happen there. I wasn't on disability benefits at the time, so I went back to work as soon as I could, out of necessity. But it has been a real blow to my system, and I'm still in shock and have a lot of emotional problems about it.

MEDIATOR: It certainly turned all your plans up on end, right?[4]

MARY: Yes.

MEDIATOR: Now, I understand that when it first happened, Ron, you moved back in to help out.

RON: I stayed around when Mary came out of the hospital until her mom came.

MEDIATOR: And how long was that?[5]

MARY: It was about a week or so. Ron offered to, I didn't invite as such, nor did I refuse. It was just that he offered to be around my place, and it wasn't my invitation. It wasn't as though I was planning it or looking forward to it.[6]

MEDIATOR: So it was something that you accepted, you didn't ask for?

RON: But I think it turned out more detrimental in the long run, with me offering assistance.[7] Because when we went to Kent, Mary showed a lot of hostility pertaining to me trying to assist in such a way, that she said that I did nothing at all and I just slept. It turned out to be not the way I expected it. I offered it from my own generosity and tried to assist by whatever possible means, and it turned out differently.

1. The opening reviews the information received from their regular mediator and helps to establish the current picture.
2. One of the behavioral assignments given to Mary is checked out with a directed/closed question.
3. I continue to check out the data, even though I respect the other mediator. Mediators take nothing for granted, preferring to check everything with the parties.
4. I empathize with Mary, without getting caught up in the drama of the accident.
5. Quantifying helps the mediator to be more specific.
6. This is the first indication that there has been a change in Mary's attitude toward Ron. She declines all responsibility for his actions. At this point, my hypothesis—based on Kent's information—is that Mary no longer wants to reconcile with Ron. Mary's answer tends to confirm this.
7. This is Ron's view of the situation; note that in 6 and 7, each viewpoint lays responsibility for the problem on the other party.

MEDIATOR: Sometimes things don't work out the way you think they're going to work out, but also, perhaps, it tells us something about getting back together. As I recall, it seemed when we met before that one of the possibilities seemed to be that at some point in the future you might get back together again. But it looks like it didn't work out that week, and you may not be looking at it in quite the same way?[8]

MARY: Well, one statement that bothered me was when he commented on Homemaker's Services being paid for. It really did bother me, because I wasn't intending on reimbursing him. I had hired a lady to come in—I was eligible for Homemaker's Services at a very low rate and she came in one day, and then he said "Well, when do *I* get paid?" It just bothered me.[9]

MEDIATOR: Was he serious?[10]

MARY: I took him as serious. It wasn't a joke when he said it. He didn't laugh when he said it.[11]

MEDIATOR: Because he's laughing now.[12]

RON: Well, I meant it as a joke, and it was just a matter of the opportune moment. She could have taken it seriously, but I didn't mean it seriously. Knowing that she was going to get this homemaker in, and she was going to the government, or whoever. So when am I going to get *my* salary?

MEDIATOR: So you spent a week there, and it didn't work out?[13]

RON: Well, the way she said that, you know, I don't know what she was expecting, but I tried to help out.

MARY: I wasn't expecting anything. All I can say is that he came, he offered, but I can't see that it was anything extra special or anything. I don't owe him.[14]

MEDIATOR: Let me just see, now—the other part of the agreement was in terms of the money. Kent said that when you met with him in September, you had paid the first part of September. What happened from there?[15]

RON: Well, so far, she has been getting the—like, I said I was going to get fifty at the first and fifty around the mid, and so far I have kept my promise. The only thing is so far that she hasn't got this month's fifty, the mid fifty for November.

MEDIATOR: So, since we met, you have been receiving one hundred a month until now; we're a little bit behind on the mid-November one.[16]

8. Normalize and check the hypothesis developed from the wife's answer at 6.
9. Mary's version reinforces my observation that she is distancing herself from Ron, which confirms my working hypothesis.
10. A check to see the depth of Mary's position.
11. Mary reiterates her view.
12. BL: The husband is smiling. In the first session, we learned that Ron frequently looked for money from Mary, and this may be a continuation of that old behavior.
13. A neutral statement, accepting each version without taking sides.
14. Mary continues to distance.
15. The neutral statement is followed with a question designed to check out the positive. I knew Ron had paid the agreed-upon amount, and I wanted him to claim credit for it. If he could report that he had kept the agreement, his self-esteem would rise.
16. The delay is placed in the context of his having paid according to the previous agreement.

MARY: But it hasn't been a hundred at the beginning of the month, it has been split fifty and fifty. On occasion, I have had to remind him.[17] But, I must say, that hundred was arranged before the accident, without taking into consideration what needs I might have then. That's why I really feel that we need to put attention on my ability to handle domestic life with Lee Anne, in view of what has happened to me physically and emotionally since then.[18]

MEDIATOR: So we've got one big step in a sense, because when you came to see me before, there was no money passing between you, right?[19] Now there's a hundred a month passing between you. The order says it should be two hundred a month. Now, the other thing, Ron, that Kent said was that you had discussed and had agreed that you would continue to look for a job in heating and ventilation through the end of October, and if nothing materialized, then you would take some other work. What's happened?[20]

RON: I didn't take another job, because when I worked out the take-home salary, I could get jobs paying up to six dollars an hour. If I take a job on a forty-hour basis at six dollars an hour, I, at the moment, would be taking home less than I'm receiving right now, after deductions, taxes, and everything.[21]

MEDIATOR: So that's two hundred and forty bucks a week?[22]

RON: That's before deductions.

MEDIATOR: And how much are deductions, approximately, from two hundred and forty dollars?

RON: I would say you're looking at maybe sixty dollars.

MEDIATOR: Is that your experience, Mary?[23]

MARY: I can't really say what they would be. All my comment is that when you do work on a temporary basis like that, with unemployment benefits, you are allowed to keep that first well, it varies according to salary; sometimes it's one-quarter or 25 percent of your benefits from the government. I know I worked that way a lot myself in the last couple of years, and it was an advantage for me to work. I would be getting my salary, as well as partial benefits from the government. Another thing is then, a year from now, I would have those worked weeks to fall back on, in case I needed the unemployment insurance benefits again. So you're building up your unemployment, you know. So, in my eyes, there isn't the disadvantage to working that he seems to think.[24]

MEDIATOR: [to Ron] So, carry on. Where are you now, in terms of looking at work?[25]

RON: Still looking.

MEDIATOR: Still looking—for . . . ?[26]

17. Mary redefines the problem, belittling Ron's actions regarding the one-hundred-dollar arrangement. (Remember that when she first stated a figure of support, it was only seventy-five dollars a month.) She also indicates that her changed situation has called for a new deal.
18. Mary warns the mediator. Always listen to these warnings, as they often signal or underscore significant changes in position.
19. A restatement of the positive, so as not to negate the gains of the previous session, while noting that the payment is still one hundred dollars short of the court order. Thus a balance is maintained between the couple's positions.
20. The search for data continues.
21. This was a hard argument to accept without comment.
22. I avoid commenting on it, but I question the math. (If deductions are 25 percent, that would be seven hundred and eighty dollars a month net, which is twenty dollars less than the unemployment compensation.)
23. Mary, who had been quiet for a time, is engaged by my asking her to comment and add data.
24. She provides additional data and uses the question to comment on the morality of her husband's position, pointing out that he could work and keep the money if he wanted to. At this point, she is back into the old marriage behavior of criticizing Ron, rather than solving her own problems.
25. I continue to question the husband about his activities . . .
26. . . . and work to make Ron more specific in his answers.

RON: Heating and ventilation and air conditioning.

MEDIATOR: At what point do you stop looking?[27]

RON: That's a good question.

MEDIATOR: Yes.

RON: Because I think I'd look at—maybe by next year.

MEDIATOR: How long does the unemployment benefit run?[28]

RON: My unemployment benefit will be until March of next year.

MEDIATOR: Until March of next year, and when that exhausts, how much time do you have to put in at work until you're eligible again?[29]

RON: I don't know. There's some new laws or something that came in here. It used to be something like twenty weeks before you're qualified, but they were talking about maybe trying to go fifty-two weeks. I'm not too sure of the figures. It would have been about twenty weeks before you requalify.

MEDIATOR: So you're still on unemployment compensation, which, if I remember rightly, was about eight hundred dollars a month? The other thing I understand is that your friend moved in as a lodger.[30]

RON: He didn't.

MEDIATOR: He didn't move in?

RON: No. That was in September he was planning on. He just stayed less than two weeks, and then he moved in with his cousin.[31]

MARY: Isn't he coming back?

RON: He's thinking about it, because his cousin is moving back to where he came from, so he's thinking about it that way.[32]

MEDIATOR: In a sense, then, we're in the same position as we were in August, except for the payment of one-half of the court order, right?[33]

RON: Yes, on Mary's part, but on my part it's different, really.

MEDIATOR: What's different?

RON: Because I was looking towards that extra two hundred, and they didn't show up. When we had the interview, I was looking at the two hundred, and I still somehow try and swing things to keep the promise of the hundred per month, fifty at the first and fifty around the middle.[34]

27. He could look forever, so a future-oriented question helps keep his focus on change. This is also based on information from Kent.
28. The future focus is maintained during data gathering, to move Ron to a point where he has no unemployment benefits, which is both future-oriented and a testing of reality.
29. Picking up on Mary's point, so as to preempt Ron's using a new benefit period to avoid looking for real work.
30. The boarder income is checked out, since it was not clear how much money the boarder had contributed.
31. I checked this in my mind against the earlier briefing by Kent. We had not discussed how long the boarder had stayed, and it was my impression that the boarder had been there most of the time.
32. Ron moves on the issue, indicating that the boarder is available as a source of income.
33. I am trying here to establish the status quo regarding the one hundred dollars, so as not to have to renegotiate the August agreement.
34. Ron states a commitment to the August agreement. Now I can avoid any discussion that might lead to renegotiating the basic one hundred and focus on the second hundred. Ron is also looking for approval for keeping his end of the bargain.

MARY: You must understand that I lost most of my earnings for August, because I got no benefits while I was off work. So that sure cut my situation up.

MEDIATOR: Mary, now that things have changed for you—unfortunately, for the worse, in terms of the accident—what is it you would like to see come out of these discussions, in terms of some settlement?[35]

MARY: I really feel that the issue of maintenance should be addressed, because there is a court order, and in fact it wasn't honored even prior to our first meeting with you.[36] For most of this last year, it hasn't been honored. So there is money owing,[37] and in light of what has happened to me and the state I'm in right now, I really feel I deserve compensation.[38] This matter of not being able to provide, I don't really accept, because this last year and a half, Lee Anne and I have found ways to survive. We were living on five hundred and forty dollars there for a while, but we had to find ways. We had second-hand clothes, week-old bread, whatever it is, green meat we were buying. I really don't feel we should have to continue like that.[39] It's not for her health at all.

MEDIATOR: Okay, so tell me what you want.[40]

MARY: Well, in matter of settlement, the court order is there. We have a facility now that allows the spouse to have this[41] enforced. I don't know if you saw the front page of the paper yesterday, but they're enforcing it to the extent that even a man was put in jail—was given a jail sentence for not paying.

MEDIATOR: [to Ron] They wouldn't need to do that, in your case. They could take it off the unemployment benefit, right?[42]

MARY: There are ways, or assets that he has. He has these two vehicles. My feeling is either supplement what he's earning or sacrifice something he owns.[43]

MEDIATOR: What do *you* want?[44]

MARY: I want monies owed to me.

MEDIATOR: Okay. One of the nice things I thought that came out of the last discussion was to get clear what it was that you each wanted, and then to leave each other alone about how to do it.[45] [to Mary] If you remember, you get the hundred bucks. How Ron got that was his problem, not yours. Yours was to receive the money. What I would really like to do today is to talk about what you think is right, and then see if we have an agreement around that.[46] Then you don't have to worry about how it comes, as long as it comes, right? [to Ron] And then, in that way, you don't have to worry about anything other than how to raise it, whatever you agreed to, okay? So I'm not clear, now—if I remember correctly, the order was for two hundred.

35. Having gathered the basic data, I begin to establish an agenda for the session by asking a future-oriented question about what Mary *does* want. I am beginning to act on my working hypothesis.
36. Mary demands payment of 100 percent of the court-ordered support . . .
37. . . . and indicates that she is raising the issue of the unpaid arrears.
38. She adds a new equity standard to her case, based on her new condition that has resulted from the auto accident.
39. Mary closes with a new "needs" case and a "best interests of the child" statement, increasing the equity of her claim.
40. The question asked at 35 is repeated, to confirm the hypothesis and determine whether the negotiations are to be about raising the one hundred to two hundred dollars only, or also about the back payments.
41. Mary indicates that she has been doing some homework and knows about the support-enforcement agency. This is a veiled threat to her husband. In this session, Mary is using Ron's strategy of threats, indicating a further change in her behavior, resulting from her changed goals.
42. Ron's counterthreat—that he could go to jail—is preempted by a reminder to him of other possibilities. This

way, Ron and Mary do not get into a fight about who is the tougher or the more "chicken" on the issue of jail.

43. Mary raises the issue of the automobiles. I ignored it in the first session, believing it to be part of their marital behavior, and continue to ignore it in this session.
44. Seeking a more specific demand from Mary (see questions 35 and 40).
45. I remind them of the understandings reached at the previous meeting, to underscore for Mary why I have ignored her demands regarding the cars and will continue to do so. I continue to feel that the auto issue is a way for Mary to punish Ron and therefore remain entangled, rather than meeting her own legitimate needs.
46. I try setting the agenda again.

MARY: Yes, it is, and there's a lot outstanding in that, and there's a debt that has come up through the government I heard about this week—the back income tax for two years ago.[47] Ron used to handle all our finances in the home, and when 1983 and 1984 went by, he was supposedly handling this income tax. In anger one time, he set it aside, and finally I was able to locate it all. When I went back, I took it to a lawyer—a volunteer—and they sent it in to the government. But now the government claims that I owe them almost a thousand bucks.

MEDIATOR: So now you're in the hole for approximately one thousand to Internal Revenue?

MARY: Yes, and I really feel that could have been prevented if the income tax had been done properly.[48]

MEDIATOR: So now the issues, then, are—because I'm trying to figure out exactly what the issues are—I'm going to ask you in a moment what your issues are, Ron.[49] [to Mary] But, at the moment, they are the full payment of the two hundred . . .[50]

MARY: Dating back to what is owed, yes.[51]

MEDIATOR: Okay, well, let me take it in three pieces: the full payment of the two hundred from now on, the repayment of the unpaid monies, and the Internal Revenue bill. Now, are there any other money issues?[52]

MARY: There are things in the home that I would like to get hold of. You know, I'm living out of cardboard boxes. I don't have enough furniture, and whatever. There have been promises to help me on that, and I would really hope he would carry through on that, because I need . . . [53]

MEDIATOR: Help me understand that, because my recollection was that when we talked about it in the last session, you said you didn't have space to take the stuff.

MARY: Well, I'm in new quarters, and there is space there, but right now I'm using cardboard where I could be using little bits of furniture.[54]

MEDIATOR: So you would like to be able to identify and take items of furniture from the family house.[55]

MARY: Yes, at least what I can make use of right now.

MEDIATOR: Okay, so then it's those four items?[56]

MARY: Yes.

MEDIATOR: Are there any more?[57]

47. Mary reiterates the point about the arrears and then expands the conflict by adding a new issue.
48. She does not say by whom, but implicitly blames Ron.
49. The issues are classified and listed according to priority, as I continue to attempt to set the agenda for the session and gain control of the problem statement.
50. Before the summary is finished . . .
51. . . . Mary restates the arrears issue, reinforcing her new toughness.
52. The issues are listed, as I understand them, and I check for agreement on the agenda.
53. Mary raises the furniture issue again. I remember it from the previous session. This is another example of the wife's enlarging the conflict.

54. Mary explains the changed circumstances.
55. A summary of the issue, honoring it and adding it to the agenda.
56. I clarify that all the issues are on the table and . . .
57. . . . double-check.

MARY: Well, I feel that he should make an effort on his employment, but now that's not for myself, that's for himself.[58]

MEDIATOR: That's right, Ron will make those decisions. So those are the four issues for you? Is that right?[59]

MARY: Yes.

MEDIATOR: Ron, what are the issues for you?[60]

RON: Well, right now, the biggest concern that I've got is trying to get employed again.[61] And right now I'm seriously thinking that I wouldn't like to change trades. I would like to stay in the heating and air-conditioning business and, in the last week, I've got five applications out.

MEDIATOR: I just want to try to clear my head, Ron. How you do these things is really for you. It is your piece.[62] What I would like to know is what you would like to negotiate today?

RON: I didn't come with anything specific. I just came open. I didn't even sit down and think about it, and I came and I'm just going to go with the flow.[63]

MEDIATOR: So, if that's the case, the first thing I propose to look at is the money owed to Internal Revenue, because Internal Revenue is not interested in your problems.[64]

RON: No.

MARY: No.

MEDIATOR: And I assume that Internal Revenue is not saying that it's all yours. It's a joint bill.[65]

MARY: No, it's in my name.

RON: No, it's her private . . .

MARY: We file separately, but I'm saying how that could have been prevented.[66] I feel that it could have been prevented if he had handled it back at the time it was due. By letting it slide, I left it in his hands, I trusted it to him, and then he put it aside and refused to do it in time. Finally, I went back in this last year, and I obtained all these materials and had them set up and sent in. But the point is, I was eligible for deductions in those days that I didn't know about. If I had been familiar with it, if he had set it up at the time, this thousand dollars wouldn't be owing.

MEDIATOR: So you need some expert advice on how to deal with that income-tax piece, right?[67]

MARY: I'm more familiar with it now. It was just that it was a matter of day care. I was teaching part-time, but I wasn't getting receipts from the neighbor who babysat, and I didn't realize at the time that I was eligible for this deduction.[68]

MEDIATOR: Can you go back and get that?[69]

58. Mary begins to respond by talking for Ron and corrects herself on the basis of the agreements of the previous session.
59. Checking once more that the wife's list is complete. When it is confirmed, . . .
60. . . . I turn to the husband.
61. Ron opens by staking out a "good boy" position, which in the past would have triggered Mary's rescuing behavior.
62. I return to the task of gaining agreement on a common list of issues to be resolved in the session.
63. Ron's claim that he has no issues is a defensive negotiating position designed to limit the conflict. He is clearly satisfied with the status quo regarding the money and would like to maintain it. As we discover later, it is also an indication that he no longer sees mediation as the arena in which to settle.
64. Once the agenda is accepted by the couple, I unilaterally determine the order of the issues.
65. This is an attempt to mutualize the issue.

66. Mary provides more data and then drops back into the old marriage fight.
67. I explore the use of experts, being careful not to get in over my head on a technical issue.
68. Mary provides more data.
69. Looking for solutions already available to the couple.

MARY: No. No, you can't. Apparently, if they didn't give it to you at the time, I'm not aware that you can force it. But it's just the fact that here's this thousand dollars over my head, and it really bothers me.

MEDIATOR: Now, my sense is that, first, we should understand the dimensions of that, because with a little expert advice you could probably avoid some of the penalties and probably avoid some of the tax if you can get back in to the appropriate deductions.[70]

MARY: I don't know if that's allowed. I'm not aware that it is.

MEDIATOR: What I'd like to do is put that one aside for a moment and ask if we could pursue it with Kent, in getting an accountant to look at that to see if he can minimize it.[71] We should try to minimize it, so you pay the least, and then decide how to deal with whatever you have left to pay.

MARY: Yes.

MEDIATOR: Okay. If you were still living together—how did you pay that when you were married and living together?[72]

MARY: I don't know if it ever occurred; do you recall?

RON: Each took care of their own personal income tax.

MARY: He claimed Lee Anne and me. No, because I filed separately. I had my own, and he claimed Lee Anne.

MEDIATOR: Was there an economic advantage to doing it that way?[73]

RON: Anyway, when I was on salary, it was more to my benefit, really, and I wouldn't even think that I ever claimed Lee Anne.

MEDIATOR: I don't want to get into those details, because I don't know enough about it.[74] But I have to say, if you work on it, you could probably get it lower. What I really want to focus you on is, whatever figure you arrive at, how would that normally get paid?[75]

MARY: It would be a matter of scrimping and saving until it would be paid, grocery money or whatever.[76]

MEDIATOR: In 1984, how would you have paid it?[77]

MARY: At that time, I had some savings put away. I would probably have resorted to my own savings or something. But it was always my rescuing, you know. That's the way a lot of things were done. Paying for appliances, it was always me that did it.[78] And one thing is that I was almost ready to go to court about it with the neighbor, because I don't think I was treated properly there.[79]

70. A definition of what can be achieved in mediation and what requires outside expert help.
71. This issue is best put aside for the other mediator.
72. This question has an embedded suggestion in it: They deal with this problem in the way they would have dealt with it in the past.
73. I am puzzled by this and ask a question to clarify why they filed separately.
74. Another attempt to isolate the issue for the other mediator or the tax expert.
75. I return to the idea that they share the expense now, in the same way they had shared similar expenses in the marriage.
76. Mary provides no new ideas.
77. I try again, with a specific year.
78. No solution is forthcoming.
79. Mary sends a threat to Ron, who was a good friend of the neighbor.

MEDIATOR: In regard to getting the receipts?

MARY: Yes.

MEDIATOR: But you may be able to reconstruct that if you have some expert advice.[80]

MARY: If there's a hope in it, yes.

MEDIATOR: Let's not figure on the detail, but rather on the . . . whatever happens, you're going to owe some money. The issue is whether we can keep that down to the minimum, but you're going to owe some money. The issue is: When we get it down to the least possible, how are you going to pay it?[81] How would you have paid it if you were still living together, and how are you going to pay it now that you're living apart?[82]

MARY: I don't have any available funds for it now, myself, so I know it gathers interest, that there will be interest there[83] from 1984 also, that's the way it works. We were putting ten bucks aside a month, or something, until I could get rid of it, but I don't have the funds available right now to handle it.

MEDIATOR: What's your view about that, Ron?[84]

RON: Well, I think the only thing that—maybe I'm responsible for is, maybe the procrastination part of it.[85] You know. Maybe the procrastination. But, okay, if the procrastination was there, and this way, you could have at least solved the problem without this procrastination. That's the only thing that I am in a way responsible for, the procrastination.[86]

MEDIATOR: If you said, "I'm responsible for the procrastination piece," as a percentage of the whole, what would that be?[87]

RON: I think it would only be 12 percent.

MEDIATOR: 12 percent?

RON: Because I have inquired into it, and they said that you're charged on the unpaid balance 1 percent per month, up to a maximum of twelve[88] months, and that debt should be taken care of in a five-year period.

MEDIATOR: So then you get it down to as low as you can, right?[89] If you pay the interest part on it, which is the cost as a result of not filing the taxes, which is the 12 percent, and you pay the tax part about it, which you would have paid anyway in 1984, would that work it out appropriately for you?

MARY: I don't know. I'm still tempted to go back to the neighbor.[90] It so happens that they have split up since, too, so she's not really in a position, but he's a very wealthy person. I don't know, it really bugs me, because we were saving them income tax at the time, and yet I end up now with the problem. I wasn't aware that I was eligible for such a deduction.

80. I again try to put it aside for the experts.
81. This defines the problem in such a way that it can be solved in the mediation session: the development of a formula the couple can use to resolve the issue, once they know the exact details.
82. I keep suggesting a formula.
83. Mary clearly sees it as her burden and looks to Ron to share it in some way.
84. I throw the ball into the husband's court.
85. Ron acts to minimize his exposure and liability.
86. Ron points to Mary's role in the delay.
87. An attempt to quantify the husband's responsibility, since quantities are always negotiable.
88. Ron defines it as one year at 12 percent, arguing that Mary is responsible beyond that time.
89. A suggestion of a way to assign responsibility between them: the basic payment to Mary, and the interest to Ron.
90. Mary again raises the threat of going back to the husband's "friend," to embarrass Ron.

MEDIATOR: If the experts can help you get that . . .[91]

MARY: If there's some way, I don't know. It's just that one thousand bucks sitting over me really bothers me. I don't feel responsible for it.[92]

MEDIATOR: You are responsible for the taxes for '84, right? You're not responsible, in a sense, for the interest, and you're not responsible, in a vague sense, for the fact that you didn't take the deduction to which you were entitled.[93] So I don't know whether or not we should get into that, because I don't know if you can work it out. You may be able to work that out with an accountant. If you can do all of that and reduce your tax down to what it would have been in 1984, would you be comfortable paying the tax if, Ron, you paid the interest?[94]

MARY: It depends on the amount of tax I'd have to pay, but if it stays at a thousand dollars, then I certainly don't feel comfortable about that. But maybe if it was a couple of hundred, then I wouldn't mind.[95]

MEDIATOR: Let's do this, then. See if you can get it down to the minimum. Look at the principle of the idea of [to Mary] your paying the tax, [to Ron] your paying the interest, and see how it works at that point.[96]

RON: Right now, maybe I should talk more about the interest. Let's say if I procrastinated, then there is still means of having it done by taking it to an accountant, or whatever, and having it done. So there is where I'm only guilty for procrastinating by putting it aside.[97]

MEDIATOR: For how long?[98]

RON: Okay, well—there, if you know, you figure that—okay, if there's certain things that I'm not doing, then you could get someone else to do it.

MEDIATOR: How long would you be responsible for it?[99]

RON: Maybe until the first of April, if nothing is being done there, you know.

MEDIATOR: The first of April . . . ?[100]

91. Another suggestion to use experts.
92. Mary wants to shift total responsibility to Ron.
93. I establish reality while continuing to partialize the issue into the basic payment and the interest.
94. A reiteration of a possible solution.
95. Mary defines areas of possible agreement.

96. The task of working with the experts is assigned, to get the problem down to a manageable size, and then a suggestion is made concerning the formula they can use.
97. Ron limits his responsibility to one year's interest, sensing that I am talking about all the interest, rather than just one year's.
98. An attempt to quantify.
99. Another attempt to quantify Ron's responsibility, so that the couple can negotiate over specifics.
100. I seek a better definition, since only specifics can be resolved.

RON: 1984.

MEDIATOR: Of 1984? Okay.

RON: If it's an '83 return, it's supposed to be in.

MEDIATOR: You're way over my head on this one, because you're talking about particular details of the tax code that I don't know enough about, other than to figure out in principle how to move.[101] I'm always more comfortable with solid data. I would like you to work with Kent and have him figure out exactly what it is we're talking about and then go from there. Okay?

MARY: Yes.

MEDIATOR: Let's now switch for a moment and talk about the money. You have been paying the one hundred dollars a month since we met in August?[102]

RON: Yes.

MEDIATOR: Mary says, Ron, that she wants you to pay the full two hundred dollars, and she wants you to pay the unpaid amount.[103]

RON: Uh huh. (Nods in agreement.)

MEDIATOR: Okay, so let's break that into two parts.[104] I suppose it's not really a question of whether you're going to do it, it's when you're going to do it, right? I mean, it's not a question of whether you're going to repay it or whether you're going to pay what the court ordered. The issue is when you're going to do that, because at some point you're going to have to pay it, right?[105]

RON: It could be a possibility that I might or don't have to pay it.[106]

MEDIATOR: Under what circumstances would that be?[107]

RON: Because—let's put it this way. Although there is the law of the state that there is a court order, you have to take into consideration for that period that the guy was unemployed, and they go by a percentage. Like, okay, that two hundred dollars that was supposed to be the court order was taken into consideration at that time there was this salary that was coming in, and these expenses. So maybe, let's say, I go to court right now and reappeal that order, it might even be coming down to fifty dollars a month, because they go by percentage.

MEDIATOR: So your feeling is that you would prefer that, rather than work it out here. You would prefer to take your chance in court.[108]

101. I admit to a lack of knowledge about taxes while maintaining my expertise as manager of the negotiations.
102. At last I can move on to the next of the four issues. The fact that it has taken so long indicates that Mary did not want to let go of the grudge. She avoided any specifics or solutions. She wanted to air a grievance.
103. Mary's position is restated without the emotional aspect, in the hope of achieving a response from Ron to its content.
104. The issues are partialized, and . . .
105. . . . the problem definition is restated as to *when*, not *whether*, Ron will have to pay. I then raise the consequences from the courts of not deciding it in mediation. This is a test of their WATNAs and will tell me whether their respective WATNAs still involve a court-imposed solution.

106. Ron has been doing some homework of his own and appears to have a tougher position as a result.
107. I nondefensively ask for more data from Ron.
108. I challenge Ron's new position, to see whether it is real or a bargaining posture.

RON: If Mary wants to, it's up to her, because she should realize that there is a certain amount of genuinity in me trying somehow.[109] After that session we had here, that I was going to get fifty dollars somehow, where I got it was up to me—I've kept my promise. I didn't see her this month around the fifteenth. Today is the first day I've seen her for a week and a half—two weeks—and I didn't get the check over to her. So if this is going to be such an issue, I'd say to hell with it, and if she wants to go into court and do that, that's fine.[110] Right now, I'm in a situation that I think there is too much hostility where the money is involved, and I can't afford to pay more than one hundred dollars as the situation is right now. If the situation improves, we could talk about it there and then.

MEDIATOR: So, that's fairly clear for me. Mary, let me ask you a question, because I'm interested in this one, it's one of those funny questions. Why did you come back?[111]

MARY: To see you?

MEDIATOR: Yes.

MARY: I was very impressed with our first encounter, and I really enjoyed meeting you. I was hoping that I would be able to settle the matter of maintenance by coming back again.[112]

MEDIATOR: It's not very often I mediate whether or not one abides by a court order. Because that's normally not the subject for mediation.[113] Normally, I help you negotiate that original two hundred or whatever, not whether or not you should pay a court order. Obviously, there's a whole mechanism for enforcing court orders.[114] I'm wondering, given what Ron says, whether you would both be better off testing it out, to see whether you're right or not?

MARY: Maybe we should let it slide?[115]

MEDIATOR: No.[116]

MARY: That I should push the issue?[117]

MEDIATOR: Yes. I mean, you've got no choice, right? Your choice really is to get the money here or to get it somewhere else.[118]

MARY: Well, okay. I'm willing to take the action, because once the order is established, the alternatives will be there.[119] If he is employed, they will garnishee salary from there, and if he isn't, they can take other assets, like he owns the two vehicles.

MEDIATOR: Don't worry about it; they'll figure out a way of handling it.[120]

MARY: Or there's the jail, okay, if he's not ready to accept one of those alternatives.[121]

109. Ron switches responsibility for court action to Mary. This strategy worked for him in session one but is not successful in this session.
110. Ron threatens Mary and at the same time rejects the pressure from the mediator, while stating his bottom line of not paying more than one hundred dollars.
111. I recognize Ron's firm position and turn to Mary, to see what she has anticipated from this session. Here, I am testing a developing hypothesis: that mediation is no longer the appropriate arena.
112. Mary maintains her interest in mediation as the arena to gain a settlement, even one that merely enforces the court order.
113. I point out the paradox of her position, and . . .
114. . . . check to see the extent of Mary's new resolve.
115. Mary is not clear about my suggestion and appears to drop back into a rescuing mode.
116. I clarify it.
117. She understands it. My hypothesis tests out. I will now act on it, to see how the couple reacts.
118. The problem is defined as *how* she gets the money, rather than *whether* she gets it. I inject some reality while also

educating her. This strategy involves taking an ambivalent word, such as *whether,* and substituting an action word, such as *how.*

119. Mary indicates her new resolve and adds to it some of the old marriage issues.
120. I focus her back on the real issue.
121. In this move, Mary rejects the various threats Ron has made about going to jail and asserts her new-found strength.

MEDIATOR: Mary, you're talking for Ron again, and you're not telling me what Mary is going to do.[122]

MARY: But my point is, right now I'm going to work every day in pain, physically. Yesterday I couldn't even make a fist with this hand. I take physiotherapy three times a week, but these hands are getting so bad, and my work is on a computer right now, and I can't even use these fingers.[123] And the depression, the shock. I took a week off last week. I finally got on benefits, and I went to the doctor, and I said, "Why are my emotions like this?" She said, "Well, finally, they caught up with you. They didn't have a chance to come up off your shock." You know, I jumped back into work so fast, she said, "It's finally coming over you." Do you know what it's like to sit over a computer, my hands aching and tears running down my cheeks over depression? What do I do? Last week, I took the week off. I had to get out of there. But the point is, I don't have two healthy limbs, my head isn't that healthy right now. He has a healthy body. I don't accept unemployment as his only alternative. I don't![124]

MEDIATOR: Let him worry about that. [to Ron] What do you think a judge would say to that?[125]

RON: I think it would be better for a judge to say things about this as the situation is.[126] Because—let's put it this way. Okay, the court order is two hundred dollars, and that's on the matter of being separated. Like, whatever debts she incurs is her responsibility, in such a way.

MEDIATOR: I'm just talking about the two hundred right now, Ron.[127]

RON: Because they went on two hundred dollars when I was making a salary. This way, they would have to read how much is cleared, and if I'm living in a deficit. So I think,[128] personally, that to get this thing–you know, let the judge maybe . . . I would be willing to go in front of the judge.[129] If the judge said, "here it is," you know, that's a chance I've got to take.

MEDIATOR: Do you think Mary doesn't have the nerve to do that? To go to court?[130]

RON: I wouldn't comment on that. It's a matter of whole general opinion. At least she should take into consideration, and not only be selfish, to a certain extent, but look at the other individual's situation, too.[131]

MARY: Selfish, sure. Ron, if I was a paraplegic or[132] quadriplegic today out of that accident, would you still speak that way? Thank God I'm not, but . . . ?

MEDIATOR: The issue, I guess, for you, Mary, is which way to move, right?[133]

122. Pointing out to her the way she weakens this resolve when she does not state clearly what *she* will do.
123. Mary responds with a listing of her new condition, suggesting that she either has not heard the intent of my statement or that it has triggered a new round of uncertainty for her.
124. This is the first real anger Mary has displayed toward Ron in the two sessions and is therefore a major step forward for her.
125. A warning signal to Ron, reminding him of the possible outcome in the alternative arena. This is another WATNA check.
126. Ron rejects my warning and sticks to his new position.
127. Ron is reminded of the content of the warning.
128. Ron reveals new information he has obtained from some-

where: that he may get away with one hundred dollars or less in the courts.

129. Ron has staked out a new, tough position.
130. Ron's resolve and his understanding of Mary's current position are tested, so as to further check my new hypothesis.
131. In answering this question, Ron suggests that Mary could be more considerate. In the past, she would have fallen for this.
132. Instead, she responds with hostility.
133. Mary's resolve is tested.

MARY: Well, I really think I'm going to have to take some action, because I can't keep pushing myself.[134]

MEDIATOR: See, you're stuck in a[135] position here now. [to Ron] You feel put upon in terms of . . .

RON: No.

MEDIATOR: You don't feel put upon?

RON: No.[136]

MEDIATOR: Okay, then what's the resistance to paying the two hundred dollars?[137]

RON: I don't have the funds. It's that simple.[138]

MEDIATOR: You do have, because, right, you get eight hundred dollars. You've got the money.[139]

RON: No, I don't, because when I—look at it this way. When I finish paying utilities and get this and that done, yes, I'm at a deficit, because my income is only eight hundred.

MEDIATOR: Okay. Out of the eight hundred, you allocate that to pay certain bills, right?

RON: Yes.

MEDIATOR: You could allocate that differently, because the deficit could fall in some other area rather than the support. The decision is yours. I'm not arguing with the decision, at this juncture. We're saying you make the decision. You don't have enough to do all the things that you need to do, so you make a decision about what not to do.[140]

RON: Well, so far, the situation that I'm in, I can't let anything slide more than where it is.

MEDIATOR: One decision you made is that you would cut off or reduce the child support. That's the decision. So, you see, that's your decision. That's okay, as long as you're willing to stand by that. [to Mary] Just as it's your decision whether or not you accept that, or[141] whether you say, "Wait a moment, I thought that the two hundred dollars was a contract and enforceable, and I'm going to enforce it." Now, obviously, you're not going to enforce it here. I can help you arrive at solutions. I can help you focus on how to work together, but I can't sit and say, "This is what you must do."[142] That's not my job, right, and I'm not going to do that. So that, if the gulf between you now is such that the funds are not there, that they have to be allocated elsewhere than to the child support, then [to Ron] I think you have to make some decisions about that.[143] You may have to have somebody say to you, "Sorry, Ron, you're going to have to allocate your money differently." Or somebody might say, "Yes, you're right, you're having a tough time. You ought not to have to pay this." My sense is, [to Mary] if somebody was looking at that scar on your arm, it's going to be a different ball game than when we talked in August, right?[144]

134. Mary backs off a little, . . .
135. . . . so I suggest to Ron that it is partly an emotional issue.
136. Ron rejects this interpretation, . . .
137. . . . so I move to the concrete problem.
138. Ron defines the issue as a lack of funds.
139. I point out that it is an issue of priorities, not availability.
140. Note how I nail Ron but do not comment on his position as I try to get Ron to accept responsibility for his decisions.
141. An attempt to sharpen the issues for the couple by pointing out how they make decisions and how they must accept the consequences of their decisions.

142. A reminder of my role.
143. Clarifying Ron's responsibility for how he allocates his money.
144. I remind both of them of the reality of Mary's accident and identify the risks to Ron in the other arena.

MARY: Yes. There are pins and plates in here, and the doctor told me that it is very likely that it might go stiff. Okay, what do I do, how do I support my daughter and myself?[145] I applied for welfare last year when I was on my own, and I was told that with one child you don't qualify. Now the same old story. But I know one thing—they won't give it to you if there's a husband available who can, or whatever.[146]

MEDIATOR: Am I clear? Let me just know, now. Am I clear that there is no way you're going to pay the two hundred dollars?[147]

RON: Let's put it this way. I think it would be a matter that could be settled in court, and we'll leave it from there onwards.[148]

MEDIATOR: [to Mary] Are you clear?

MARY: Yes.

MEDIATOR: [to Mary] You know what you have to do in that regard?

RON: I think Mary knows. That shouldn't be an issue, because it's pretty easy in picking the phone up and getting information pertaining going to the courts and have this matter taken care of, without other incurred expenses like lawyers and so forth. I think that will be really the best way to solve this piece of problem that's in the air.[149]

MEDIATOR: [to Mary] Okay, I think it's clear, right?

MARY: Yes, seems so.

MEDIATOR: And you're clear?

RON: I'm perfectly clear.

MEDIATOR: Okay. So, you're going to go back now to court, to get the order enforced. Okay, what about the back payments?[150]

RON: Well, we'll leave all that to the courts to decide.

MEDIATOR: So, what you have to do, then, is go back to court, not only for the enforcement of the current rate but also the collection for the back stuff, right?

RON: Because all could be done at the same time. It's all in maintenance, and where this guy wasn't keeping his word in having the two hundred dollars, and it could all be taken care of in one matter, anyway.[151]

145. Mary restates her condition and reinforces her position.
146. She also restates her threat to use the child support-enforcement agency.
147. I clarify the situation and check on Ron's position.
148. Ron stands by his position: that he can get a better deal in court.
149. It becomes clear that Ron has received advice about the courts that has made him very confident about shifting arenas.
150. A check to see if they want to deal with the other three issues. (Do not accept that a stalemate on one issue means the mediation is over.)
151. Ron switches his confidence to the courts on all issues.

MEDIATOR: I suspect you believe that she won't do that?[152]

RON: I think I would try to encourage her to do it, because this way, at least, you could get that out of the air. I would encourage her 100 percent: Let's do this. At least this way, she'd know where she stands, and I'd know where I stand, instead of having this thing being brought up every single time there is this type of discussion. I think—let's let the law decide what's to be done. Let's put it this way. I'll stand the consequences of the law, whatever judgment is passed on me.

MEDIATOR: Okay, I think that makes sense, in terms of how

to proceed. [to Mary] Are you clear and comfortable about being able to do that?

MARY: Yes.

MEDIATOR: So, I would suggest that you do that and proceed along that way, and the court will make the decision, in terms of what has to be done. Then, if there are any outstanding issues between you, Kent can work with you on that and certainly work with you in terms of finding out how to minimize that tax liability. All right?[153]

MARY: If there's any possibility.

MEDIATOR: There may not be. There may be no possibility of reducing it, but it would be worth looking at it, to see whether there is. Okay. So you can stay in touch with Kent, in terms of what's happening, and if I can be helpful sometime—maybe, maybe not? Thank you very much.[154]

MARY: Thank you very much.

152. A challenge to Mary through a question to Ron.
153. I assign tasks and bring the session to a close, . . .
154. . . . leaving open the possibility of their working on a specific issue later with Kent or myself.

Analysis

The Mediator's Assumptions

My behavior in the second session was completely different from in the first session. Ron had paid the support, although late and in two parts; this was a marked change from the previous nonpayment. I wanted to support this behavioral change. Strachen (1967) points out that relapses are likely during the recovery stage, between the cessation of drinking and the return of self-esteem. Ron's self-esteem would return more quickly if he paid his share of the support for his daughter and if he received outside recognition of this action.

Mary made it difficult for me to support Ron's payments,

because she saw his lateness as another indicator of his lack of good faith. She was now looking at the "half-empty glass." She also wanted to raise the ante by demanding not only the full two hundred dollars—a reasonable goal—but also all the missed payments. The latter demand was unrealistic, given Ron's continued unemployment and limited funds. I had hoped to use the second session to endorse Ron's behavior—payment of the one hundred dollars—setting the stage for Mary to negotiate for the full two hundred. This strategy was determined by my concern that the process be consonant with his recovery program.

Ron also had a new position: that, because he was unemployed, the court would not make him pay the two hundred dollars. He resented not receiving recognition for having paid the one hundred dollars. He also strengthened his resolve not to move on the other issues that Mary brought up. It now appeared that he saw mediation as the less attractive arena; the courts might do better by him. Thus, his commitment to mediation waned during the session, in direct proportion to the increasing toughness of Mary's demands.

Given Ron's shift from the previous session, so that he now thought he could get a better deal in court, his BATNA in mediation was to take his chances in court. Mary's best deal remained in mediation, however, because she shared Ron's new belief that she would get a worse deal from a judge. I felt that her assessment was incorrect: She would at least have the two hundred dollars enforced, and she would probably also get the back payments.

As long as Ron felt he could do better in court and there was no hope for reconciliation, mediation could proceed only by wringing unfair concessions from Mary. Therefore, if she did not review her beliefs about where she would get the best deal, she might choose the wrong arena for settlement. I proceeded in the latter part of the second session under the assumption that her BATNA lay in the courts, rather than in mediation. I needed to help her consider court as a reasonable option. Thus, the focus of the mediation became the choice of an arena, rather than the terms of a settlement.

I conducted the second session according to the behavior,

goals, and information I received in that session. I no longer needed to protect the spousal relationship. I no longer needed to prevent Ron from threatening Mary with dire consequences, so that she would rescue him. I did, however, want to create an atmosphere that would anchor the changes in Ron's behavior and enhance his continued recovery.

Once I accepted their decision not to reconcile and measured Ron's intransigence and Mary's new toughness, I knew the court was as suitable for this couple as mediation. Mary's eventual determination made the court suitable for her. I checked to see if mentioning the court alternative was a bluff on Ron's part, but it did not seem so. Therefore, I suggested that they change arenas to settle the issue.

Mediation is the best arena in most situations. When a mediator determines that the court is a better arena for a couple, however, she must help them move to the court, because it is more appropriate for their case.

The Mediator's Strategies

Before meeting with Ron and Mary in the second session, I was briefed by their mediator on the events of the intervening three months. This information led me to change my hypothesis about their reconciling. Nevertheless, I always check out whatever information a third party gives me. At the beginning of session two, I reviewed the data with the couple, to see whether my information was correct and whether my new hypothesis, based on that information, was also correct.

I reviewed the agreements we had made at the end of the previous meeting and reminded Mary of her agreement not to rescue. I then moved to confirm the new data that Kent had provided. Mary's description of Ron's moving in when she returned from the hospital indicated a change of attitude on her part. She declined all responsibility for Ron's actions (6), and the content and the tone of her message confirmed what Kent had told me.

I tested this again at 8: "You may not be looking at it in quite the same way?" Mary's response (9) reinforced that she was distancing herself from Ron. I revised my hypothesis at 14, when Mary continued to distance herself from Ron.

The new hypothesis was that, while they would not reconcile, they still wanted to work out an agreement on the money issues, and that they both still saw mediation as the desirable arena in which to accomplish this goal. From this point on, my questions were designed to elicit information and move the couple toward bargaining over increasing the one hundred dollars to two hundred.

The information regarding the boarder income suggested that the hypothesis was valid. Ron stated his commitment to the August agreement of paying one hundred dollars a month. (34) Although there had been a shift on the wife's part regarding reconciliation, there was no corresponding shift on his part concerning the money. The task of moving them toward a higher figure seemed reasonable.

Working under this hypothesis, I turned to Mary to get the bargaining going. (35) I asked her, "What is it you would like to see come out of these discussions, in terms of some settlement?" Mary responded by demanding not only the full two hundred dollars but also all of the arrears. (36, 37) At 42, I preempted a threat by the husband, while continuing to prevent the wife from making sale of the autos an issue. (44)

Clients' Negotiating Behavior

Conflict Expansion. Mary added a new strategy: conflict expansion. This is a ploy whereby one party expands the conflict, making it more difficult for the other party to negotiate on the core issue. In this case, Mary set the bargaining parameters at two hundred dollars' payment each month and payment of the arrears. She then expanded the issue to an Internal Revenue debt of one thousand dollars. If this was a bargaining strategy, then she could hammer away at the one thousand dollars and retreat once Ron had agreed on the two hundred dollars and back payments. Conflict expansion can have another motive, however: maintaining the conflict. If Mary had designed this expansion to maintain the conflict or continue to work off old grudges, then focusing on it would prevent agreement on the basic money issues.

The mediator has two choices when one party expands the conflict by introducing a new issue. The first is to ignore it and return to task. The second is to deal with it and eliminate it as a problem, if it appears to be easily solvable. In this case, my task was compounded. Mary was engaging in both strategies—expanding the conflict to reinforce her position on the basic two hundred dollars, and expanding the conflict because she was working off an old grudge.

I had to explore the basic information about the issue, to determine whether and how to deal with it. As I did so, I became more and more sucked into the old marriage fight. When I clarified the issues and attempted to establish an agenda (52), Mary enlarged the conflict again by adding the issue of the furniture. (53) This conflict enlargement was clearly an old marriage fight, since there was no difference between them; it was simply a matter of Mary's taking whatever furnishings she needed.

Mary was now "on a roll" and began to add the issue of Ron's getting a job. She checked herself, however, remembering the work we had accomplished in the previous session with respect to Ron's responsibility for his own decisions. (58)

My efforts at setting the tax issue aside for experts did not meet with much success. Therefore, I decided to see if I could develop a formula for solving the problem, once the data were known. Fighting can be sustained only in the absence of facts. Once the data are available and agreed upon, the parties can only solve the problem. Thus, when the parties want to fight, they will tend to obscure the facts, in order to protect the fight. In this case, Mary could hold the grudge and maintain the conflict as long as the precise amount of the debt was unknown. Obviously, it would have been a very different fight if the back bill had been one hundred dollars, rather than one thousand. She repeatedly rejected my proposals to find out exactly what the debt was. Given that I could not get the precise figure, I turned my attention to developing a formula that could be applied regardless of the amount.

My experience tells me that people can let go of a fight

(grudge) if they know how the issue will be resolved, even though they may be unaware of the precise scope of the problem. Therefore, I try to develop a formula for resolving the issue if a specific proposal cannot be made because of missing data. I tried to develop the formula by relating the issue to their past behavior. (72, 75) I thought that if they could remember how they had handled similar problems in the past, they might be able to use the same process now. I repeated this idea at 82, but the wife viewed it from the negative standpoint of the past and saw the debt as her own burden.

Mary's reluctance to develop a formula for solving the problem came partly from her inductive thinking style (which clashed with my mediator's deductive style) and partly from my failure to adapt my own approach to Mary's inductive style. I was concentrating on the big picture (a formula for agreement), while Mary was concentrating on the details (how much she would have to pay). I spent a lot longer on the tax bill than the issue warranted, because of my failure to shift my language to match Mary's inductive thinking.

I finally made a specific suggestion for solving the problem. (94) Mary would pay the back taxes, and Ron would pay the interest. Without agreement on the formula, however, Mary was unwilling to let go of the matter. I finally persuaded the couple to deal with experts and lay the issue aside for now.

Equity Versus Equality. It may be a mistake to characterize Mary's reaction only as conflict expansion. She was also changing her position from equity (seeking less than equality on the support payment) to equality (payment of the full two hundred dollars). Ron maintained an equity position: He needed all his money to meet his other obligations. In the first session, Mary went along with this premise; indeed, she asked for only seventy-five dollars of the two hundred Ron was supposed to pay. In the second session, Mary raised a new standard of equity: her accident. After the accident, Mary claimed that her injuries justified a new standard of equity, and she raised her demand to the full two hundred dollars.

In the second session, Mary moved from her equality position (receiving the two hundred dollars) to an equity position:

She demanded not only full payment of the court-ordered support but also full payment of the arrears. Clearly, she was entitled to both. The question here is why she chose to enlarge the area of conflict. She may have added the issue of the arrears to make negotiation over the second one hundred dollars more realistic. What Mary appeared to be doing in the second session was enlarging the conflict in an effort to obtain a more generally equitable settlement, which would not unfairly benefit Ron. Her accident had changed her rescuing behavior; indeed, she needed rescuing now, or at least substantial help, to deal with the pain of her injuries and her loss of income as a result of the injuries.

When Mary returned home from the hospital after her accident, Ron moved in to take care of her. He wanted credit for that, but Mary, sensing that this would cost her in terms of support money, dismissed Ron's generosity: "I wasn't expecting anything. All I can say is that he came, he offered, but I can't see that it was anything extra special or anything. I don't owe him." (14) As part of her changed needs, she now dismissed Ron's actions, so as to avoid having to make a concession in return for them—something she would not have done before the accident.

When I returned to the support issue, after settling the tax question, I was still working under the hypothesis that they both wanted to settle in mediation, and that my task was to help them find the agreement. The husband's behavior changed, however, causing me to review my working hypothesis.

Conclusion

I restated the problem in terms of *when* Ron would pay the court-ordered support, not *whether* he would pay. (105) This change of wording implied movement toward a future focus and a concrete action. Ron switched his position, suggesting that he might not have to pay the court-ordered support. (106) He had been talking to friends and learned that the court was favorable to unemployed men. Whatever advice he had received had led him no longer to fear the court. He shifted from *when* to *whether* he would pay.

This caused a change in my hypothesis. Given Mary's difficulty in letting go of the tax issue, and given Ron's statement, I had to review whether mediation was appropriate. Mediation works only if both parties want to settle in that arena; if one party wants to settle elsewhere, then mediation will not work. I proceeded to check my new hypothesis, because if it was correct, I would have to change my behavior dramatically.

I tested the hypothesis by asking the husband directly whether he would prefer to work it out in mediation or in court. (108) Ron responded in terms of the old marital behavior, by putting the responsibility for the choice on Mary's shoulders. (109) He then threatened that he would go to court unless he got recognition for the one hundred dollars he had paid. (110) At this point, Ron remained committed to paying the one hundred dollars.

I then checked my hypothesis with Mary, to see why she thought mediation was the appropriate arena. (111) Mary held to her view that mediation was the preferable arena. (112) I tested her further (114) by asking whether they might not both be better off testing the issue in court. I reinforced this by telling the wife that her options were to get the support paid in mediation or through the court. (118) Mary then announced that she was willing to take action in court. (119)

This led me to take a more confrontational approach with Ron. I pointed out that his claim—that he did not have the money to pay the child support—was untrue: He had the money, he simply did not want to allocate it to his daughter. (140)

I thought it was important to warn Ron of the possible WATNA that still existed in the court, in view of Mary's accident and the condition of her arm. (144) This did not seem to have any impact on his resolve to change arenas, however. As I did that, Ron became clearer on going to court. I accepted his choice and checked to see if they wanted to settle any of the other issues and leave only the child support to the judge. (150)

Ron had clearly switched his confidence to the courts. This stance was probably bolstered by Mary's new and tougher position. I challenged Mary, to be sure that she understood what was happening and that she would be able to go through with it (152), and I brought the session to a close.

The hypotheses changes helped me to be most efficient with the couple at each stage and to accept their right to settle in an alternative arena. In the first session, I accepted their right to work out an agreement that enhanced the possibility of reconciliation. In the second session, I accepted their right to change that goal and to change arenas for resolving the basic money differences between them. The mediator controls the process; the parties control the content and the outcome.

7

TOM AND PAT: MOVING ONE HUNDRED MILES APART

In this chapter, you will meet Tom and Pat, who have been married for fifteen years. They have a daughter, Heather, twelve years old, who was diagnosed five years ago as diabetic. They separated six months ago. All the details of the separation agreement have been worked out but not yet filed with the court. An important event has taken place, throwing the previous agreement into disarray.

Pat is the residency parent. She is an assistant bank manager in Edmonton and has been offered a promotion as a bank manager in Lloydminster, a town about one hundred miles away. She wants to take the job. Tom, who thought he had an agreement, has just been told this and is very angry. He does not want Pat to go, since it means that Heather will move with her mother. Their lawyers thought it would be useful if Tom and Pat could mediate just this issue, to save the rest of the package.

The behavior of a mediator is situational: He responds to conflict in different ways, according to the behavior of the parties. In this case, the issue is relatively simple: What arrangements will the couple make for parenting their daughter when the wife and the daughter move to the new town? However, the dynamics of the couple complicate the situation.

Tom does not want Heather to go; neither does he want her to live with him. Thus, his opening position—trying to prevent the move by his wife and his daughter—is unrealistic. The task for the mediator is to help Tom accept the move and define the problem in a way that meets his legitimate self-interest. Tom could try to prevent Pat from moving with their daughter, but such an attempt would have only a marginal chance of succeeding in court. It could also tear the family apart and result in one or the other parent's losing his or her relationship with Heather. The mediator's role is to help the couple find a solution acceptable to them both.

Although Pat wants to move, she has an underlying fear: that once she moves, Tom will try to woo Heather to stay in Edmonton with him. Added to this is her concern that even if Tom accepts the move, Heather may not want to stay in Lloydminster if she makes frequent trips to her home town, her father, and her peers. Until this underlying issue is resolved, Pat cannot focus on a reasonable agreement that meets her other legitimate interests.

The mediator misses the importance of this issue until later in the session. When an underlying fear or an issue remains unstated or is ignored by the mediator, resolution of other issues will not result in an agreement. Indeed, the mediator discovers that as one practical issue is resolved, it is quickly replaced by another. Agreement is not possible until the underlying issue is dealt with.

Another issue found in this chapter is dealing with multiply defined problems. (This is part of the conflict-expansion issue, discussed in Chapter Three.) The essential problem is defined in a number of ways, and the mediator must decide which problem to work on first. This case also demonstrates how the mediator avoids the marital (spousal) issues and focuses on the future (parental) issues.

Conflict expansion, multiply defined problems, and marital issues are all part of the underlying issue. The wife's legitimate underlying fear is not taken seriously for some time. To deal with her underlying fear (issue), she expands the conflict, making the central problem multifaceted, and frequently returns to the marital fights. This case demonstrates how, once the underlying issue is dealt with, other issues raised in connection with it are dissolved.

The assumptions found in this chapter include the situational nature of mediation, the fact that almost everyone wants to settle, and the idea that conflict over issues is resolvable in mediation while conflict over dynamic behavior is resolvable in therapy. The mediator's major strategies include defining the problem, summarizing, and orchestrating the negotiations. The clients' negotiating behavior involves underlying fears, conflict expansion, and (a variant of this) multiply defined problems.

Transcript and Annotations

MEDIATOR: Well, it's good to see you both, and, as I understand it from counsel, there really is one issue—although you must correct me if I'm wrong—that we're going to work on today.[1] Let me just double-check now. As I understand it, you have an agreement about the whole package.

PAT: Well, we've had discussions, yes.

MEDIATOR: You've had discussions, and there was sort of a tentative understanding about the money, and the assets, and the support, and those issues.

PAT: We're not too concerned about those things right now.[2] We haven't been separated that long, but we've sort of worked out access. Actually, it isn't even down in writing, but it seemed to have worked out all right up to this point.

MEDIATOR: Okay, and the problem is?[3]

PAT: The problem is that I am now going to be a bank manager in Lloydminster.[4] I've been transferred there, and it's about one hundred miles from Edmonton to Lloydminster, and I'm going to move there with my daughter.

MEDIATOR: Okay. When are you supposed to take up the new position?[5]

PAT: Well, they've asked me to be there by at least the first of October, but if I could be there by the first of September it would be better, and since it's . . . The first of September would be the beginning of school for my daughter, Heather, and that's when I would like to go.

MEDIATOR: And the issue, then, is that now you have the promotion, you need to move, and that throws the whole issue of access into dispute? Is that your view, Tom?[6]

TOM: Well, that's right. And let me say off the top that I'm not particularly happy to be here. I thought we had an understanding when we separated that I would have access each and every weekend to my daughter. Now my wife is telling me that she intends to move away one hundred miles, and it upsets the whole situation at home. She's living in the home now; my daughter has friends there, associations that I want to continue, and she's going to simply uproot her, take her to Lloydminster.[7] Quite frankly, I don't know what's going to happen if that takes place.[8]

PAT: Well, I mean, quite frankly, I don't have any choice in the matter.[9] The bank transfers you, and you just have to go. In this case, I'm getting a promotion, so it means more money as well. So, I mean, you ought to be happy about that.[10]

TOM: Well, I don't particularly care how much she makes; money is not a problem for us. We're able to work out those things.[11] Frankly, I can't see why she has to move. There are positions available in Edmonton if she waits for them, but she's jumping at the first opportunity to get this managerial position.

1. The opening gives the couple permission to correct me, while I check that the referrer is their attorney. This enables me to check the information that counsel has provided and, if it is correct, define the problem quickly.
2. Pat responds in generalities.
3. A specifying question.
4. Pat provides the basic information and her definition of the problem—the bank made me do it. This is the strategy of making a third party—the bank—responsible for events beyond her control. In defining the problem, she announces, "The problem is that I am now going to be a bank manager in Lloydminster." The claim is offered

as if the person advancing the position had no control over whether the bank moved her.

5. I seek data about when Pat must move, to determine how much time the couple has to work on the problem.
6. The question is directed to Tom, to engage him in the process.
7. Tom expresses discomfort at being in mediation, but he is also concerned at the prospect of the agreement's coming apart. BL: Tom is sitting very stiffly, arms folded.
8. Tom makes what could be considered a vague threat, from not wanting to be in mediation. By his definition, the whole problem rests with Pat.
9. Pat again frames the issue to remove responsibility from herself: It is the bank's fault. This is her problem definition, which places the solution out of her control. In support of her position, Pat says, "I don't have any choice in the matter. The bank transfers you, and you just have to go." If accepted, such a claim would preempt a large area of discussion and any movement by the person advancing the claim. It would mean, therefore, that the only way to solve the problem would be for the husband to change his position and accept the wife's move.
10. I wonder whether Pat's statement about the money is a hint to Tom: that she might trade support for the freedom to move.
11. Tom rejects the suggestion regarding the money. He is not willing to trade dollars for time with Heather. Instead, he reiterates his problem definition.

MEDIATOR: The issue is not whether or not Pat moves, right? Because, as adults, you can move wherever you want to move. The issue, I suppose, is for Heather.[12]

PAT: Heather can come with me. I'm perfectly happy to take her with me. I intend to take her with me, so I don't think there's a problem at all. The problem is that her father, you know, wants to see her all the time, that's all. And what he said to me, the suggestion that he's made, is that he wants to see her every single weekend. That's ridiculous. It just won't work.

TOM: But that's what I've been doing for the last two months, since we separated. I've been seeing her—well, not for the full weekend, but I've been seeing her for portions of Saturday and Sunday each weekend, and that's worked out just fine, and I don't see why it should have to change.

MEDIATOR: Well, let me just clarify one issue, if I could. Are we now talking about whether or not Heather should go to Lloydminster with her mother, or are we talking about how to arrange the parenting of Heather when she moves to Lloydminster?[13]

PAT: No, she's coming with me. That's not the issue.

MEDIATOR: I know that's your view. I want to know what Tom's view is.[14]

TOM: As I said, I don't think it's necessary that she has to move, and I'm opposing the move in itself.

MEDIATOR: You can't oppose your ex-wife moving, right? You can oppose your daughter moving. But your ex-wife has a right to move wherever she wants. It's a free country.[15]

TOM: I suppose so. I want my daughter to be with her. I realize that, and so I am opposing the move because it's going to involve both of them.[16]

PAT: Look, the bottom line is this: He doesn't want her. He wants to be a sugar daddy every once in a while . . .

MEDIATOR: Why don't you let Tom talk for what he wants, Pat, and you tell me what you want, because I really do want to know what you want.[17]

PAT: I want to take my daughter with me. I want to move up. I want to move ahead, and I want to make more money. I'm the only one who can look after her, in any case. I don't know if you're aware, but she has diabetes.[18] She has to have insulin every day. She's on special diets, none of which he knows anything about. I mean, he's never taken an interest in that aspect of Heather at all.

MEDIATOR: Just check this out, now. So we're talking about when she moves, what kind of access and time she'll have with her dad. Is that right, Tom?[19]

TOM: Well, it's obviously going to be very difficult for me if she's a hundred miles away. I mean, how am I going to be able to see her each and every weekend?[20]

MEDIATOR: Well, our task is to focus on that, if that is the issue, you see. I mean, the issue is one of two issues. Either you don't want Heather to move to Lloydminster with her mother, or you want to work out a reasonable arrangement for you as the father in terms of access to Heather, if you're living one hundred miles apart.[21]

12. I clarify the problem by separating the right of the spouses to move from the question of where Heather lives. This educates them to the fact that this is an adult decision, to be made by them as parents. I also state my definition of the problem, which is a mutual one.
13. The repetition of earlier statements is designed to sharpen the conflict by clarifying and separating the issues.
14. Tom's need to respond to Pat is preempted by my asking him to respond to me. His response is task-focused and untainted by the marital interaction, but his statement is what he does not want, rather than what he does want. Thus, it is also unrealistic.
15. A challenge to Tom to separate the issues, in the hope that he will develop a position that is realistic and in his own legitimate self-interest.
16. Tom's response reveals his strategy: He wants to defend his access to the daughter while leaving residency with Pat.
17. A process interruption is used to help Pat speak for herself.
18. Pat states her needs clearly and adds new information about the diabetes. In creating a second component to the problem definition, she also expands the conflict.
19. A more mutual problem definition tests whether it would be acceptable for Pat and Heather to move, if the access arrangements were satisfactory. The question is directed to Tom, to engage him.

20. Tom does not provide a specific response. BL: His arms are still folded.
21. In clarifying, I frame the issue in a way that precludes the right to prevent Pat from moving. Tom still has not developed a good position for himself. He wants Heather to live with Pat, but in Edmonton, not Lloydminster. Therefore, I inject reality about Tom's options and define the problem as one of access, not one of residency.

TOM: I guess there's obviously no way for me to stop her from moving. As I said before, I want her to have custody of my daughter. I simply cannot look after her myself, given my work schedule and the fact that I'm out of town so much. So, if we can arrange something, some system whereby I can see her regularly, I would be happy with that, but I want to know a lot more about where she's moving and what facilities there are for her.[22]

MEDIATOR: That's fair, that's fair.[23] Okay, so let's then focus for a moment now: that if she moves with you, Pat, to Lloydminster next month, what kind of time would she have to share with Tom?

PAT: Well, she would be going to school, she's going into grade seven, and she would be starting school early in the morning and would be going for the regular school time, and really the only times that are available to him is in the evening.[24] It's a long drive. It's—you know, a hundred miles away, so he couldn't do it unless he wanted to fly out and on the weekends. That's the only time she would have. But then she has the problem of moving to a new place and trying to meet new friends and establishing some roots there, too.[25]

MEDIATOR: Yes, and those are all problems we will have to deal with.[26] What I would like to do first is get some general sense of what you each think would be an appropriate arrangement for the parenting. Then we can look at helping her integrate into the new community with her peers and also having a good strong relationship with her dad.

PAT: Well, it's worked out well to this point, because he's seen the child on a daily basis. He hasn't had Heather overnight or for long weekends, or anything like that, because she takes insulin every day, and I look after that.

TOM: That's not really true. The problem is that I only have a one-bedroom apartment, and that causes problems for accommodation. There's never been a problem with the diabetes. She's had this condition for five years, and there hasn't been any . . .

PAT: How many times did you give her insulin?

TOM: I haven't had to give her any insulin. She's twelve years old; she knows how to deal with that problem herself, and there hasn't been any insulin shock or anything of that nature. It's a problem she's coped with. She's now twelve years old; she's had it for five years. She's a healthy young girl. I can't see that as being a problem.

MEDIATOR: How will that work for you in the future? I mean, you say you have a one-bedroom apartment, so what will happen?[27]

TOM: Well, as far as weekends, you know, if I have to get a larger apartment, I'm certainly prepared to do that. We've only been separated a short period of time. I just wanted to find something quickly, and that's what I have. But I'm perfectly willing to get a two-bedroom apartment.

MEDIATOR: Okay. You know, lots of kids like to sleep on the living-room floor with a sleeping bag. I mean, for the short run, that might work.[28] I can see you're not comfortable with that, Pat.

PAT: All you have to do is ask him what kind of foods she has to eat. Ask him how much insulin she takes every day. He doesn't know, he has no idea of any of those things. He's shown no interest in that at all.[29]

MEDIATOR: All right. I'm not running medical tests here, right? I'm just trying to help you figure out how you can make your move to Lloydminster in a way which meets your career needs and your mothering needs and also meets Tom's fathering needs.[30]

PAT: The thing is, though, if she doesn't take her insulin, she could die.

MEDIATOR: Uh huh. Tom, Pat has expressed some real concerns here about the medical aspects for Heather. What does that all mean for you?[31]

22. Tom finally accepts this problem definition, which is also acceptable to Pat. In doing so, Tom also provides some key directional information. While he is arguing against Pat's moving from Edmonton, he also states, "So, if we can arrange something, some system whereby I can see her regularly, I would be happy with that." This indicates where Tom is willing to settle, and the session can proceed, with this information guiding me in managing Tom's and Pat's negotiations.
23. I acknowledge Tom and, given his movement, turn to Pat for a time proposal. This is the first attempt at a reciprocal concession.
24. Pat gives data and . . .
25. . . . indicates an underlying concern regarding the daughter's settling in at the new place.
26. I acknowledge Pat's issue and tie it to Tom's concerns, to focus the couple on how they can meet both sets of needs in the future. This linking of issues is future-focused. While working on linked, mutual issues, the couple is more likely to find mutual solutions.
27. I move to the apartment's size first, sensing that it is the easier of the two issues raised by Tom.
28. In suggesting ways of making the one-bedroom arrangement work, I educate the parents about the new situation and normalize it.
29. Pat returns to the diabetes issue, where she feels in total control. When one party has control of one issue, he or she frequently returns to it when faced with the possibility of movement on another issue.
30. Reestablishes my role, so that I can avoid being sucked into the marital fight about care of the diabetes, and em-

phasizes that Pat's career needs have been heard and suggests the need to meet them as well as Tom's needs.

31. I do not comment on the validity of Pat's concerns but ask a broad question of Tom. Avoiding a "how does that feel," open question, I use the term *mean,* which helps Tom focus more on the practical aspects of the issue.

TOM: Well, as I said, I just don't see it as being a real problem. She's had this condition for some time, and there haven't been any serious problems.[32]

MEDIATOR: Okay. How would you then answer Pat's concerns?[33]

TOM: What are they?

PAT: You see, that's the position he's always taken.[34]

MEDIATOR: Share them with him.[35]

PAT: He doesn't—he hasn't shown any interest at all in the diets. He hasn't shown any interest.[36]

MEDIATOR: I'm sorry. I asked you the wrong question. What I really wanted you to do was share with Tom what the issues are that concern you about Heather's medical circumstances.[37]

PAT: Well, the issue is she has to have insulin every day, a certain amount every day. It has to be given in a certain fashion, and she's learning how to do it now, but she isn't doing it all the time, and she has to do it under supervision. She has to give herself the shots under supervision, and they have to be carefully monitored. You have to measure a certain amount of insulin out every day and make sure you don't give too much, because, you know, she can die from that kind of thing.

TOM: I can do those things. I can do those things.

PAT: No, you can't. You've never done them. You don't know how to do them.

TOM: Well, I can learn. I'm not stupid.

MEDIATOR: Pat, would you like for Tom to be able to do them?[38]

PAT: I would be worried about him doing them, because he has just never done them in the past, and I would . . .

MEDIATOR: Would you like for him to do them in the future?[39]

PAT: Well, I—if she were going to spend any time with him, he'd have to do them. That's all there is to it. He'd have to do them, and he'd have to show some interest in it. But he hasn't shown any interest, and that's the problem. He doesn't know anything about her diet, either, and the kinds of food. She just can't take any kind of food. She has to have those snacks at certain periods of time, and he doesn't know any of that, and he's just never shown any interest in that.

MEDIATOR: Tom?[40]

TOM: I can learn these things, obviously. I'm sure Pat can write these concerns down on a piece of paper, so I know how to give an insulin shot. She's right. I haven't ever given Heather anything like that, but I just didn't see it as a big problem.

PAT: I had to take a special course in it when she was diagnosed. I had to go to the university hospital every day for a week and learn how to give shots and about the diet, and I read up on those kinds of things. He just doesn't care; he's left it to me entirely, and I've taken that role. I look after my daughter, and she's all right now.

MEDIATOR: One of the problems in marriage is that we tend to take on certain responsibilities and roles in the marriage and then leave the other one to take care of it. And that's true in a whole range of areas, and then when you separate, you suddenly realize there are things you have to learn to do for yourself.[41] I'm sure there are things around the house that you're learning to do at this juncture, Pat, that you've not bothered to do in the past. [to Tom] There's things that you've not done in the past that you each will have to now learn to do. Let me see, if I may[42] put up on the chart here some of the concerns, and then let's plot out how to deal with those concerns, right? So that if, in a sense, I understand this correctly, what we're looking at here is, you have a concern that she needs the insulin.

PAT: Right.

MEDIATOR: And so there's the issue of the amount of insulin and the issue of how it's given.[43]

PAT: That's correct, and when it's given, how often it's given.

MEDIATOR: How, when, and frequency.

32. Tom denies the problem, and so . . .
33. . . . the question is repeated in a slightly different form.
34. The marriage fight takes over.
35. Since Tom does not respond, I ask Pat to restate her concerns, and . . .
36. . . . she uses the question to return to the marriage fight and the diabetes.
37. I accept responsibility for the confusion and restate the task, almost in an instructional manner. In response, Pat digs in her heels. The practical aspect of the diabetes must be dealt with, and so I decide to concentrate on the medical issue.
38. This yes-no, future-oriented, parenting question cuts through the marital fight. It is the type of question that rarely gets a negative answer. Once Pat accepts that she would like Tom to deal with the diabetes, her control of the issue is diminished.
39. A move from the past to the future. Future-oriented questions open the clients to more options, or mental pictures of the situation in a different way. In this case, the question keeps Pat from drifting back into the past and into a situation that she did not want.
40. Since Pat is determined to stay in the marriage fight, I go to Tom.
41. This comment normalizes role specialization, which also, in a way, comments on how their relationship is complementary: They are always one up–one down. The monologue educates them about the changes during divorce.

42. The chart displays the issues, providing a focus for the couple's attention.
43. The content is extracted from each point, and the extraneous material is ignored. The content is put on the chart as part of the summary.

PAT: And then there's also the thing, [to Tom] which you didn't even know about, the monitoring of the insulin. There's a special monitoring device, so that there has to be blood tests taken, depending on what kind of activities she's in, take blood tests, measure the blood-sugar level.

MEDIATOR: So there's the diet issue.

PAT: The diet, too.

MEDIATOR: That is, understand what she may or may not eat.

PAT: And how often she has to eat.

MEDIATOR: Okay. We've got the frequency there, and then we have the monitoring.

PAT: And how to react in crisis.

MEDIATOR: Okay, in crisis. All right. Those are the critical issues, the critical medical issues, right? Those are the critical medical issues.

PAT: That's right. [Mediator sits.]

MEDIATOR: Now, let me ask you: Assume for a moment that Heather did not have diabetes. Assume for a moment that you could turn the clock back to five years ago, when she didn't.[44] Would there be any serious issues of parenting between you?

TOM: None, other than this move she's contemplating.

PAT: Well, I suppose the other major issue is if he wants to take Heather every weekend, that means I won't have a chance to see her at all, because I work, too. It means also that we have the problem of her trying to fit into a new place when she's spending time at her old house.[45]

MEDIATOR: So is there a problem of sharing the good times, the fun times, which are the weekend times?[46] That's number one, and number two is the whole medical issue. Let me just see if I can focus for a moment on the medical issue. Let's see what it would take to solve that problem, and then let's look to see how, if you can get that out of the way between you, you can then focus on how to organize the time. Then how we can plug in what's obviously right for Heather, in terms of her making her new entry into peer groups, etcetera, up in Lloydminster. Okay, so let's do it in that order–one-two-three. Let's focus for a second on the medical issues. Now, let me see if I understand, Pat. What you say is, there's a problem of knowing the amount and frequency with which to give the insulin on a normal, regular basis. There's a question of monitoring her need for insulin. There's a question of the diet–not only what it is that she eats, but when and how frequently she eats, and then there's the issue of crisis management–what do you do if things go wrong, if she overexercises or something like that.

PAT: If she doesn't take enough insulin, or if she takes too much.

MEDIATOR: Okay, and clearly, for her as she grows up, she has to be able to take more and more control for those things as she moves into adolescence and adulthood.[47]

44. Having completed the work on the chart, I change the subject, to give the couple time to digest this information. This also checks to see if this is the real and/or only parenting issue, by isolating it from the divorce.
45. Pat uses this opportunity to raise another real concern, repeating a point she made at 25. This is her important underlying issue.
46. By identifying and numbering clusters of issues and then setting the order in which to work on them, the mediator controls the agenda and the process. Ideally, a monologue should state each person's dilemma aloud.
47. The daughter's progress is normalized, and the developmental issues are separated from the divorce, giving the subject a future focus.

PAT: And she's starting to take control now. She's lived with it for five years. She's just on the verge of being able to do it, and sometimes she takes too much responsibility herself, and somebody has to be watching her and monitoring her all the time.

MEDIATOR: She's in that in-between stage, right? She's a young lady one moment and a child the next. If she didn't have the diabetes, she'd still be in that space of one foot in each camp.[48] Okay. Tom, for you as the father, how would you like to deal with those problems up there?[49]

TOM: Well, I think I could easily educate myself to take care of those concerns. I mean, this is a common disease. A lot of families have to deal with it.

MEDIATOR: Where would you get that information? Is there a Diabetes Association?

TOM: Sure, there's . . .

PAT: Or there's classes at the university. You can go to those classes for a week.[50]

TOM: Full week?

PAT: Two hours every day. It means having to . . .

MEDIATOR: That may not be the only way.

TOM: There may be a night course I could sign up for.

MEDIATOR: I'm sure they have something for working parents, don't you think? But, okay, there's the possibility of that, and you would do that?[51]

TOM: I would try.

PAT: Try!

MEDIATOR: Pat, when you got through with your program, did you get a little certificate of completion, some indicator that you were now . . .

PAT: No. They just watch you to make sure you can do it properly, and at the end of that period of time, you just manage all right. If you have problems, then you can call her doctor up. But, you know, it's pretty comprehensive, and they have you doing it over and over again, so you know how to do it by the end of the week.

TOM: If she can do it, I can do it.

MEDIATOR: So you would be willing to do whatever it takes to get a handle on all of this stuff.[52]

TOM: I don't have any problem with that.

MEDIATOR: Okay. All right.

TOM: Like I said, I never saw it as a big problem.

MEDIATOR: Okay. [to Pat] What would you need, to be comfortable?[53]

PAT: I would need to know she was safe.

MEDIATOR: How would you know that?

PAT: I wouldn't. I would never believe that she would be safe with him. That's my problem. I mean, he says, "I'd learn somehow." Or "I'd just learn. If she can learn, I can learn." I mean, that's not taking . . . making the steps toward doing it. It's just talk. It's just more talk, that's all it is. And if he had–why doesn't he go and take the course right now, and the next time we meet he'll have finished this course.[54]

MEDIATOR: You have a problem, right? Which is that you want to move to Lloydminster, and if you wanted to, you could probably get engaged in a nice little piece of litigation now. It could really mess everything up, right?[55]

48. Through normalization of the developmental issues, the stage is set for change in the whole family, with talk about the future and how Heather will grow up. If the couple can reduce their conflict, there is evidence that the lower level of conflict might help Heather control her diabetes (Minuchin, 1974). If this is true, then increasing Tom's competence will reduce the tension and enhance Heather's control of her illness.

49. This demonstrates the value of the chart. When Tom is asked to respond, the list is in front of him, and there is less chance of his wandering.
50. Pat demonstrates her high level of expertise, to maintain control of their daughter.
51. I rescue Tom from this marital issue by suggesting possible alternatives. At times, the mediator intervenes in a dispute with a specific suggestion that might favor one or the other party at that moment, as a way of breaking out of the cycle of conflict that the couple is developing. In asking whether Pat had received a certificate at the end of her training, I was hoping that she would have a statement of competency that Tom could also earn. Thus, they would be autonomously equal in their debate over whether Tom could take care of Heather.
52. The argument is reframed into a positive commitment by Tom.
53. The use of the word *comfortable* provides greater space for a flexible answer. It also gives Pat control of the outcome, which, if reached, she would then own. Therefore, she should then be able to back away from her original problem definition.
54. Pat attacks Tom and rejects his commitment. This is an example of dismissing a concession in order to avoid having to reciprocate. Pat is using this strategy when she makes it appear that Tom's failure to be involved in caring for Heather's diabetes in the past precludes his doing so in the future. Once she has Tom on the defensive about the diabetes, she keeps pushing the issue whenever she feels that her underlying concern is being ignored.
55. Pat is reminded of her self-interest, since ultimately it is legitimate self-interest that will define the outcome. Tom defines the conflict in adversarial terms. He also recognizes that, given the win-lose framework of the courts, if his position were to be sustained, he would win the battle—that is, prevent his daughter from leaving town with his wife—but he would lose the war, because he could not care for Heather on a full-time basis. Thus, I remind them

of their WATNA: Moving to the courts is in each party's worst interests, and settling in mediation is in each one's best interests.

TOM: The only reason I'm here today is because I realize what it's going to cost for me to go through the courts.

PAT: Well, I'll be gone. That's it. I mean, I'm leaving in September.[56]

TOM: Well, that's fine. You can go. I'm here to talk about Heather.

PAT: I'd never give Heather to you.

TOM: I don't think she's thought through the disruption that this is going to cause in Heather's life. This is a twelve-year-old child. She's got friends; she's been in school here for years and years. She's involved in recreation here. She's got ballet classes. This whole thing is just to be thrown into disarray, like you said.

MEDIATOR: Do you have a good relationship with Heather?[57]

TOM: Absolutely. Fantastic.

MEDIATOR: Do you want Heather to have a good relationship with Tom?

PAT: She has a good relationship with him, actually.

MEDIATOR: Would you like to get your job and keep your job, and grow as a manager in the bank system, move up?[58]

PAT: I would. But I don't know how to do it.

MEDIATOR: So part of the issue is to resolve this issue between you, so that Heather can continue to have the best that she gets from you, Tom, and the best that she gets from you, Pat, on the one hand, and, on the other hand, so that you can continue in your own career, growth, and development.[59] Because it's a burden to have a child that has those kinds of medical problems. It's obviously one that you've met very well.[60] It's also one that you will want, over the next few years, to free yourself from as much as is reasonably possible.

PAT: Well, she'll take on that burden herself, in time.

MEDIATOR: Yeah, okay, and in a sense—as a matter of fact, moving between you may help facilitate that assumption of responsibility, of taking it on and doing it in that way.[61] So, the question is: How can you let go of each other, in the sense of knowing that, between Tom and Heather, they'll do what's right? You're obviously not going to get a certificate to say each weekend, "We did what's right." Some weekends they ain't going to do what's right from your perspective, and that's not unusual. Parents have different ideas.[62] But how can you feel comfortable, so that Heather can have time with Dad and maintain that good relationship and at the same time assume more and more responsibilities for her own medical care? That Tom can do what he has to do as the father to guide and to monitor it, and that you can then enjoy those weekends when Heather is not with you and not sit up at Lloydminster worrying all the time.[63]

PAT: I think he has to show some genuine ability to cope with the diabetes problem, and he hasn't shown that. That's the bottom line. That's the problem. [Mediator uses hand movement to ask the husband to respond.]

TOM: I can't believe she makes comments like that—she is worried about the safety of Heather when she's with me. That's just absurd to me. I mean, I've been looking after this child since she was born, and this is just ridiculous.

56. Pat makes a bluster threat, which I ignore; but note that Tom does not counterthreaten. He simply states that he is here to talk about Heather, indicating that he has fully grasped the implications of his WATNA.
57. I ignore Tom's counterattack and use a process-interrupting, positive question regarding his fathering, to bring him back on track.
58. Pat's legitimate self-interest is reinforced by embedding a suggestion in a future-oriented, clarification question.

59. This mutualizes their parenting needs and highlights their overlapping self-interest.
60. Projection to the future and to Heather's growth is part of my continual attempt to educate the couple about their daughter's development, thus normalizing the matter.
61. This points out how the access arrangement can aid in Heather's development in the future.
62. This normalizes their potential differences.
63. Pat is helped to let go by a reminder of the reality of Heather's absences.

MEDIATOR: And you feel comfortable that you could take whatever training was necessary to get these pieces into control and then be able to monitor that.[64]

TOM: I can do it. If there is a course available, I'll take it. I have no problem with that.[65]

MEDIATOR: See, because if you don't work it out, the chances are you can get yourself a court litigation, and Heather could get stuck here while you're up in Lloydminster, until the issue gets settled out, right? You don't want that, right? [to Tom] You don't want that, right? Heather doesn't want that.[66] So it's really up to you to try to move on between the two of you and let go of some of that stuff in terms of . . . hold that for a moment. Assume that you get this worked out, right? Because there's no way in which Heather is not going to come down and spend time with Dad, right?[67] [to Pat] So that's not the issue, right? The question then becomes, assume you're now living in Lloydminster, how would you share the time between you?[68] [to Tom] What would you like?

TOM: The only time I have, because of my employment, is the weekends. That's the only time I have to spend with Heather. You know, I can appreciate what she's saying—that's the fun time, that's the time they can go out and do things on the weekend and travel around. I can appreciate that. But she's got to appreciate my needs, too. I don't get to see the child at all during the week. I can phone her, but it's just not the same thing.

So I want to see her. We're used to seeing one another on the weekends. She needs me, and I need her, too.

MEDIATOR: Would you see that Pat would also need some of that fun time?[69]

TOM: I see what she's saying there, but it works both ways.

MEDIATOR: How about you, Pat?

PAT: Well, I think that we both need to spend time with her on the weekends, and that's what we've done up to this point.[70] We've both spent time. But he's spent every weekend with her for periods of time. She'd go over there on Friday evening for a few hours or Saturday for a few hours, or Sunday she'd go out for a few hours. There was all those periods of time that was spent. Now, with the distance, it means sort of taking her for these long extended periods of time. What he's proposing now is, he wants her every weekend, and that just leaves nothing for me, nothing at all.

MEDIATOR: What would you like for you?[71]

PAT: Well, I think, you know—once, or maybe twice, if he could deal with these problems—maybe once or twice a month is—the weekends is, you know—maybe even alternate weekends.[72] You know, maybe that would be all right. But it still is a problem for her right now, because she doesn't know the place, and she's gone half the time when she has free time. I can see it eventually, possibly working itself into every second weekend, or something like that. But right now, it would be really difficult for her, because she wouldn't get a chance to develop relationships with other kids in the neighborhood or anything like that.[73]

MEDIATOR: That's true for most kids whose parents are divorced.

TOM: Who's creating that problem?

64. Tom's attack is reframed into a positive.
65. As a result, Tom recommits himself to learning how to handle the diabetes.

66. This lets the couple look at their WATNA and reminds them of the need to find a mutual solution in mediation.
67. Testing and explaining reality.
68. A move to quantify the dispute.
69. Tom is asked to reverse himself and think of Pat's needs. This approach uses dissonance theory. It also tells Pat I have heard her underlying concern.
70. Pat makes a substantial move and agrees that they both need weekend time. This movement is a product of our dealing with the diabetic issues completely and acknowledging Pat's need for time at 69.
71. I ask Pat what she does want.
72. Pat makes her first quantified proposal.
73. The situation is normalized.

MEDIATOR: [to Pat] So you're saying you feel that if the situation gets worked out, that for you, you would like to have her at least one weekend a month.[74]

PAT: No, no, at least two weekends . . .

MEDIATOR: Or perhaps alternate weekends.

PAT: I'd like to have her at least two weekends a month, at least two weekends a month. I mean, that's the close time for us; that's the time that we're really close.

MEDIATOR: [to Tom] So if you had alternate weekends, right? What would you do? I'm not asking you to buy this at all, for the moment. But if you had alternate weekends, what would you do with the rest of the year?[75] Because we're looking at when she's in school, and she's in school approximately one hundred and eighty days a year, which means she's out of school one hundred and eighty-six days. Well, one hundred and four of those are weekends, so there's another seventy-odd days a year that are not weekends and she's not in school. For example, what are the important holidays in your family?

TOM: Well, Christmas is an important time. Christmas Day and the way we celebrate it, and Christmas dinner, and we have Christmas Eve . . . [76]

PAT: Actually, I don't think that Christmas is going to be a major problem, since our families don't live too far apart. We could both see the child over Christmas and share a bit, because we won't have a hundred miles to worry about, since both our families are in Edmonton. So that isn't going to be a major problem, and I don't see the summers as being a major concern. If we can sort out all the other problems, I mean, I just think we could share those . . .

MEDIATOR: Share the summer.

PAT: Summers. I'll tell you another problem that I have, and this is . . . this is this: If Heather starts coming back and spending a lot of time in Edmonton again on the weekends, you know, she may not want to come back to Lloydminster.[77] I mean, this is where her friends are. So I, you know, we have to give her a chance to develop in Lloydminster, too. That's the problem that I see, and, you know, she's going to have to develop out there.

MEDIATOR: Yeah, you're both going to have to be supportive of her in making the move. It's not easy for a twelve-year-old to make the move, and in her particular case, the move is complicated by the fact that you two are separated.[78] If you were both moving up there, she would still have trouble. A twelve-year-old has trouble making moves, and you have to cooperate in terms of helping her integrate that. But my sense is that while Heather may not want it, that you both are clear that her primary residence should be [to Pat] with you.

PAT: Yes.

MEDIATOR: Because Tom is very clear about that, too.

TOM: Well, as I said, I think Heather should be with her mother, but, of course, I'd sooner it's here in Edmonton. There isn't a need for this move, and that's where I'm coming from.

MEDIATOR: What would you do if Heather comes down and begins saying, "Gee, Dad, I really would like to live with you, and I want to stay down in Edmonton and I want to be closer to my friends"?[79] It certainly will happen the first three months or so, because she won't have close friends for the first three months, and there will be a lot of tears and a lot of sadness. That would be there regardless of whether you two are getting divorced. Just simply moving is difficult for a twelve-year-old.[80] And I guess the question is: Would you be supportive of Pat when those things come up?

74. The dispute is quantified, in the belief that numbers are easier to understand, compromise and agree on.
75. An elaboration of the alternate-weekend idea that looks at the holidays. Tom is not asked to agree to one piece of it until he sees the whole package.
76. BL: Tom looks to Pat for confirmation of this statement, tending to indicate a low family role in the past.
77. Pat clearly states her underlying issue.
78. Heather's possible reaction is normalized, and a suggestion is made that Pat's fear has already been dealt with.
79. I finally act on Pat's underlying issue by trying to get Tom to make a commitment that would ease her concern.
80. The child's reaction to the move is normalized, to relieve some of the burden from the mother and from the divorce.

TOM: That's where I have some difficulty, because I just don't see the move as being necessary.[81] The child has great connections here. I know her friends. I like her friends, and I want her to maintain those friendships. She's moving somewhere where I don't know what her friends are going to be, and she's getting to that age where she's becoming interested in boys, and I won't even get to see these people. I trust Pat's judgment, and I'm hoping she'll do the right thing, but . . .

MEDIATOR: In a sense, the only recourse for you would be to have her live with you, right?[82]

TOM: That's the problem I have. It would be very difficult at this time.

MEDIATOR: Yeah. I mean, you've got the job where you travel, and all those responsibilities, etcetera. It just doesn't make . . .

TOM: It just doesn't make any sort of sense.

MEDIATOR: So, given that the move is inevitable, right, the issue is how you can be supportive of that move for Heather, in a way that frees you up so that you can enjoy your relationship with Heather and continue with your work, so it doesn't all get messed up.[83]

PAT: Really, one of my major concerns was that he would sabotage the move somehow or other by saying, "You like it here, don't you? It's too bad you had to move with your mom. Why doesn't your mom stay here in Edmonton?" I mean, it would be so easy for him to do that.[84]

TOM: Yeah, but it's so easy for her, you know, when she moves to Lloydminster, to just start cutting back on my access, making it difficult for me to see the child. I don't know, maybe she's going to end up moving out of the province or something. What do I do then? This is just the first step.[85]

MEDIATOR: Yeah. I don't think you have to trust each other, by the way. I don't think you have to trust each other, but what you've got to know is that there's a consequence for what you do. If you're supportive of Tom, Tom will be supportive of you, because that's in your best interests, and [to Tom] it's in your best interests. But if either of you are not supportive of the other, then the other won't be supportive back, and you're both in trouble.[86] So that, ironically, at this stage, your best interests lie in being supportive of each other in the parenting roles, because if you're not, the consequences are that you can each unravel this.[87] And if you do—and it's very easy to unravel it—you're both going to be in duck soup, right? So you don't have to trust. You have to know that cooperation is in your individual self-interests and in your mutual self-interests.[88] You've got to do it, therefore, for yourself, not for each other, because you're past doing things for each other, right? But you can do things for yourself that represent mutual interest. Because if you don't, you're in real trouble, both of you.[89] Because you'll get a situation that neither of you will want or be able to handle. If you cooperate, then you can have a situation where you can make the best of what is not a good deal for either of you, in that sense.[90] So we're looking at some of the other holidays, right? What other holidays are important? Christmas is an important one.[91]

81. Tom does not respond to Pat's underlying issue. Instead, he uses her concern as a weapon.
82. He is disarmed with a reality statement that could also be a threat, in that Tom stated earlier that he could not have the child living with him.
83. Using Tom's movement, achieved through reality testing, I try to gain support for Pat regarding her concern over Heather's not wanting to move.
84. The underlying issue is completely in the open now.
85. Tom's underlying fear emerges as Pat's is made clear.
86. Self-interest is the key to making a deal work. Trust is based on consequences, based on action, which leads to overlapping self- and mutual interests, which force trust.
87. Their overlapping self-interest is highlighted.
88. BL: The couple is thinking about this seriously. The wife's eyes roll up, and the husband's eyes are down.
89. A reminder of their WATNA.
90. Holding out hope and . . .
91. . . . returning to the task.

TOM: Well, the summer is important, you know. I'd like to have her for at least a month, to maybe travel to Vancouver, visit relatives, that sort of thing.

MEDIATOR: So you might be able to divide the summer vacation. What other big days are there?

TOM: Well, they get a spring break. I sometimes arrange to have a holiday at that time of year, so . . .

MEDIATOR: Spring break. Any national holidays that you all share . . .

PAT: Labor Day weekend. Yeah, there are holidays like that.

They usually fall on a Monday, so there might be a long weekend from time to time.[92]

MEDIATOR: Would you want to share . . .

TOM: That's another thing, too. I sometimes—you know, on long weekends, we're talking about weekends, [to Pat] that includes the extra day, too.[93]

PAT: You know, the thing is, it means if you were to have her for a month, [to mediator] that for a month he'd have to be worried about this problem every day. It's not a little problem, it's a problem every day that you have to live with, diabetes, every single day.[94]

MEDIATOR: Yeah. It's really a question for both of you, because it's something for concern for Tom, but it's also a question of whether or not you're going to be up in Lloydminster and enjoy that month, or sit up there worrying about it.[95] It's whether you want to take control of it or give control to Tom.

TOM: She can telephone every day and make sure it's done properly.

MEDIATOR: Okay. All right. So what are we looking at now? [to Tom] We're looking at your taking whatever action is necessary for you to gain the medical expertise and control. [to both] We're looking at alternate weekends for the parenting.[96]

TOM: I don't know if that's enough. I've got a problem with that.[97]

MEDIATOR: Okay, so . . .

TOM: I mean, are we talking about the full weekend, like Friday night right through Sunday night?

PAT: I don't know. How soon can you get up to Lloydminster to pick her up?

TOM: That's another problem—transportation back and forth.

MEDIATOR: I assume you're going to share in that, aren't you?[98]

PAT: You mean, that I would drive her part of the time, and you would come and get her the other part of the time?

MEDIATOR: That's what's most common. Sometimes you might do it by weekends, or sometimes just one of you might come. [to Pat] You might bring her down to Edmonton, and Tom may take her back to Lloydminster, or vice versa.[99] It would give you a chance to visit some of your friends.

TOM: That's a lot of driving back and forth.

MEDIATOR: It's a two-hundred-mile round trip, right?

TOM: It's about a four-hour drive. I'm sure not going to do that in a one-day turnaround.

MEDIATOR: What is it, two hours each way?

PAT: Yeah.

MEDIATOR: The way I see most people drive out here, it's probably . . . [100]

PAT: . . . shorter

MEDIATOR: . . . an hour and a half, yeah. Okay.

PAT: Yeah. I mean, when she's older, she would be able to go by bus or, you know, some other means.

92. Pat smiles at Tom. Obviously, this holiday has some family meaning, which does not appear to be relevant to the mediation; therefore, I ignore it.
93. Tom returns to the weekends, to be sure he gets the extra days on long weekends.
94. Pat counters by returning to the diabetes to balance control.
95. A return to reality for the couple. The issue of control for Pat is raised in a different context. Thus, she can have a new control, if she gives up an old control.
96. The discussion is narrowed back down to two issues.
97. Tom expands the issues.
98. A third alternative is offered, which introduces an idea

that they may have not thought was normal, since the residency parent tends to think that the other parent should do all the driving. In this case, however, the extra burden is being thrust on the father by the mother's move. Therefore, sharing the driving seems a logical way of handling it.

99. Educating them about the options available, to speed up the negotiations.
100. Humor can be used to break the tension.

MEDIATOR: Yup, and the next year would be a good year of development, in terms of her taking more responsibility. She may also may be able to do that trip up and down by bus.[101] I guess what you'd need to think about, Tom, is whether what you were looking for was every weekend. If it was not every weekend, could you deal with alternate weekends, if those alternate weekends ran from Friday evening through Sunday evening, and then sharing the major holidays and vacations in the way that we have talked about?[102]

PAT: Do you know, I still think it would be nice to give me a little bit longer time with her, to get used to living in a different place without being whipped back and forth.[103]

TOM: See, see, this is . . .

MEDIATOR: [to Pat] I think you're pushing it now.[104]

TOM: See, this is a concern I have, you know, that my access is going to get—*whoosh* . . .

PAT: I mean, the concern I have is about the insulin, do you see?

TOM: Yeah, we've dealt with that.

MEDIATOR: You've both got concerns, and they're real concerns. I wouldn't underplay any of those concerns. They're real. But the question is whether or not you're going to work something out that's right for Heather.[105]

PAT: Here's another problem that could arise: What do we do if Heather decides she wants to do some sports on the weekend?

MEDIATOR: Oh, I think she's . . . [to Pat] if she's with you that weekend, she negotiates it with you, [to Tom] if she's with you that weekend, she negotiates it with you. She's old enough now where she can negotiate those things directly. [to Pat] She comes to you for certain things, [to Tom] she comes to you for certain things right now. Kids are very smart. They know when they get the best deal from you, and they know when they get the best deal from you. She knows that already, and she knows how to deal with you. My sense is, she gets a square deal from each of you in different ways. So those issues—she'll have to talk to her dad about them, and she'll have to talk to her mom about them, and that's true for every kid, whether or not you're getting separated.

TOM: I have no problem with that, because I want her involved in athletics and things like that on the weekends, and there will be times when neither of us will be able to see her because of these sporting things.[106]

MEDIATOR: Okay. What I would like for you both to do between now and next week—and next week we should put all the flesh onto the idea. But what I'd like you to think about is how the arrangement would work on an alternate-weekend basis.[107] Who would bring her down, who would take her up? Whether you would take the whole weekend, or whether you would each take half—you know, one way, up and down. I would like you to identify the major holidays. Look through the calendar and see if there are any other big weekends. Recognize that if it's a long weekend, and [to Tom] that's your weekend, then Heather spends the long weekend with you. If it's your weekend, she'll spend the long weekend with you, and then think about the vacations. How you'd like to divide the summer, and perhaps the spring break from school. Then, when we get back together again next week, we can put these details into a coherent framework, so that you'll be able to know that. Tom, you have one other task between now and next weekend, which is to get the details on this plan, so that you would have knowledge of what it is you're going to do in terms of the medical piece. Very good. Then we'll get back together next week at the same time, and put the package together neatly.

PAT: Good. I'm looking forward to seeing him taking this information to heart.

MEDIATOR: All right.

101. The problem of transportation is tied to a positive statement regarding Heather's development, which offers hope. All situations are frozen only for that moment. All children grow and change, and it is helpful for parents to be reminded of this reality.
102. A return to the specifics.
103. Pat raises her underlying concern again.
104. Given the reality that Tom will not try to triangulate the child into moving back to Edmonton, I send a warning signal to Pat, to prevent her from dismissing his proposal.
105. I acknowledge and legitimate the concerns and turn the focus back to the parenting issue.
106. Tom's response relieves some of Pat's fears.
107. With the broad agreement apparently reached, I assign tasks for the next session.

Analysis

The Mediator's Assumptions

The assumption that conflict over issues is resolvable in mediation, and that conflict over dynamic behavior is resolvable in therapy, leads me to avoid dealing with marital issues. When a couple have ongoing dynamic marital issues that reflect their marriage relationship, they will bring that relationship with them to the mediation. In Chapter One, I discuss when the mediator should refer the parties to therapy. Frequently, however, the parties to the dispute engage in marital behavior that is dysfunctional in that it impedes the process but is not destructive enough to prevent the process from working at all. The mediator must decide when such marital conflict can be permitted in the session. The general rule is to allow conflict as long as it does not prevent the process from working. Since a significant amount of relational behavior will take place between the parties, the mediator must choose strategies for containing it. The most useful strategy seems to be to ignore it, as we have seen in the case of Michael and Debbie (Chapter Four).

The Mediator's Strategies

Avoiding the Marital Fight. Pat revealed that their daughter is diabetic, and she claimed that only she could take care of her. As I gathered data on this question, I discovered that the father had had a minimal role in Heather's medical care. However, Tom expressed willingness (albeit reluctant) to learn how to provide this care. Thus, I attempted to solve the issue through the husband's willingness to learn how to handle the diabetes. Pat would not accept this, and she tried numerous strategies to avoid reaching an agreement on the daughter's medical care. This was, in part, the old marriage fight—that is, in the marriage, the mother took exclusive care of the daughter; in the divorce, the father wanted to share in this care. Indeed, he would have to share in her care, if he was to share in the parenting after the mother and the daughter moved.

In this case, I used numerous strategies to avoid getting caught in the marital issues. When the couple engaged in a spousal fight, I separated their spousal (past) roles from their parental (future) roles. (12) For example, early in the session, Pat made a nonnegotiable statement: that Heather was going with her, and that this was not an issue. She asserted a marriage role of sole decision maker. Normally, such a statement from a wife would elicit a marital response from the husband. I prevented this by asking Tom to respond to me, not to Pat, thereby avoiding a marital fight. (14)

Sometimes I asked a clarification question, which was also future-focused. (19) At other times, I used a future-focused comment to create doubt about the husband's position. (21) Each time the fight looked as if it were breaking out again, I used a future-focused question (27) to avoid taking sides in the marital fight. (30) I also used future-oriented questions to break up squabbles and get one or both of the parties to think about the issue in a different way. (39) Other past-to-future conversions can be found at 41, 47, 48, 57, 58, 61, 71, 83, 95, and 101.

Another complicating factor in this case was Pat's underlying fear. It controlled her negotiating behavior and challenged the mediator as well. The underlying fear also needed to be dealt with as a legitimate issue conflict, not as a dynamic behavioral conflict. Each time Pat raised her underlying fear, however, I gave it less priority than she did.

I was operating under a general rule that priority should be given to the problems that are a function of the divorce. Problems that are not a function of the divorce will probably continue; knowing that the problems are not divorce-related may allow people to use their normal problem-solving skills. Pat's move to a new town would present Heather with problems that all children of moving parents have to deal with; the problem of settling into a new home and with new peers faces all children who move. Therefore, when Pat first raised the issue, I assigned it a low priority, since it did not fit my model of dealing with the divorce-related problems first.

I continued to ignore it for the first half of the session, even though Pat raised it a number of times. Finally, I sensed its importance and dealt directly with her concern. Once the concern was dealt with, the divorce-related issues were quickly resolved. I am reminded of an old professor who told me, "Rules are made for the guidance of wise people and the adherence of fools." I had allowed a rule to become rigid. Had I allowed the rule to guide me, I might well have dealt with the underlying fear earlier in the session.

Moving from Past to Future. The problem lies in the past; the solution lies in the future. Most participants in a dispute seek to dwell on the past, not recognizing that the past is unchangeable. They can control their futures, however. Therefore, the mediator frequently tries to move clients from a past (problem) to a future (solution) focus. Obviously, the parties cannot negotiate a solution while still engaged in the past.

Mediation is not an arena in which to settle past marital issues. It is the arena for establishing a workable future. Thus, the mediator tries to avoid dealing with the marital issues because, in the context of mediation, they are not resolvable. Clients in therapy may be able to gain insights into the past, but the goal of mediation is to help establish a new, future relationship.

Defining the Problem. When two people believe that they have an intractable dispute, the mediator's primary task is to gain control of the problem to be solved. He must redefine the problem, moving from two individual self-serving positions to a mutual problem statement that requires action from both parties and that, if the problem is solved, provides benefits to both. The mediator must orient the couple's thinking from defining the problem as intractable to defining it as a problem that has not yet yielded to a solution.

When the mediator joins the disputing parties, he takes over the management of the negotiations. A significant part of the problem of the disputing parties is their inability to agree, either on the process of resolving the dispute or on the content of the dispute. Indeed, the two parties often have quite different versions of the nature and history of the dispute.

Thus, each party has a unilateral problem definition, and the parties are in dispute about process and content. Their inability to develop a joint and mutual definition of the problem is itself a major part of their problem. This means that the mediator's role in the early stages of negotiations is to define the problem to be solved. The mediator attempts to find and control a mutual problem definition, whose resolution benefits both parties.

If the mediator accepts either spouse's definition, he will also "buy into" a solution that benefits that spouse. Therefore, the mediator attempts to create legitimate doubt about the certainty of each party's position, as a step toward taking control of the problem definition, to ensure its neutrality. In this case, the husband's opening position was unrealistic: He wanted to stop his wife from moving to a new job a hundred miles away. Since this was an unattainable goal in this jurisdiction, the mediator had to help him face reality and develop an alternative goal that protected his self-interest.

As long as the mediator accepts and works with two disparate problem definitions, no agreement is possible. The mediator attempts to recast the problem statements as mutual definitions of problems that can be solved by movement on both sides. The mediator moves to create a mutual problem definition, using strategies that match the clients' behavior. In this case, I normalized the couple's experiences. When one spouse states a unique and therefore not easily solved problem, the mediator restates it as a normal and therefore solvable situation.

Tom's first problem definition was vague. The problem could be solved only by a return to the status quo. (7, 8) Later, he defined the problem as Pat's unwillingness to wait for a promotion in the town where they were then living. (11) His solution was for her to wait for a promotion in Edmonton. Tom repeated his call for a return to the status quo, which required change only on Pat's side.

In her first problem definition, Pat denied any responsibility for the problem. It had just happened to her; therefore, she had no power to help its resolution, and the solution had to come from a change by Tom. (4, 9) Pat characterized Tom's demand to see Heather every weekend as ridiculous, saying that it would not work. She did not say that the couple ought to share weekends, since this would have weakened her problem definition, and she was not ready to let go of her original position. She added the issue of their daughter's diabetes, to further complicate the conflict and to make it unique and therefore less easily solved. (18)

My role, up to this point, was to try to obtain a mutual problem definition. In a summary to Pat, I added her need, so as to lay some responsibility for the problem on her. Believing that some of the couple's conflict was a confusion between parental and spousal roles, I also distinguished between these two roles. I followed this by testing a mutual problem definition: "We're talking about when she [Heather] moves, what kind of access and time she'll have with her dad." (19) Most of the first part of the session was devoted to obtaining a mutual problem definition, so that the couple could bargain realistically. Although Tom did not actually reject my definition of the problem—that it was not whether he saw Heather, but how often—he also did not operate under it for some time.

Up to this point, each party had stated a problem that was resolvable only by movement on the part of the other. I sharpened the problem definition, to help Tom be realistic in his own self-interest and to make it clear that the problem was solvable by cooperation between both parties. In doing so, I raised the possibility of a solution that did not involve winning or losing. (21)

Summarizing. I frequently summarized the situation for the couple, to help them stay on task, to clarify that my understanding was correct, and to let the couple know that both had been heard and understood. Summaries take the content of each person's position and play it back to the couple. By stripping away the emotional aspects of a message and focusing on the content, the mediator helps each spouse hear what the other has said. Each party listens to the mediator more carefully, and often hears more clearly.

As the session proceeded, I tended to direct more and more of the summaries toward the couple, whereas in the earlier stages, the summaries tended to be directed toward an individual. As a mediator works on gaining a mutual problem definition, he needs to move each party separately. When the mediator is working on a solution to the mutually defined problem, however, he needs to move the parties jointly.

Clients' Negotiating Behavior

Conflict Expansion. When Tom finally accepted a mutual definition (22), Pat, who should have been pleased with Tom's movement, expanded the conflict and the problem definition. In retrospect, my suggestion of what he thought was a mutual problem definition did not adequately deal with Pat's concerns regarding Heather's settling into her new life in Lloydminster. (25) Tom responded with a different expansion (the size of his apartment), to complement Pat's expansion and provide him with a defense against his wife's argument.

Multiply Defined Problems. Pat's opening position was related to the residency of their daughter, Heather. Pat wanted Heather to move with her. As I clarified this issue, Pat developed a new problem definition: Heather's diabetes. This was a more complex issue, and as I was working on it, Pat raised a third issue: distance, and the time Heather had available. At this point, Pat hinted at another, hidden problem. Thus, at one point in the mediation, the wife presented three problems. I could not work on all three at once, for then nothing could have been solved. Rather, I chose to settle the issues one at a time. The issue of residency was resolved, then the issue of the diabetes, and finally, while we worked on the details of the parenting arrangements, the issue of Heather's ability to settle in Lloydminster.

Faced with a number of mixed issues, a mediator must choose the order in which to deal with the problems. A general rule is that the mediator works first on issues that do not need prior agreement and then moves on to the issues that, in order to be resolved, must be preceded by agreement. Thus the order of dealing with the wife's issues was (1) residency, (2) care of the diabetes, and (3) the underlying issue. Agreement on issue 1 was necessary for agreement on issue 2, and agreement on issues 1 and 2 was necessary before agreement could be reached on issue 3.

When the parties raise a number of issues, or aspects of the same problem, the mediator cannot deal with all the issues at the same time; therefore, he separates them. In deciding whether to move on the practical or emotional aspects, the mediator isolates the issues into independent components. Starting with the practical issues, the mediator isolates the emotional components for solution later, when the problem-solving climate improves. In starting with the smallest or easiest practical issues, the mediator begins to build trust in the process while gaining cooperation on the smaller practical issues. From this first level of cooperation, the mediator is able to tackle the more complex practical and emotional (underlying) issues in a better climate.

In this case, the practical and the prior-agreement issues coincided. The wife created multiple issues by complicating the access question. The question started with her move to a new job. She then added the daughter's diabetes. Further, she brought up the size of the husband's apartment and the factors of time and distance. Pat moved among these issues whenever she felt pressure to move on an issue—before the emergence of her underlying fear. Thus, the complexity of the issues was partly a defensive strategy of the wife, which frustrated mediation until the underlying fear surfaced. I brought order to the session with a monologue that identified all the overt issues.

Negotiation of Underlying Issues. Sometimes one party has an underlying concern, which makes agreement more difficult. Indeed, an agreement is not possible unless the underlying issue is dealt with. An underlying issue is a dilemma, concern, or need of one party, which is not announced but which pervades the discussion and is usually built into that party's position. In this case, Pat was concerned that if she moved to Lloydminster and Heather visited her father and former peers in Edmonton, she would not want to return to Lloydminster. Thus, Pat's dilemma was how to make the move without losing her daughter.

Since Pat also had two other issues on the table, I could not deal with the underlying issue until the two prior problems were resolved. Each time Pat raised the issue of Heather's not wanting to stay in Lloydminster, I attempted to normalize the problem by pointing out that Heather would have had the entry problem regardless of whether the couple were divorced, and I continued to work on the other problems defined by the wife. Another part of Pat's underlying concern, however, was that Tom would try to woo Heather into staying in Edmonton with him, and that Heather would be receptive to this proposal.

People frequently do not deal openly with underlying issues, perhaps because the issues are embarrassing or make people feel undefended and in a weaker bargaining position. Perhaps they also feel that keeping something hidden will give them an advantage in the negotiations. An underlying issue often controls the negotiations, and until it is discovered and dealt with, its existence prevents agreement on other issues. Therefore, the mediator is sensitive to underlying issues and attempts to uncover them as soon as possible.

One clear indication of an unidentified underlying issue occurs when the mediator successfully helps the couple resolve a practical issue, only to find that movement on the total agreement is blocked, or perhaps the party with the underlying issue continually blocks reasonable, practical solutions to other issues: The closer the mediator gets to the underlying issue, the more likely is resistance on other practical solutions.

Here, the underlying issue was slowly revealed. The first

indication of it (in hindsight) occurred with Pat's statement that her husband wanted Heather every weekend. The "sugar daddy" allegation was another indication (evident only in hindsight). Given the centrality of the diabetes issue, this could also have been a statement of Tom's parenting ability: A "sugar daddy" would be most dangerous to a diabetic child.

Later on, Pat was explicit about part of the problem of moving: Heather's making new friends. (25) I acknowledged the concern but suggested that it be dealt with later. (26) Pat raised it yet again, adding new information and thus creating a theme. My response was to normalize the problem. While acknowledging her fears, I suggested we deal with them in sequence, putting the underlying fear last. As a result, while I moved toward a practical solution of Pat's overt fears, the underlying issue dominated Pat's behavior. The underlying fear—Would Tom sabotage the move?—was not yet clearly articulated by the wife, nor did I understand it. With this impediment, practical solutions to the other issues evaded the couple.

I tried a strategy of imagining the future, by asking them how they would want to organize their time with Heather if she were living in Lloydminster. This allowed each partner to fantasize and risk making suggestions that were not offers of compromise, thereby creating movement. Pat made the first movement, on sharing weekends with Tom. That movement followed my articulating her need as legitimate, and the husband's response that he understood but that "it work[ed] both ways."

Pat made a practical proposal, specifying the number of times Heather would go to Tom. She was now dealing with the practical issues, but the underlying fear was still strong. She reiterated her concern, indicating that I needed to do more work before the underlying fear would emerge and be dealt with directly.

Pat finally stated specifically the first part of her underlying fear: that Heather would want to stay in Edmonton. (77) I tried to normalize, ending my comments with an embedded suggestion: that while Heather might want to live in Edmonton, both parents had a mutual interest and agreed that she should reside with Pat. I finally dealt with the possibility of Tom's sabotage by asking him about it directly. (79) This was the key point in the session with respect to the underlying issue.

When Tom attempted to use Pat's underlying issue as a weapon against her, I quickly tested the reality of Tom's threat, as a way of warning him about the consequences of this strategy. (82) Pat then openly identified her major concern: that Tom would sabotage the move. (84) From this point on, I focused on self-interest and overlapping self-interest, to move the couple toward an acceptable agreement.

Once the hidden fear was in the open, I was able to deal with the issue by restating the concern and gaining Tom's commitment not to engage in that strategy, thus demonstrating that Tom did not want to have Heather live with him full-time. Pat was then able to let go of the underlying issue and come to an agreement on sharing the parenting in a way that also would help Heather developmentally.

8

NEVILLE AND CHERYL: WHO *DOESN'T* GET THIS CHILD?

Every case is unique. Every couple has their own idiosyncratic view of life in general and of the presenting problem in particular. This is one reason why mediation is so challenging. The tasks of divorce mediation may appear uniform in each case—settle the amount and duration of support, divide the assets, and establish the future parenting for the family—but the dynamics of the couple make each case different.

Just as each couple's dynamics are different, each mediator's dynamic differs from that of any other mediator. Our professional training provides us with the means to prevent our dynamics from intruding into the mediation—when we are aware of them. There are times, however, when the dynamics of the mediator intrude so subtly that even the most aware mediator may not sense the intrusion. Neville and Cheryl's case is such an instance.

Neville and Cheryl have been married for eleven years. They have three children—Ken, age eleven; Ashley, age nine; and Michael, age seven. When they came to see me, they had been separated for six months and were locked in a dispute over custody of the three children. The presenting problem was to determine the parenting of the three children, but as the session proceeded, the presenting problem changed. It appeared that both parents wanted custody of their daughter. Neither was particularly involved with the elder son, Ken, and neither wanted the younger boy, Michael. This was an interracial couple; the husband came from the Caribbean region.

Neville was quite hostile toward mediation and the mediator. Cheryl seemed to have difficulty following some of the process. The couple did not fight overtly, but there was a lot of tension between them. My first problem was to understand and accept that they had radically different interests in the children. In the early part of the session, I focused most of my effort on the invisible son, Ken. It was not until the latter part of the session that I finally accepted and began working on the idea that neither parent wanted the youngest child.

This session clearly tested the validity and practicality of my assumption that there is "that of God" in each of us. The behavior of both parents tested my balance. That behavior was also exacerbated by Neville's continued rejection of me. He challenged me and my work at each step of the way, and it was only by working under that assumption that I was finally able to connect with him. I discuss that assumption, as it applies to this case, after the transcript.

The strategies that appear in this chapter include summarizing and using the flip chart. In this case, I missed an important issue, but the process rescued us. My own dynamics caused me to turn a blind eye to the couple's rejection of Michael; instead, I focused on Ken, their other son. However, the process and my own task focus rescued me, so that real progress was made in the session. I discuss the way I missed the issue, and how the process worked, after the actual transcript, where I also discuss the problems of the mediator's bias.

Finally, I discuss how one deals with sensitive issues. The color question is important to Neville and Cheryl. I ignore neither the interracial nature of their relationship nor the role of color in their family. I deal with both issues in the same way I would treat any other significant factor in the case.

The client's negotiating behavior includes examples of triangulation.

Upon reading this transcript, you will discover that no

actual negotiations take place in the session. Indeed, I discouraged an attempt by Neville to negotiate over Ken. This session was a preparatory session, clearing the ground for later negotiations. It demonstrates the importance of timing and of the willingness to understand and deal with dynamic issues, to ensure that the parents are ready to move on to actual bargaining. The transcript of the session follows.

Transcript and Annotations

MEDIATOR: Well, it's good to meet with both of you, Neville and Cheryl. As you know, your judge has asked you to come and see me, to see if we can work out some understanding between you and for you in relationship with the three children—Ken and Ashley and Michael.[1] As you know, the judges have asked you to come over to see me because they have a basic philosophy: that you're the ones that really know best what's right for your three children. Of course, the judges care about your kids, but they don't love your kids. You love your kids, and they think that you probably have a better chance of doing what's right for them than asking the judges to impose a decision for you.[2] Although, obviously, if it doesn't work out, then they will impose a decision on you.[3] But my expectation is that you're going to be able to work out what's right just for you. Now, if I understand, you have been living apart for about six months.[4] Why don't you tell me what the current situation is in regard to the children?[5]

NEVILLE: Well, whenever we talk about the children—the current situation is . . . quite frankly, I would like to have Ashley. Let me put it that way.[6]

MEDIATOR: Uh huh. And Ashley is how old, Neville?[7]

NEVILLE: Ashley is nine years old.

MEDIATOR: She's nine. All right. Ken is how old?

CHERYL: Twelve.

MEDIATOR: Twelve. And Michael is?[8]

CHERYL: Seven.

MEDIATOR: Seven. Okay. Twelve, nine, and seven. [to Neville] So, when you talk about this, you would like to have Ashley, the middle daughter, live with you.[9]

NEVILLE: Yes.

CHERYL: And I feel that, you know, she should be with her mother.

MEDIATOR: Uh huh. All right. How about the other two?[10]

CHERYL: Well, I think Michael should be with his father. I think he's at an age now where, you know, he needs a father.

MEDIATOR: He's a seven-year-old. Okay. So, how do you feel about that, Neville?[11]

NEVILLE: Well, Michael is very demanding and . . .

MEDIATOR: Seven-year-olds always are, right?[12]

NEVILLE: . . . unlike the other two when they were passing through seven. He is somewhat spoiled by his mother, too.[13]

MEDIATOR: I'm sorry. I was trying to understand what your feeling was about where you think it would be better for Michael to reside.[14]

NEVILLE: I think it would be better for him to be with his mother.[15] They're quite close, and not only that, because he is so demanding . . . . As a technician myself, working on my own, sometimes I work sporadically, and so on, and the type of attention he needs, I think he would get better from his mother.

1. The opening statement is designed to empower the couple to make their own decisions and to establish mediation as the arena to settle the dispute.
2. This is a positive statement about their parenting, to further empower them.
3. The threat of the alternative arena enhances the attraction of mediation or at least makes mediation the least unattractive option.

4. A positive assumption and a "here and now" statement start the session off in the present.
5. The question is undirected, to enable me to learn who will answer it and how. BL: My hands are turned, palms up, to indicate that either party may answer.
6. Neville provides a partial response, but the point uppermost in his mind comes out.
7. I note this and continue to gather data.
8. Data gathering expands to include all three children.
9. Having completed the preliminary data collection, I use a summary to check my understanding.
10. A neutral response to Cheryl, while I continue to enlarge the data collection.
11. Cheryl's response is checked with Neville's, to see that it coincides.
12. A clumsy attempt to normalize, which instead sounds more like a criticism of Neville, who . . .
13. . . . implicitly criticizes my lack of knowledge of his family.
14. I quickly apologize, to get back into balance and redirect the question. Here, I offer the first definition of the dispute in a neutral, nonjudgmental way.
15. Each parent wants the youngest child, Michael, to live with the other. This is difficult for me (a youngest child), and I miss the point, dealing only with the surface issue.

MEDIATOR: I see.

CHERYL: I think that's just an excuse. I work, too.[16]

MEDIATOR: An excuse for what?[17]

CHERYL: For not taking him.

MEDIATOR: Uh huh. Because you're a nurse, right?[18]

CHERYL: Uh huh.

MEDIATOR: All right. So, now, let me see if I understand, then. The first disagreement between you, if I understand it, is that Neville, you would like Ashley to live with you, and Cheryl, you would like Ashley to live with you.[19, 20]

NEVILLE: No way!

CHERYL: Uh huh.

MEDIATOR: And the second dispute between you is that you would like Michael to live with Neville, and Neville, you would like Michael to live with Cheryl.[21, 22]

NEVILLE: Yes.

MEDIATOR: All right. What about Ken? Where does he fit in?[23]

CHERYL: I don't really have a strong stance one way or the other about Ken.[24]

NEVILLE: Ken can live with his mother.

MEDIATOR: All right. Tell me a little bit about each of the kids. Tell me a little bit about Ashley.[25]

CHERYL: Ashley?

NEVILLE: She's a bright young lady, and we are quite close. We're quite attached. And, funny enough, sometimes I call her my right-hand man.

MEDIATOR: Uh huh. Yeah. Yeah.

NEVILLE: She's a scientific sort of person: She just gets involved in technology, and she's generally bright. She's good in the arts as well in sports.

MEDIATOR: Uh huh. Uh huh.

CHERYL: I think she's quite pretty.

MEDIATOR: Pretty! Uh huh.

CHERYL: She's quite well behaved, very helpful and considerate, and so I call her "mother's helper" kind of thing.

MEDIATOR: I see. Okay.

NEVILLE: [derisively] Mother's helper.

MEDIATOR: So, on the one hand, she's your right hand, and she's also your right hand.[26]

CHERYL: Uh huh.

MEDIATOR: Okay. All right. Tell me a little bit about Ken.[27]

NEVILLE: [deep sigh] He tears around all the time. One thing, he's a pretty poor loser. When we're playing games at home—table games—we don't have to get very far before he realizes that he might lose. He cries, and his mother goes on his side. He goes out to play baseball or play ball with the kids. He comes in screaming. I try to toughen him up . . .

MEDIATOR: What does he do well?[28] [long pause][29]

NEVILLE: [turning to Cheryl] What does he do well?

CHERYL: Ken? He's a quiet boy, really. More of a serious sort of boy.[30]

MEDIATOR: How is he as a scholar?

CHERYL: He's average.

MEDIATOR: Average. Sports?

CHERYL: He's not really one for sports. He's more of a book person.

MEDIATOR: He reads a lot?

CHERYL: Reads a lot and watches T.V.

MEDIATOR: He's a good reader?

CHERYL: Uh hum.

MEDIATOR: Enjoys reading?

16. Cheryl makes a global statement.
17. A specifying question.
18. Having gained some clarity about the conflict through that question, I check my understanding that they both work outside the home.
19. I define the first issue by summarizing what they have told me and by honoring each position. The playback is used to edit their versions into a positive form.

20. BL: I use my hands, circling toward the left when talking about Neville's position and toward the right when talking about Cheryl's position.
21. I use the same language to summarize the second issue.
22. BL: To complement this, I use the same hand gestures.
23. This undirected question is designed to help me find out about the third child. It moves the clients away from a potentially explosive situation, where I could polarize the parents regarding Ashley.
24. In talking about Michael, each party is firm about his living with the other. He is not wanted. Their responses about Ken indicate a low investment in him. He is invisible. This response and the mediator's dynamics provide the basis for developing a hypothesis: that their low investment in Ken—or, rather, in the two boys—is the problem.
25. Redirects the family back to the three children via Ashley.
26. Mutualizes their responses regarding Ashley and . . .
27. . . . returns to Ken.
28. I make no direct comment on Neville's negative response, while redirecting him with a positive question.
29. There is a long silence, while Neville tries to think of something good about Ken. I am comfortable with silence and make no attempt to rescue Neville by filling the silence.
30. Neither parent responds with positive information. Therefore, I embark on a series of questions, to try to find some positive statement about Ken. There is, of course, an embedded suggestion in these questions: There are some good things about Ken. Note that Cheryl answers all the questions.

NEVILLE: I don't think he's really . . . think he's up to par.[31] We have our differences in that I think he should be doing a lot better than that for his age.

MEDIATOR: Okay. [to Neville] Does your par differ from [to Cheryl] yours?[32, 33]

CHERYL: Yes.

MEDIATOR: In terms of expectations from Ken?

CHERYL: I think he's way too hard on Ken.

MEDIATOR: [to Cheryl] And how about you?

CHERYL: What is the question?

MEDIATOR: You thought that Neville was too hard on Ken? How about you?

CHERYL: I think I'm more understanding of him.[34]

MEDIATOR: All right. Tell me a little bit about Michael, the youngest.

CHERYL: He's a typical seven-year-old boy. He gets into trouble and mischief. He's very curious, and he likes to get into things.

MEDIATOR: Okay. [to Neville] And you find that a little difficult to deal with.

NEVILLE: He's kind of carefree.[35]

MEDIATOR: Carefree. Okay. So, let me see if I understand correctly. Your feeling, if I understand, is that you would like Ken to live with his mother.[36] I wasn't sure that I fully understood, Cheryl, what you wanted for Ken.

CHERYL: He can live with me or with his father. I don't have a strong . . . like, I think he would be fine with either.

MEDIATOR: Uh huh. All right. So, then—so you feel that you would like Ken to live with his mother. You feel that he might live with either of you.

CHERYL: Uh huh.

MEDIATOR: You feel that Ashley should live with you?

CHERYL: Definitely.

MEDIATOR: And you feel that Ashley should live with you?

NEVILLE: Precisely.

MEDIATOR: You feel that Michael should live with Cheryl? And, Cheryl, you think Michael should live with Neville?[37]

CHERYL: Yup.

MEDIATOR: All right. Pretty complex, huh? Pretty complex.[38]

NEVILLE: I don't think so. It seems pretty easy to me.[39]

MEDIATOR: Uh huh. Yeah, I guess if you got exactly what you wanted, it would be easy. [to Cheryl] If you got exactly what you wanted, it would be easy. So the problem is that you've got to incorporate what each other wants, as well as what you yourself want. Right?

CHERYL: Well, it seems sort of reasonable that the daughter should go to the mother and the son should go to the father.

NEVILLE: They fight like cats and dogs, she and her daughter.

MEDIATOR: Okay.[40]

31. When Cheryl finally comes up with a positive statement, Neville interjects with a clear negative.
32. An attempt to separate the couple on the apparent negative agreement about Ken. Until now, they have presented a fairly solid wall against me, and I try to provoke some differences, to see if I can enter their dispute through the conflict.
33. BL: I circle my hands toward each of them individually, to reinforce the question. Note that the use of the term *par* mirrors Neville's.
34. A small difference emerges regarding Ken, so I move to Michael, hoping to complete the family profile in an atmosphere where their differences are clearer.
35. A neutral response from Neville.
36. I summarize my understanding regarding Ken (Neville nods assent) and seek clarification from Cheryl, leaving Michael aside. I am still having difficulty dealing with neither parent's wanting him.
37. This series of summaries checks each situation for each child with each parent.

38. This is an attempt to join the couple through gentle humor.
39. Neville's response indicates that I have yet to engage him in the process.
40. I ignore this bickering.

CHERYL: No, we don't.

MEDIATOR: So, tell me a little bit about this. . . . What are the reasons, what would you say, [to Neville] if I were to ask you the two most important reasons why Ashley should live with you? And then I'll ask you the same, Cheryl, the two most important reasons. What would they be?[41]

NEVILLE: I think that Cheryl doesn't give Ashley love, the mother-daughter relationship . . . [42]

MEDIATOR: Oh, I'm sorry. Let me just intervene for a moment, Neville. It wasn't so much that I was asking what you didn't want, but what you did want. That is, from your perspective, what are the positive reasons for you in terms of Ashley living with you?[43]

NEVILLE: I think it would break her heart if she weren't living with me. We're quite close to each other, and we get along quite well together. The child is so spontaneous when she is relating to me.

MEDIATOR: Okay. What is the current arrangement in regard to Ashley? [to Cheryl] I'll come back to the question I asked you in a moment. How much time does she currently spend with you, Neville?[44]

NEVILLE: Sometimes, even when she comes home from school, she comes down to the shop and spends some time down at the shop with me. She spends quite a bit of time with me, on odd occasions. The weekends, we spend time together. I have been going in rotation with the children, taking them out on occasion on their own, like any good father would do.

MEDIATOR: Yeah.

NEVILLE: Quite often, the boys think I'm out to lunch, but not Ashley. When we go out together, we might go to see a movie or go to the mall.

MEDIATOR: [to Cheryl] Is she currently living primarily with you?[45]

CHERYL: Yes.

MEDIATOR: [to Cheryl] All three children are currently living with you? Okay, good. [to Neville] We come back, then, to the question: the two reasons why Ashley should live with you.[46] I was trying to think of sort of positive reasons. I suppose if she were to lose either of you, it would break her heart, and that's true for all children, and particularly true for special children. But let me ask you for two positive reasons why she should live with you.

NEVILLE: Okay. One of the reasons is, she is quite spontaneous with me. She comes to me with her homework and things beyond her homework. The child's a genius. She works beyond what is given her, and I'm able to help her. Her mother, all due respects to her, . . . [47]

MEDIATOR: Don't tell me about Cheryl. Tell me about Neville.[48]

NEVILLE: Aren't they connected?[49]

MEDIATOR: I'm not sure. I really want to know what you want, you see, because then I can be the most helpful. If I know and understand what you want.[50] [to Cheryl] If I know and understand what you want, I can be most helpful. I'm not particularly helpful to you until I understand what it is you disagree with your spouse about.

41. While asking for positive statements from each parent regarding Ashley, I tell them both that they will have a chance to speak. This assurance limits the need of either to interrupt, and each can think of his or her own response to the mediator's question, not to what the other is saying.
42. Neville responds with a negative reason designed to augment his position.

43. I apologize for the misunderstanding, to avoid alienating him further, since I am aware of Neville's distance from the process. This redirects the question, to focus Neville on the task at hand.
44. I suddenly realize that I do not know the current access arrangements, and therefore I have nothing to measure their responses by. The switch to data gathering is temporary.
45. The access data is shared and will need to be double-checked with Cheryl before we return to the original line of questions. This demonstrates the importance of tracking the interview, to be sure that the mediator stays on task and is balanced in his or her interaction between the parties as evenly as reasonably possible. It also helps the mediator decide why and how to pursue a specific line of questions. I chose not to pursue any questions regarding Neville's relationship with Ashley once I knew that she lived primarily with Cheryl, on the basis of a belief that a "surrogate boyfriend" relationship between a father and a daughter is normal. (See discussion following the transcript.)
46. I remember Neville's nonresponse at 41 and redirect the question to him. Another example of tracking.
47. When Neville begins to wander into an attack on Cheryl, . . .
48. . . . the interjection refocuses him on the question and on himself.
49. Neville continues to challenge my every action.
50. A nondefensive response places the responsibility back on the couple, to help the mediator be helpful to them.

NEVILLE: I would like to give Cheryl [sic]—to give . . . to give Ashley the best that she can get in terms of education, in terms of culture. I would like to be able to give her the emotional support she needs as well, because I think she gets very good—and here I have to make some comparison—she gets good emotional support from me.

MEDIATOR: From you. Great.[51]

NEVILLE: She also spontaneously attends to me, which shows her love and closeness.

MEDIATOR: Okay. So, the principal reasons, then, for Ashley living with you are that she's spontaneous with you, she's open with you, she gets good support from you, she gets help academically from you and in other matters, and that she can be more spontaneous when she's with you.[52] Those would be the reasons. Okay, good. That's helpful.

NEVILLE: And she's planned out her—she talks about what she wants to do later on in her career, et cetera. We're in sync on that.

MEDIATOR: Okay. Good. [to Cheryl] Ashley, tell me two reasons . . .

CHERYL: Cheryl.

MEDIATOR: I'm sorry. Cheryl, tell me two reasons why Ashley should be with you.

CHERYL: The primary reason is that she's nine years old. She's a little girl, and I think she needs a mother and should stay with her mother, you know, in the sense that we're both girls, both women, that sort of thing. And the other reasons are, you know, I think I could say the same, in terms of the homework and emotional support and closeness, that's true. But there's other reasons, too.[53] I think she's at an age where it's not good to change schools and where she lives. Her friends. She has a lot of friends, and they're all in the neighborhood.

MEDIATOR: Okay. Those are sort of negative reasons. Stay with the positive, if you would, at this juncture.[54]

CHERYL: Well, just—she does have a lot of friends in the neighborhood, and I wouldn't want to see her move.

MEDIATOR: So she has a good peer relationship, lots of friends, right?[55]

CHERYL: Uh huh.

MEDIATOR: And that she's—your feeling is that, for a nine-year-old girl, there are developmental reasons for them being with mothers, and you can provide that support?

CHERYL: Yes.

MEDIATOR: Okay. All right. So, you see, you both very much care about her. Right? Do you see? [to Cheryl] You care a lot about Ashley and what's right and best for her, and [to Neville] you care a lot about Ashley and what's right and best for her.[56]

NEVILLE: May I say something?

MEDIATOR: Please do.

NEVILLE: This business of what you call developmental, or whatever it is. The fact that she's a woman, and Ashley is a girl. It's a load of bosh. I have seen guys who have brought up their daughters beautifully.[57]

MEDIATOR: Um hum. Yeah. The professional literature indicates that children need both parents, of course.[58] They need the best from their father, and they need the best from their mother, and only you two can, in a sense, give that. There are times when the children are closer with Dad and closer with Mom, and that differs, actually, by sex. Sometimes the boys are closer to Dad and sometimes the girls are closer to Dad, and sometimes the boys are closer to Mom and sometimes the girls are closer to Mom, in terms of their changing needs. They need good role models; [to Neville] they need to role model from you, what it's like in terms of dealing with men, and [to Cheryl] they need to role model from you, in terms of what it's like to deal with women. My sense is that you can both give that to the two kids.[59] I'm now clear in my head about what the issues are between you around Ashley. That is, you both love and like her a great deal, and you both have a lot to give to her and offer to her, and you each feel that you can do that. Therefore, you'd each like her to live with you. I'm not so clear about Ken and Michael. And I wonder if we could now turn our attention to them for a moment, and if you would help me understand that a little bit better.[60]

51. A positive response, to reinforce Neville's positive comments.
52. A neutral summary of Neville's content.
53. Cheryl moves from positive comments to negative ones, and so . . .
54. . . . I redirect her back to the positive.
55. This is another content summary, which keeps me in charge of the process and the couple focused on the task.
56. Mutualizes the issue and makes it a positive, joint concern for Ashley, as preparation for moving on to the more difficult situation with the two boys. BL: I use my hands to reinforce my comments.
57. Neville confronts me again.
58. The nondefensive response reviews the children's need for both parents, thus validating and educating each parent.
59. The reference to *two* children is revealing. Obviously, I am still blocking the total picture.
60. I ask for help in understanding the issue. A plea for help is rarely ignored by clients.

MEDIATOR: [to Neville] What are your primary reasons—give me a couple of reasons why Michael should live with you.[61]

NEVILLE: Why Michael should live with me?[62]

MEDIATOR: Yeah.

NEVILLE: I don't want him.

MEDIATOR: At all?[63]

NEVILLE: Well, you're putting me on the spot, not that I don't love my kid. But the way things are, we've separated, and . . .[64]

MEDIATOR: . . . and . . .

NEVILLE: Well, I don't want the kid. He's got to grow up.

MEDIATOR: Let's assume for a moment that he was living with his mother. Would you want him to spend time with you?[65]

NEVILLE: Oh, yes. Oh, yes. I'll take him out. Oh, yes.

MEDIATOR: So it's not really a question that you don't want him. It's a question that you don't want him to live with you.[66]

NEVILLE: I don't want him to live with me. That's right. Oh, I would take him out. Oh, I love my son. I love my child. I love all my children.

MEDIATOR: Okay. Cheryl, how about you?

CHERYL: I would rather he take Michael, and I'll take Ashley.[67]

MEDIATOR: Stick with Michael just for a moment, because I think I have an understanding and a fix on where you both stand in regard to Ashley. I'm not clear that I fully understand where you both sit in terms of Michael. So help me understand that a little bit more.[68]

CHERYL: Well, I mean, I guess I could keep all three kids, if it comes right down to it, but I just think it would be nice to have Michael to have his dad.[69]

MEDIATOR: Uh huh. What does he get special from you?[70]

CHERYL: Michael? Time, attention, love.

MEDIATOR: All right. What do you think he gets special from his dad?[71]

CHERYL: Well, I guess—I guess him and his dad need to get closer, really, I . . .

NEVILLE: That doesn't mean we have to live in the same house, though.[72]

MEDIATOR: Uh huh. Okay.

CHERYL: I just kind of think that probably wouldn't happen on visits.

MEDIATOR: So you would like to see him have a better, closer relationship with his father.[73]

CHERYL: Uh huh.

61. A repeat of the question format used when discussing Ashley, . . .
62. . . . much to Neville's surprise.
63. Seeking the parameters of Neville's position.
64. Neville becomes more defensive.
65. The question is designed to put Neville back in a positive light again by providing him with an opportunity to express interest in Michael.
66. A reframing summary of the situation regarding Michael.
67. Cheryl uses the opportunity to expand the issue and include Ashley, in order to propose a trade.
68. Redirects the focus to Michael in a noncritical way. I don't like parents trading over children in the same way they might trade over money. In addition, a trade proposal over Ashley at this point in the session would only lead to more entrenched positions.
69. Cheryl turns the question against Neville, and so . . .
70. . . . I redirect with a specific positive question.
71. This question is designed to see if Cheryl will comment positively on Neville's parenting.
72. Cheryl's response leads to bickering.
73. Reframes the bickering into a positive statement, while avoiding the basic dispute.

MEDIATOR: Okay. Ken! Help me understand Ken. You both have been quiet about Ken, and I'm not sure I understand where he fits into the picture.[74]

CHERYL: Ken is so quiet himself that its almost easy to forget about him.

MEDIATOR: Uh huh. Neville said a little earlier that he was sort of tearing around. Does he tear around quietly?[75]

CHERYL: I don't think he tears around.

NEVILLE: We always have these differences. I don't know, she doesn't have a logical brain, she doesn't see.[76]

MEDIATOR: What do you see?[77]

NEVILLE: Sorry?

MEDIATOR: What do you see? In Ken!

NEVILLE: He tears around outside with his friends, and even when he's tearing around—all the other kids who tear around, they don't mind getting bumped every now and then. But when he gets bumped, he gets pampered by his mother.[78]

MEDIATOR: Does he get pampered by his dad?

NEVILLE: No way!

MEDIATOR: What does he get from his dad?[79]

NEVILLE: I take him out.

MEDIATOR: What happens when he gets bumped, cuts his knee, falls off a bicycle? What does he get from you?

NEVILLE: For his age, when he gets bumped on a bicycle—I got so many bumps on a bicycle when I was a kid![80]

MEDIATOR: Didn't we all?[81]

NEVILLE: I fell off trees. I can show you some scars I got from falling off trees, walking in streams, and stuff like that, wading across . . . the kid's soft.

MEDIATOR: Uh huh. What does he get from you?[82]

NEVILLE: He gets my attention. We go out and go shopping.

MEDIATOR: What does he get from you when he comes in with a bloody knee?

NEVILLE: I tell him to toughen up.

MEDIATOR: Okay. All right. You'd like see him more of a man.[83]

NEVILLE: Sorry?

MEDIATOR: You'd like to see him more of a man?

NEVILLE: Sure.

MEDIATOR: Okay.

NEVILLE: Because the world is pretty tough out there, you know!

MEDIATOR: Yes, that's true. Let me put up on the chart here what I think it is we've talked about so far. Let's all check it out, so it's up there and we can all see it. I think it might be helpful if we did that. Let me just see this, now.[84] We've got the three children. We've got Neville and we've got Cheryl and we've got the three kids. We've got Ashley, and Ashley is quite close to both of you, and you would both like her to live with you. Then we have Michael. Michael, a little further—and, actually, you would each like Michael to be with the other. And then we have Ken, and Ken's further away, and you would prefer that Ken live with his mother, and you [to Cheryl] would prefer that . . . [85]

CHERYL: That's fine.

MEDIATOR: That's fine. One way or the other, no great feeling. Okay, all right. So, Ken is twelve, Michael is seven, and Ashley is nine. Is that right?[86]

CHERYL: Uh huh.

NEVILLE: Yes.

MEDIATOR: Okay. Ashley is bright, articulate. Michael is a bit of a daredevil, hellraiser. Ken is off somewhere. Is that right?[87]

CHERYL: Uh huh. [Mediator sits down.]

74. An open question regarding Ken, with a statement of how I am feeling.
75. Picks up on the parents' different characterizations of Ken, with a little humor that is totally missed by the couple.
76. Neville attacks Cheryl.
77. Use of the same language, *see*, to redirect.

78. BL: At this point, Neville relaxes and leans forward in a more open manner.
79. I continue my search for the positive.
80. Neville's voice tone indicates a rising level of anger.
81. An attempt to join Neville by universalizing his experience.
82. As Neville continues, I try to keep him on track with another question about Ken.
83. This is a slight positive reframing.
84. In complex cases, it is useful to chart. The mediator can illustrate her view of the family in ways not usually seen by the parents. In this case, the location and size of circles would have told the observer something about the mediator, as well as about the couple. For example, I placed Michael in the middle, close to Ashley and closer to the parents than Ken was. The order of the children was chronologically incorrect. This summary also avoided the real issue, since my own pain caused me to focus on the invisible child, Ken, rather than on the unwanted one, Michael.
85. BL: I ask the question with hand movement, circling each hand toward the respective parent I am addressing.
86. Confirms the ages . . .
87. . . . and confirms the characteristics they have described for each child.

MEDIATOR: Let's assume for a moment that we get through this session this morning, and we don't get anywhere. Let's just for a moment assume that.[88] So you went before the judge, and the judge said, "You're right, Neville, you're right. Ashley should be with you, and so should the two boys. Boys go with their fathers." So he says, "The three kids live with you." Think about that for a moment. [to Cheryl] And let's assume he says, "You're right. Ashley should go live with you. Mothers should bring up children; all three will live with you." Think for a moment, now: What would you do in that case? What would life be like for you, Neville? [long pause]

NEVILLE: Well, is there a way to appeal that?[89]

MEDIATOR: I suppose so. Let's assume that you go all the way up. Top court says, "This judge is right; that's the way it's going to be."[90]

NEVILLE: Well, if the judge gives me all, I would try and make do. But [pointing to the circles on the board] those boys would have to smarten up.

MEDIATOR: Okay. What if the judge said to you, "You can have it all one way, or you can have it all the other way. You have all three live with you, or all three live with their mother." What would you do?[91]

NEVILLE: That's a toughie!

MEDIATOR: Yeah.

NEVILLE: That's a toughie!

MEDIATOR: Lots of judges have a prejudice that children should stay together, you know.

NEVILLE: I didn't tell you that—that I told you that Ashley needs me. I think I kind of need her, too.[92]

MEDIATOR: Yeah.

NEVILLE: I think I'd fall apart.

MEDIATOR: Uh huh.

NEVILLE: I think I kind of need her, too.

MEDIATOR: It's very tough, very tough in a divorce, because you always lose a little piece of kids.[93] It's hard enough losing your kids as they grow up, anyway, particularly when you have a special relationship with one of them. It's very tough. What would your choice be?[94]

NEVILLE: My choice would be to take them, all three.

MEDIATOR: Take them, all three. Okay.

NEVILLE: I love my kids.

MEDIATOR: Okay. Cheryl, what about you?

CHERYL: I'd take all three right now, no problem.

MEDIATOR: Take all three right now, no problem.

CHERYL: That would be great.

MEDIATOR: Okay. What do you know about the literature from the professional field, about children in divorce?[95] Have you read any of that? Anybody suggest any . . .

NEVILLE: I'm seeing some things on the television, as well as—it's a problem. Everybody knows. Everybody knows what happens.[96]

MEDIATOR: How do your three kids get along?[97]

CHERYL: Well, the two youngest ones get along pretty good.[98] Ken doesn't—well, he's older, and he finds that the little kids can be a nuisance. But underneath all that, he does care for them.

MEDIATOR: Uh huh, uh huh.

88. Use of the "what if" approach can help the couple break out of their current thinking. It also helps the couple test the reality of their positions.
89. Neville tries to wriggle out of the "what if."
90. This closes out other options, forcing Neville to stay with the original "what if."
91. New use of the "what if," to create new options for the couple to explore. Their responses indicate that the alternative arena (the court) is unsatisfactory to both of them and helps each of them identify each parent's "bottom line."
92. Neville reveals himself for the first time.
93. I empathize, normalize, and return to the question.
94. I have become increasingly disturbed by the parenting behavior of this couple. If I am to be helpful to them, however, I must keep my feelings in check and look for the good in each of them. The insincerity of the follow-

ing exchange challenges the mediator to remain nonjudgmental.

95. A change to an educator role, using the professional literature, to begin to have them consider the consequences of splitting up the three children.
96. Neville again dismisses the mediator.
97. I respond with a specific question.
98. Cheryl reveals an important piece of information regarding Michael and Ashley's relationship, which I will use to try to keep the children together.

NEVILLE: See what I said? Talking about logic! They fight like . . .

MEDIATOR: Who fights?[99]

NEVILLE: That big kid there [pointing to the board] needs to pick on kids his own age.[100]

MEDIATOR: Okay. How do Michael and Ashley get along?

NEVILLE: They get along okay. She tends to mother him sometimes, though.[101]

MEDIATOR: Yeah.

NEVILLE: Sort of a little mom.

MEDIATOR: Yeah, in a sense, [to Neville] she does a little mothering for you, [to Cheryl] she does a little mothering for you, does a little mothering for Michael, huh?[102] Is that a fair burden for a nine-year-old? Does she have much time for herself?[103]

CHERYL: I think she does.

NEVILLE: She manages.

MEDIATOR: Oh, I'm sure she manages. Because she sounds like being a superkid. I was wondering if it's fair for her to carry that burden.[104]

CHERYL: Well, I never ask her to look after Michael.

MEDIATOR: Uh huh. How about looking after each of you?

CHERYL: I think she gets as much out of it as I do.

MEDIATOR: Uh huh. All right. You know, kids have a special relationship in families that's different from the relationship they have with us as parents.[105] In the sense of confidants, and being able to share fears and hopes with each other that they can't always share with us as adults. Test things out with each other, and they get a lot of support from each other. As they're experimenting and expanding, as they grow and move out further and further. I'm wondering to what extent splitting the kids, particularly Michael and Ashley, would be difficult for them, in the sense of having that special confidence and comradeship that siblings have, as distinct from the kinds of relationships they have with each of you as parents.[106] Think about that. Give it a thought in that regard. What would you like to see happen, so that you could both feel better about Ken?[107]

CHERYL: Well, I think with Ken, it's just that he's twelve going on thirteen. It's a difficult time. He pulls away from his parents a bit. I think that's kind of normal.

NEVILLE: Why don't you tell the doctor the truth? From the beginning, when you got pregnant, you didn't like the kid, anyway.[108]

CHERYL: Well, yeah. Ken was . . .

NEVILLE: All the way along, it's the same thing, so don't give me this stuff about . . .

MEDIATOR: Are we talking now for you or for Cheryl?[109]

NEVILLE: I just told her to tell you, to tell the doctor what . . .

MEDIATOR: Uh huh. How about you?

NEVILLE: The truth about it!

MEDIATOR: How about you?

NEVILLE: I thought it was okay when she got pregnant. Like, I said we can get married, and all that.

99. Another specific question. It is easy to fight over generalities; it is hard to fight over facts.
100. Neville refers to the chart, indicating that its use has brought Ken into the room, and that the chart is a focus of the clients' attention.
101. Neville confirms Cheryl's view of the Michael-Ashley relationship.
102. Identifies the mutual aspect of Ashley's mothering to each of them.
103. This is my first critical question.
104. I pursue the question until I sense that Cheryl becomes defensive.
105. I move back to the educator role begun at 95.
106. Raises the negative consequences for Michael and Ashley if the children are split up. This is done in a way that focuses on the parents' self-interest and simply leaves the idea for them to think about.
107. Returns the focus to Ken, using *each* when referring to the couple as spouses and *both* when referring to them as parents. This helps them separate their two roles and recognize both their continued joint parenting and their separateness as ex-spouses.
108. A family secret emerges.
109. A check on whether Neville is speaking for himself but ascribing the opinion to Cheryl. I pursue it until he answers.

MEDIATOR: Uh huh. So you got married after Ken was born?[110, 111]

CHERYL: Uh huh.

MEDIATOR: Okay. [to Neville] Which of the kids looks most like you?

NEVILLE: Ken.

MEDIATOR: Okay. [to Cheryl] Which of the kids looks most like you?[112]

CHERYL: Ashley.

MEDIATOR: Okay. In a mixed marriage, like yours, they come through, right, with different colors—what shadings are they?[113]

NEVILLE: Ken is on the dark side, and the other two—they are like what we call our Puerto Rican kids.

MEDIATOR: Okay. So, in one sense, you must be a little proud of Ken.[114]

NEVILLE: He's got my flat, broad nose . . .

MEDIATOR: Uh huh. It's rather handsome.

NEVILLE: I got it from my dad, so it's kind of cute, but he's got it.

MEDIATOR: It came all the way down, a long line. A proud long line.[115, 116] So, in one sense, now, just let me ask you about Michael. Where does Michael fit in? Who does he look most like?

CHERYL: Well, I think he looks like both of us, really.

MEDIATOR: Mixture of you?

CHERYL: Yeah.

NEVILLE: He looks like her grandmother.

MEDIATOR: Grandmother. Yeah. Is that your favorite grandmother, or your not-so-favorite grandmother?[117, 118]

CHERYL: [laughs] No, I like my grandmother.

MEDIATOR: Yeah, okay. Would you agree that Michael looks a little bit like your grandmother?

CHERYL: No, I think he looks like both of us.

MEDIATOR: Like both of you?

CHERYL: Uh huh.

MEDIATOR: Okay. So Ashley looks a lot like you, Ken looks a lot like you, Michael looks like both of you.[119]

NEVILLE: Ashley is like my mother.

MEDIATOR: Like your mother?

NEVILLE: Turned pale. [laughs]

MEDIATOR: Okay, so that's kind of special.[120]

NEVILLE: You bet.

MEDIATOR: Yeah, okay. Ken, then, carries down a very important part of your line and lineage too, right?

NEVILLE: If only he would be smarter.

110. The summary is used to clarify the secret.
111. BL: Neville smiles in relation to Ken.
112. I feel I have now been admitted to the family and can therefore look more closely at issues. By not pursuing the issue of Michael, however, I conspired with the parents to keep it out of the session.
113. Although the mediator is always careful to honor the family, she must not be too shy to deal with sensitive issues.
114. Another reframing, to gain a positive comment for Ken and leave Michael and Ashley joined in Neville's definition of the "Puerto Rican kids."
115. Honors Neville's lineage.
116. BL: Neville's body language indicates that he is more involved in the process. He is relaxed, with arms unfolded, and smiles at times.
117. I am not sure whether this is a positive or a negative statement.
118. BL: Neville smiles again.
119. This summary makes Michael part of both of them.
120. I turn Neville's statement to a positive.

MEDIATOR: Okay, how did you get along with your dad?[121]

NEVILLE: Off and on.

MEDIATOR: Off and on? Anything like the way you and Ken get along?

NEVILLE: Better.

MEDIATOR: Better. You got along better with your dad?

NEVILLE: Better with my dad.

MEDIATOR: Okay, all right. If I understand correctly, the thing that you don't like about Ken is that he tends to cry a lot?[122]

NEVILLE: For a kid at twelve. You tell me. You've got kids?[123]

MEDIATOR: Yes.[124]

NEVILLE: What would you like to see? Would you like to see a twelve-year-old boy crying when he gets hurt outside with the other kids?[125]

MEDIATOR: I was just wondering if that was the most important thing about him that you didn't like.[126]

NEVILLE: That's one thing. Another thing is that I would like to see him be a better achiever, like Ashley.

MEDIATOR: Uh hum. Okay. You would like Ken to achieve more. You think that he's not reaching his potential?[127]

NEVILLE: Uh huh.

MEDIATOR: Would you agree with that, Cheryl, that he has more potential?[128]

CHERYL: Yeah, I would agree with that. I think he can do better.

MEDIATOR: Okay. What can you give him, as parents, to help him achieve that potential?[129]

NEVILLE: A clout around the ear.

MEDIATOR: Have you tried that?[130]

NEVILLE: Here? My dad used to do that back home. I wouldn't do that here. The kids would go to the school and get Social Services on you, and all that garbage.

MEDIATOR: Okay. So you've not done that? You must have been tempted to do that?[131]

NEVILLE: Yes, I've been boiling inside.

MEDIATOR: Yeah. About?[132]

NEVILLE: About disciplining him the way I got disciplined. But I've not bothered to do it, because we don't want to be dragged into court and get all the scandals and all the rest.

MEDIATOR: Okay, so you've not been able to bring some of your family values to bear in this marriage?[133]

NEVILLE: For Social Services to come and pick us up?

121. Enlarging the family profile, to see the extent to which Neville's parent-child cycle is repeating.
122. This is an attempt to specify the issue regarding Ken.
123. Neville challenges me again.
124. I ignore the challenge.
125. Neville tries again.
126. I continue to ignore it and return to the question at 122.
127. I also ignore the comparison with Ashley. This slight positive reframing gives Ken some potential, rather than just repeating the parents' generally negative descriptions.
128. I check the reframe with Cheryl, hoping that she will add to the positives.
129. I complete the reframe by asking the parents what they could give Ken, thus making it a joint, positive, future-parenting issue.
130. I check the reality of Neville's statement.
131. I empathize and normalize in a nonjudgmental way.
132. This is an attempt to get the specifics out.
133. Another positive reframe.

MEDIATOR: Well, yeah. Okay. [to Cheryl] How about you?[134]

CHERYL: Well, I think if Ken had a better relationship with his dad—I think he needs to know his dad is pleased with him, you know.[135]

MEDIATOR. What does he need to know from his mom?[136]

CHERYL: I think he needs to know that he's loved, and I think he knows that.

MEDIATOR: Would you agree with that, Neville?[137] [Pause. Neville signals yes and no with his hands.] I get the sense that you would both be a lot happier if you only had two children.[138]

CHERYL: Three has been a handful.[139]

NEVILLE: Ah . . . I . . . I . . . I don't agree with you.[140]

MEDIATOR: You don't?[141]

NEVILLE: I come from a large family, a family of twelve, and I can remember one of my sisters saying to my mother, "Why didn't you just have me?" Oh, no—she said something like "How come you have such a large family?" And my mother said, "Who do you want me to eliminate? You?"[142] I don't want to eliminate Ken. We've got him.[143]

MEDIATOR: Okay. You both, however, seem to have a low investment in Ken. Am I right?[144]

NEVILLE: You heard when Cheryl said she doesn't mind having him.[145]

MEDIATOR: I didn't see any great enthusiasm on either side . . . [146]

NEVILLE: I'll have him.

MEDIATOR: Certainly not the enthusiasm I see in Ashley, right?

NEVILLE: I'll have him. If you want it, I'll have him.[147]

MEDIATOR: Let's leave that to one side for a moment, then.[148] Let's leave Ken to one side for a moment and focus on Ashley and Michael. Ashley is nine years of age, very close to each of you. Does some mothering, not only of each of you, as we look on the board she also does some mothering for Michael. Right?[149] And I would assume, if they're like most kids, Michael does some things back that are supportive and helpful for Ashley.[150]

NEVILLE: Yes.

CHERYL: Yes.

134. I check with Cheryl, to see if she accepts the reframing.
135. Cheryl turns it against Neville.
136. Refocus back to what Cheryl can do.
137. Checking this with Neville gets a muted response.
138. A high-risk question, to provoke the couple out of their current positions. Upon reflection, however, I see that I am still blocking on Michael and focusing on Ken.
139. Cheryl seems to agree, but . . .
140. . . . Neville reacts in the opposite way.
141. This question is designed to provoke more response and obtain more information.
142. I am the youngest of five, and I empathize with this response, making an unstated alliance or connection with Neville.
143. Neville's response indicates that he is also thinking about Ken, not just Michael.
144. I restate the "low interest" question, taking into account Neville's response.
145. Neville attacks me again, . . .
146. . . . but I continue to push my observation about Ken.
147. Neville's use of "if you want it" would make the mediator responsible for the outcome. This also informs me that Neville is not serious, . . .
148. . . . and so I ignore Neville's conditional offer.
149. Instead, I return to the consequences of splitting up the children.
150. I note that while Ashley helps Michael, he probably supports her.

MEDIATOR: Okay. So now we've got: Ashley is [to Neville] close to you, [to Cheryl] close to you.[151] You both said to me that, in a sense, she acts as your right hand, and your right hand. [to Neville] She reminds you of your mother, and at times she mothers Michael, and [to Cheryl] she's like a co-mother for you. And my sense is, that's a terrible burden to put on a nine-year-old.[152] That is, what time does she have to be a nine-year-old, excited, exploring, expanding, carefree? I'm wondering what that would do, if you separate the children—what that would do for the relationship between Michael and Ashley.[153] I'm wondering how each of you can have the best relationship with Ashley and with Michael, without severing the relationship between Michael and Ashley. And I'm wondering what makes the residency so important. [to Neville] What does it mean for Ashley to live with you primarily or [to Cheryl] live with you primarily, as distinct from spend a lot of time with you, and spend a lot of time with you?[154] Maybe primary residence in one place, obviously. What does it mean to have the child live with you, that's different from having a good relationship and good access to the child living with the other parent?[155]

NEVILLE: I can't explain it in words. I can tell you how I'm feeling right now while you're talking. I'm just sort of thinking that she's not with me, and I don't know how to tell you what my feelings are.[156]

MEDIATOR: One of acute pain and loss.[157]

NEVILLE: I'm just trying to imagine her not living with me, and I'm just sitting there . . .

MEDIATOR: Yeah. And it hurts, right, to think of that void. And I wonder what that means, in a sense, that—can that void, is that void real, in a sense, because whether she lives with you primarily, or lives with you primarily, as I understand it, they're going to spend a lot of time with both of you, right?[158] [long pause] No?

NEVILLE: What happens if I want to move?[159]

MEDIATOR: Tough question. Tough question! I assume that [to Cheryl] you have the right to move, [to Neville] you have a right to move . . . [160]

NEVILLE: And I would leave my daughter behind?

MEDIATOR: But you don't have a right to move the kids without some mutual agreement between you, right? As adults, we can pick up and move. As parents, we have some obligations to keep the other parent in reasonable access. Right? Is that a real issue?

151. Acknowledges Ashley's central role.
152. This returns to the question of the burden and fairness for Ashley.
153. Weaves back to the issue of dividing the children.
154. Using the same language, to provide a link to my earlier observations, I ask why residency is so crucial.
155. Separates the residency issue from their individual relationship with the children.
156. Neville opens up with his feelings.
157. I empathize.
158. Repetition of the question at 155, to keep the possibility of movement open.
159. Neville goes on the offensive again.
160. This response is to separate Neville's right to move and his responsibilities as a parent, educating the couple about their new roles.

CHERYL: I'd want him to see the children, taking them out and spending time with them. Access is not a problem.[161]

NEVILLE: It's not a problem for me.[162]

MEDIATOR: All right. I'm going ask you each to think about something between now and next week, when we meet again, and I tell you what I want you to do.[163] I want—first, Neville, you, and then, Cheryl, you. Neville, I want you to think about what kind of arrangements you will make if Ashley is living with you, for her to be with Michael and with Ken and spend time with her mother. And Cheryl, I want you to think about Ashley's living with you, what kind of arrangements you'll make in terms of the access she can have with her dad, as well as the two boys. And I want you each to think, therefore, about what it is you each need in relationship to that. That would be question number one.[164] Question number two would be, how can you each have a good relationship with Ashley, as mother and daughter and as father and daughter, in a way that frees her up from needing to be also supportive of you, and of you, so that she doesn't feel that she has to shore you up, or shore you up?[165]

NEVILLE: Makes sense.[166]

CHERYL: Uh huh.

MEDIATOR: And the last thing I want you to think about is, what do you want for Ken? How are you going to link him back into the lineage he came from, so he carries on that name and that tradition? What do you want for him? And then, when we get back together next week, we can talk about some of those things and see whether or not we can come to some kind of a conclusion. How you can each have a good relationship with all three of the children, and all three of the children have a good relationship with you. Work well with each other, be supportive of each other, so they can develop and grow in the most normal way, and you can still have a good mothering relationship and you still have a good fathering relationship. We can work it out, so as to free them up from some of the stuff that goes on between the two of you. Okay?[167]

CHERYL: Those were good questions.[168]

MEDIATOR: Okay, so we'll meet again then, next Tuesday. Same time?

NEVILLE: Same time.

CHERYL: Sure.

MEDIATOR: Okay, good.

NEVILLE: I said I would have Ken, though.[169]

CHERYL: And I never thought about Ashley and Michael needing to be together before.[170]

MEDIATOR: Okay. We've not made any decisions, we've just made some suggestions today, right? Nothing is in concrete. Nothing's fixed. We'll think about it and come back next week.[171]

161. Cheryl signals that the issue is not whether the children will spend time with each parent.
162. Neville signals that moving is not a real problem for him.
163. Each parent is now under pressure to come back with a

plan to do better for the children than the other parent could.

164. Asking the parents to articulate positions opposite from the ones they claim causes dissonance in their behavior. It is difficult to argue for a position you do not hold. Either the position must change, or the argument must change. In either case, the respondent has thought about the other's position, which is the first step toward understanding the compromises that must be made to achieve agreement.
165. A second part is added to the assignment, for them to think about for the next week. This task assignment also creates the agenda for the next session.
166. A positive response from Neville.
167. This is a series of positively phrased questions, to end on an upbeat note and focus the couple on the next session.
168. Cheryl acknowledges the question, indicating that she will think about it seriously.
169. Neville returns to his offer to have Ken.
170. Cheryl stays with her thoughts about the value of the questions.
171. This puts the issue of Ken on hold until a later meeting.

Analysis

The Mediator's Assumptions

Personal History. Viewing this case in retrospect, I can see how my own childhood shaped my behavior as a mediator. I am the youngest of five children. Each of my siblings was born two years apart. There was a five-year gap between my next sister and myself. This has often led me to think about whether I was an accidental child and whether, if my parents had used birth control or abortion (in the 1930s), I would have been born at all. Thus, I empathized with the youngest son, Michael—particularly since my middle name is Michael.

My background shaped the lens through which I viewed this family. I believe I ignored the couple's statements about

Michael because they were just too painful to accept. They would have been painful even if they had not triggered some of my own dynamics. Given that impact, I simply blocked out any sense of the couple's abandoning Michael and focused my attention on helping the parents deal with Ken.

The value of mediation, as a process, is demonstrated in this case. Although I missed the central issue for the first three-quarters of the session, my focus on helping the parents make the decisions and on educating them about children's needs gave them the ability to develop the right answers for their family.

There Is "That of God" in Everyone. In Chapter One, I discussed the essential concept of the goodness that lies in each of us and the role of the mediator in locating and working with that goodness in each client. The search for God is strategically useful; it is a key to maintaining neutrality on the issues. If I am looking for the good, then I will not become judgmental or critical of one or both parents. I can accept them for who they are and embark on the journey to find their goodness and work with it.

In each case, the mediator controls her reaction by remembering that there is "that of God" in everyone and that the task is to find that part of the person and work with it. Thus, if the mediator cannot find "that of God," it is not because it does not exist, but because the mediator is not looking hard enough or in the right place. The mediator focuses on the positive, looks for the goodness, and then works with it. As the good part of the client emerges, it can be encouraged to overtake behavior that the mediator may find offensive.

Looking for the good is an essential part of mediation. If the mediator's bias is not so much toward one spouse as against the other, then seeking and finding the goodness in the latter spouse will bring the mediator back into balance between the couple. This concept goes beyond being nonjudgmental and becomes an active search to like and love the person with whom one is working. It does not mean that the mediator must accept and approve of the offending behavior; rather, she attempts to override this disapproval by focusing on the other patterns and values of the parties.

The mediator cannot like or empathize more with one party without having this bias work to the detriment of the other. Thus, when I find myself more attracted to or sympathetic with one party, I look to see why I am biased. As I identify my bias and the reasons for it, I can see what part of my experience is causing the bias. Once I do that, I can look at the behavior of the unfavored party to identify how it affects my biases.

In this case, Neville was overtly hostile to me, and it was easy to dislike him because he was making my work more difficult. When I realized that I was becoming irked by his rejecting behavior, however, I concentrated even harder on finding something about him that I could like, to offset the danger of losing my neutrality. I sought "that of God" in Neville, found it, and worked with it. I sought his family values, his history; I honored and worked with them. I was not judgmental about his rejection of Michael and Ken. I worked with him to find his good parenting aspects. The result was that I finally joined Neville and began to see movement on the issues.

While doing this, I also had to work on my relationship with Cheryl. She was not hostile toward me, but it would be easy to judge her mothering harshly. She did not seem to protect the boys, and she shared Neville's low investment in them. She drew on her nine-year-old daughter for emotional support. I laid all this aside: Cheryl was not in the room to receive a lecture from me or to be judged; she was there for help in making her own decisions for her children. Given this faith, she rose to the challenge and made the right decisions for her family.

Working with Neville and Cheryl, I realized that I disliked their attitudes toward the three children because I saw them as uncaring attitudes. They did not want the boys, and each parent wanted the daughter—not for what each could give to her, but for what each received from her. I controlled my feelings by remembering that there is good in everyone, and I set out to find it.

I also operated under the assumption that the parents had bad feelings about their own incongruent behavior. They were aware that their feelings about the children did not reflect mainstream values. They probably wanted to do things differently, but they just did not know how. I helped them by focusing on their positive conduct. Through careful questioning, I elicited positive statements about the children, and each time I accomplished this, I reinforced the positive aspects. I frequently reframed negative responses into positive ones. I made positive statements whenever I could. Judgment is not useful to the couple or to the process until an agreement is reached; then the mediator can judge the outcome (the agreement). Until then, judgment is liable to display the mediator's bias and interfere with the process of helping the couple make decisions. It is difficult to be partial, biased, or judgmental while seeking the good in clients.

In looking for the good, I attempted to get the father to say something positive about his son Ken. When Neville drew a blank on this assignment, I pursued the question with the mother. The purpose of this was to help the couple seek and find the good in their son and at the same time in themselves. (29–30) Neville also talked about his need for Ashley and ended by saying that she got good emotional support from him. I interpreted this positively, (51) and then I reframed the parents' dispute about Ashley as an indication that they were both good parents, noting that the dispute came from their mutual caring. (56) I also reframed Neville's not wanting Michael at all to his not wanting Michael to live with him full-time. (66)

When I raised the issue of race, I honored Ken's and Neville's lineage, to put Neville in touch with his origins, which helped him reassert his pride in his family line. (115) When Neville was self-effacing about his race, I pointed out that Ashley was like his mother (in contrast to Neville's "Puerto Rican" view of his younger children). (120) Both parents seemed to have lost touch with their positive parenting aspects. Asking them what they could do for Ken put them in touch with their good side.

I closed the session with a series of questions, putting them in touch with their goodness and their positive parenting aspects. These questions were designed to stimulate their thinking in this mode during the following week, to maintain some of the gains made at this session.

The Mediator's Strategies

Dealing with the Mediator's Bias. It is useful to review cases that are giving you problems and ask yourself the four questions discussed in Chapter Two. The answers to these questions will quickly reveal whether your bias is at work.

How can the mediator check her behavior regarding the impact of personal experiences on mediation behavior? A beginning mediator should take extensive notes in the process, to track what she is doing in each session. They may seem tedious to read and write, but process notes help the learning mediator focus on what she does and explain it. They also provide supervisors with useful commentary about the way a mediator views a case. At times, a mediator also senses that something is remiss or missing. These are the kinds of cases that stir up anxiety during and after a session. Mediators can seek out peers to discuss such feelings.

Missing an Issue: The Process to the Rescue. It could be argued that my failure to deal directly with one issue—that neither parent wanted Michael—had some positive outcomes. First, it meant that they did not have to deal publicly, in the session, with this serious weakness of their parenting. Second, at one level, I saw the issue of Michael's residence as part of the marital fight. It seemed to be part of Cheryl's disappointment with Neville as a father and a husband. It also seemed to be part of Neville's feeling that Cheryl made the decisions about the children, and that they were usually wrong decisions. By not dealing with the marital issue directly, I required the couple to deal with the parenting issues concerning all three children, rather than their marital differences. My oversight left the marital aspects of the issue outside the room.

By focusing on Ken, the invisible son, I also freed the couple from defending their untenable position of not wanting Michael. My unwillingness to define the problem in the way the parents defined it prevented a solution that would have been detrimental to the entire family. At the end of the session, both parents commented on the value of the session, noting that neither had thought about Michael and Ashley's need to stay together. This opened the way for the parents later to develop a solution that would keep all three children together. (The couple spent two and a half hours in the parking lot outside, discussing the session and hammering out a solution.)

By not dealing with the rejection of Michael in the same terms in which the couple originally had framed it, I also prevented their having to own that position. When the mediator deals with an issue in depth, the parties are forced to own their positions. They can then become locked into their positions. Here, the process took over and provided the couple with a problem-solving arena. My focus on the issues of parenting and understanding and meeting the children's needs provided the couple with the opportunity to find solutions that were right for them. My emphasis on the importance of their individual backgrounds and cultures also enabled the parents to honor their respective histories and work with the positive aspects of them. The missed issue, had it been an overriding issue for the couple, would not have been missed for long. If either parent had really had a very strong position regarding Michael, then my inability to deal with it at this session would have provoked one or both of them to raise it, in a way that would have forced me either to deal with it or to withdraw from the case.

My decision to ignore the special relationship between Neville and Ashley was deliberate. The relationship of father and daughter often has a "surrogate boyfriend" aspect. It can be a safe way for a daughter to learn how to behave with the opposite sex. When this issue is raised in the session, the mediator can either pursue it through a specific line of questioning or take note of it and see whether it emerges again, checking the context in which it reemerges and noting the other spouse's reaction. In this case, it would have been inappropriate for me to go looking for something deeper, without clearer indications of pathology. The issue remained with me. It was part of my tracking of the issues and should have been dealt with in more depth only if any indications had emerged that the relationship was more than a "surrogate" one.

One key point at which I missed the issue was when I attempted to deal with Neville's criticism of Michael by normalizing Michael's behavior. (12) Neville's first rejection of Michael was reinforced with a typical work-related reason. Since the reason seemed typical, I overlooked the underlying issue of rejection. (15) When it was clear that neither parent wanted Michael, I tried some reverse questioning–for example, asking the father to give reasons why he should do something he did not want to do (have Michael live with him). This uncovered the issue that I had to deal with. Even then, I reframed Neville's response ("I don't want him") to suggest that Neville did want him but did not want to live with him, thus missing or at least mitigating the real issue. (61–66)

When I tried the same strategy with Cheryl, on the assumption that Michael was a marital-fight issue, she strengthened that assumption by the way she turned her lukewarm acceptance of him into an assertion that Michael should "have his dad." (69) I proceeded to reframe this into a positive. My feeling of being admitted to the family by the disclosure about Ken's birth led me to focus on Ken, which kept me from attending to the couple's position on Michael. While I was willing to try a high-risk question about Ken (138), I failed to deal with Michael in the same penetrating way.

Dealing with Sensitive Issues. Mediators work with a range of people from different cultures, races, and classes. The mediator must honor those differences and respect them. One result of the civil rights struggle has been that it now seems inappropriate to ask questions about racial, cultural, and class differences. These differences do exist, however, and they often play important roles in the decision of a couple to end their marriage. As such, these differences cannot be ignored. I dealt with Neville's blackness and honored it. I mentioned Ken's need to be linked to his heritage and the couple's need to view it as a proud heritage, not as one to be ignored. Neville's behavior toward me changed as I entered this sensitive area. He dropped most of his overt hostility and shared some of his feelings with me. From that point on, the session became much more positive.

I believe that all people are good, and that every segment of every society has a unique and positive contribution to offer. I work with all classes of people and honor their class values. Likewise, when I work with people from diverse cultures and races, I note their differences in the session, honor them, and blend them into my work in a positive way.

Summarizing. This is part of the reframing technique. In the session with Neville and Cheryl, I frequently summarized, to help them focus on the content. In this case, however, I also used summaries to focus on their positive parenting aspects. (Examples of summaries in this case are found at 9, 19, 21, 36, 37, 52, 55, 73, and 119.)

Displaying the Data. I always work with a flip chart in the office, to display data and ideas. The parties always become more deeply engaged in the process through the work on the chart. The selection of the data to be displayed, as well as the way it is displayed, also affects the mediation.

In this session, I drew the children on the chart and placed them according to their current closeness to the parents, not in chronological order. Ashley was the closest, Michael was in the middle, and Ken was the farthest away. This was my view of the family. The drawing had an impact on the couple, even though they made no direct comments about the diagram.

Clients' Negotiating Behavior

Neville used a form of triangulation. When both parents were under pressure to talk about Ken, Neville turned to his wife and said, "Why don't you tell the doctor the truth? From the beginning, when you got pregnant, you didn't like the kid, anyway." (108) This strategy had two purposes. First, it put Cheryl in a bad light—she did not like her son. Second, Neville tried to align himself with me by claiming to be the truth teller, to help me be a better mediator. I turned this comment back to Neville: "Are we talking now for you or for Cheryl?" (109)

Conclusion

Neville and Cheryl did not do any negotiating in this session. Neville did offer to take the oldest son, but this was merely a strategy; Neville was negotiating with me rather than with Cheryl at that point. A superficial look at the session could suggest that it was more therapy than mediation—that is, most of the session dealt with relationship and dynamic issues, for the couple and for Neville and Cheryl individually. However, this work took place in the context of negotiations preparation. We did not reach the point of negotiating the specifics of residency and access, but I laid the groundwork for the couple to begin dealing with those details at the next meeting. I also gave them the task of thinking about the consequences of separating Michael and Ashley, an assignment meant to prepare them to consider the best arrangement for all three children.

This case demonstrates that measurable movement is not always obtained in the first session. The mediator often must lay the groundwork, clearing away some of the marital dynamics and misunderstandings between the couple. I used most of this session to develop a relationship with the couple, and I believe that no negotiations could have taken place before I developed a relationship that allowed the parents to trust me as a partner in solving their problems, rather than seeing me as an arm of the court. Such work may take up all of the first session, but the next time the mediator meets with the couple, they will be more ready to deal with the issues and negotiate.

9

NORMAN AND TERRI: WHO MAKES THE DECISIONS?

Norman and Terri were sent to me by the local court system. Terri is an advertising executive, a very successful professional. Norman is an aviation consultant, also very successful in his field. They have been divorced for three years, sharing custody of their daughter, Susan. Susan spends one week with Terri and another week with Norman, rotating back and forth. They live in different parts of the same town. Susan, now six years old, will enter public school in September. The parents have to decide which school she will attend and with whom she will live during the week once she enters school. Each parent wants Susan to live with him or her during the school year. The judge sent the couple over to me, to see if Norman and Terri could work it out in mediation.

The first ten minutes of working with clients are important. The mediator sets the stage for the relationship and takes control of the process. I like to set the stage by approaching the situation with an absolutely clear mind. I try to think of my mind as a tabula rasa; the couple will "write" on the slate through their behavior and reactions. They will meet with a nonjudgmental, open professional who has no preconceived notions about them or their situation and no idea of the outcome.

The couple comes to the session with some heavy baggage. They have probably been fighting for years. Over this time, they have built up an impressive folder, containing evaluations and commentaries of various professionals. I conduct my work with a future focus, however, because that is where the couple will find the solution. I ignore the past information, for three basic reasons. First, the mediator avoids being influenced by the past or by one particularly well-written or well-reasoned piece. Such information is useful if the mediator is being asked to make a decision. If the mediator is to help the couple make the decision, then he needs to remain neutral. Second, the solution lies with the couple at the present and in the future, not in the past. Not knowing about the past helps the mediator work unencumbered for the future. Third, the action sends a clear message to the couple. The mediator is working with them in a fresh way that does not link them to their unsuccessful past. This increases the opportunity for success in the future.

Each party comes to mediation with a version of the story to tell the mediator. That story is about the past, but the solutions to problems lie in the present and in the future. Since the mediator cannot change the past but can influence present and future decisions, he tries to avoid getting too deeply enmeshed in the past. Thus, in this session, I laid aside the documents that detailed the past and, in so doing, wiped the slate clean for the couple. This sent a powerful message: I was not going to judge or be influenced by past behavior. Most people entering mediation have something in the immediate past that they would prefer not to discuss, and my action relieved Norman and Terri of the need to expose their past.

This case illustrates when and how to intervene in the marital fight. As we have seen, most couples have a story to tell about the marital fight and will try to inject a version of it into the mediation. This version has usually been carefully rehearsed beforehand. When the story is continually raised, the mediator must decide whether to intervene and control resurrection of the marital fight by forbidding it or focus on the issue to maintain control of the process.

This chapter focuses on managing the dynamics of the couple's relationship. A comprehensive analysis of the management of these dynamics follows the transcript. It also deals with the special problems presented by one's family-of-origin history. The clash of this couple's loyalties to their respective families of origin was a major cause of their divorce and continually intruded into the session.

This case also demonstrates the use of a working hypothesis. The development, testing, confirmation, and use of the hypothesis are identified in the annotations and are discussed in detail after the transcript.

An obvious alternative presented itself early in the session. Subsequent discussion analyzes the obvious alternative, as well as the way I used it. Since timing is a key element of this strategy, timing is discussed in the post-transcript analysis. The analysis closes with a short discussion of the use of language and process management, as they appeared in this case.

Transcript and Annotations

MEDIATOR: Well, good to see you both. As you know, I have seen your folder here, and I have got just the barest of details from it.[1] I have really not read all of the reports that have been compiled over the years, because it seems to me that it is most helpful if I put that down and ask you to tell me what the situation is.[2] Let me see. If I understand correctly, the real issue between you is how to reorganize the parenting and the residency of your daughter, Susan.[3] So, why don't you tell me what the situation is? Perhaps if you could begin, Terri,[4] and then I could ask you to tell me your position, Norman.[5]

TERRI: Well, as you know, John, my ex-husband and I are having difficulties regarding what school Susan is going to go to. There is a school adjacent to my home that is a very liberal-thinking school and has very liberal teaching philosophies. The school is modeled along the lines of the open classroom, and it provides an enriched environment that I would dearly like to see Susan attend.

MEDIATOR: Yes, I see; and so you'd like her to live with you during the school week, while she is attending the school.[6]

TERRI: Yes, I think that that's only fair. It is close to the home.

MEDIATOR: Okay. Thank you. Norman?

NORMAN: Well, I think that Terri's use of the word *school* is a more generic one.[7] It's not really a school, in my estimation; it's more of an elevated game preserve for children. It is very progressive; I give her that. It is unstructured—no curriculum, and all that sort of thing. But I want my child to get back to the basics and have a broad experience with every walk of life and kind of people. I don't necessarily want an urban brat. You know, we have had three years to think about it, and I guess what's happened—in the intervening three years, our expectations have been individually developing.

MEDIATOR: Let me interrupt you for a second, Norman, because I wasn't quite sure that I understood. What is it that you would like for Susan?[8]

NORMAN: Well, I live on just the fringe of town. I live on a beautiful, sprawling acreage, and there is a school district within a very short distance of our home. When I'm there, I can drive; when not, there is a bus system very nearby. It gives a very broad, human experience to the children. There are rich kids, there are the yuppie kids, but there are farm kids.[9] There are whites, blacks, Oriental, the whole experience, and that, frankly, is what I want for my children. That's what I had.[10] Dr. Haynes, I am a self-made man and brought up in a small town. My father was a miner, and he gave me the basic opportunity to have an education, and so on, and I have succeeded. Not that Terri hasn't. But I feel I have gone up through the ladder, and I am a better person for it.

1. This couple's folder from the local court was three inches thick, filled with reports from professionals who had seen them in the past.
2. The opening statement was designed to tell the couple that the past was not important and would not influence me. It empowered the couple to make their own decisions.

3. Defines the issue and suggests a future-oriented problem statement.
4. The question is directed specifically to Terri, to avoid a contest over who will answer, because this is a powerful couple. The closed form of the question limits the response to her and helps avoid opening the marriage fight.
5. This tells Norman that his turn is next, to reduce his need to intervene while Terri is talking.
6. While summarizing, I redefine the problem as the real one between them: Susan's residency.
7. Norman does not respond to my question; rather, he responds to Terri. This is the first indication of the level of the power struggle and of the way they relate and fight.
8. I intervene, taking responsibility for the confusion, and redirect Norman to what he wants for Susan, which focuses on Norman's needs and his future parenting of Susan.
9. This digression is not cut off, since Norman's initial response is positive and provides useful information. It maintains a balance between data gathering and ventilation.
10. The issue of Norman's strong loyalty to the values of his family of origin needs to be honored. It is also related to the divorce.

MEDIATOR: Okay. So one difference between you, then, is a sort of a philosophy of education: that you [to Terri] would like Susan to go to the school system with an open classroom and a philosophy . . . [11]

NORMAN: John, if I could interrupt, it's not a philosophy of education, it is a philosophy of living. Terri is an urban snob. I want my children to learn, for example, that [holding credit card in one hand and cash in the other] *this* isn't money, *this* is money.[12]

MEDIATOR: All right. So there are other issues between you around bringing Susan up.[13]

TERRI: Yes. As Norman has most pointedly indicated, our philosophies of life differ quite substantially. Norm feels that, because he had to work for everything that he has obtained in life, that our child must do the same thing. I would like to see our daughter have some of the things in life that both Norman and I weren't able to have as children by virtue of our family circumstances.[14]

MEDIATOR: Okay. So I guess that was probably one of the reasons that you ended the marriage, which were those differences . . . [15]

NORMAN: That's right.

MEDIATOR: . . . in terms of how to approach things. All right. The struggle here today is to see how to organize the best for Susan, so that you can have a good parenting relationship with her, Norman, and you can have a good parenting relationship with her, Terri.

TERRI: That is correct.

MEDIATOR: That's the goal.[16]

NORMAN: I think so. Over the past three years, the joint custody has been fine. I mean, it has allowed both of us an opportunity to preserve our relationship with Susie, and that's fluffy and all the nice things that really stroke Terri.[17] But it is time to get down to basics. I don't care if the child is musically inclined and realizes herself. I want her to read.

11. Beginning to redefine the issue, while testing my early hypothesis.
12. BL: Norman's left hand holds a credit card; in his right hand is cash. Obviously, he has thought about this action and rehearsed it before the session.
13. A nondefensive response normalizes their differences.
14. Terri confirms that Norman's family ties are a marital issue. I must respect it, without trying to resolve it or allowing it to divert the focus.
15. This acknowledges the marital fight as part of their unresolved past and closes it out by defining the issue in parenting terms.
16. This is the first agreement on issue definition.
17. Norman takes it back to the marital fight.

MEDIATOR: Tell me a little bit more, then, about the geography, because I need to get that understood now. [to Terri] You're in the school district downtown.[18]

TERRI: That is correct.

MEDIATOR: [to Norman] And you're in a school district in town.

NORMAN: On the fringe of town.

MEDIATOR: On the fringe of town. And what is between you?[19]

TERRI: The city.

NORMAN: Pollution, garbage.

MEDIATOR: How about school systems?[20]

TERRI: Oh, I believe there is another school somewhere in there.[21] I think we live about fifteen miles apart, if you had to measure it out.

NORMAN: As the crow flies.[22]

MEDIATOR: So, it's about fifteen miles apart, and you currently live in two different school systems, and there may or may not be a third school system between you.[23] Let me ask you a couple of questions, so that I can understand.[24] What do you know about the outcome of your respective school systems, in terms of the number of kids that go on to college, for example?[25] Or the grade levels? Do you have any ideas?

TERRI: Well, I can tell you about the school system in my neighborhood. I have investigated it quite thoroughly, I think. It is a rather new school. It is actually a physically older building, but the school has been revamped and designed for an open-classroom kind of setting and an enriched program for children. Susan would be attending school with children of her own socioeconomic background, which I think is very important.[26]

MEDIATOR: I'm sorry Terri. I missed—you lost me somewhere

there. You were telling me about the outcomes of the school system—what kind of results they have.[27]

TERRI: Yes. Well, the results are not yet known, because this is a new philosophy of education that has been put into what used to be an inner-city school.

MEDIATOR: I see. Okay.

NORMAN: They are still at the guinea-pig stage.

TERRI: I really resent that.

MEDIATOR: Norman, what is the outcome . . .

NORMAN: You are such an urban snob. It makes me want to throw up.[28]

TERRI: I'm so tired of this self-made-man stuff.[29]

18. The intrusion of the marital fight is easiest in a non-factual environment. By returning to data collection, I take control of the situation, refocusing the couple and collecting basic information, so that I can test the hypothesis.
19. This question gathers information and alerts the couple to the existence of a possible alternative.
20. The question cuts through the marital snipes and focuses on data.
21. An obvious alternative emerges.
22. Norman repeats his behavior of having to "top" Terri.
23. Restatement, in Terri's terms, and summary of the basic data, to double-check that they agree on the data.
24. At this point, I privately note that the couple has not thought of options—only of winning.
25. Turns to "neutral" data. Measurable outcomes are not subject to debate. They are independent of either parent and are not part of either parent's problem definition.
26. Terri responds in terms of philosophy, rather than outcomes.
27. I take responsibility for the non-answer and redirect Terri to the original question.

28. I ignore this bickering, since Terri seems able to handle Norman.
29. Terri responds to Norman's family loyalty in a way that shows it is a longtime issue between them.

MEDIATOR: [to Norman] What is the outcome of your school system?[30]

NORMAN: Well, the children—again, it's difficult to tell, because we're talking about elementary school, but I can tell you the children don't just wear pastels and skip to school.[31] There is a good mix; they don't all expect to have alligators on their sweaters. There are plaid shirts, there are ski sweaters, there are T-shirts, there are no shirts. There is a broad mix of experience, race, color, creed, socioeconomic categories.[32] Now, I would suggest that once the children evolve out of this elementary school, near to my home, they are necessarily funneled into the cosmopolitan kind of school system. And it may be that the children will ultimately be destined to Strathcona Middle School or to Harry Ainley or the like, but at that stage, their individual likes and preferences and all that sort of stuff can be accommodated.[33] But at this stage, the school Terri is suggesting is close to the university, is experimental, and . . .

MEDIATOR: Okay. I've lost you again, because you were going to tell me about outcomes of your school system.[34, 35]

NORMAN: Well, statistically, I don't think we can suggest the success rate of going to college or that kind of thing, because it is an elementary school, after all. But the natural progression would be that you would have good, rounded, athletic, scholastic children out of my school, that I am proposing funneling into the public system and being assimilated by the system, excelling if they're disposed to and not if they're [not] disposed to.[36]

MEDIATOR: Let me ask a couple of other questions.[37] You must forgive me for jumping around, because I need to get a sort of overall picture in order to be most helpful to you. Terri, tell me a little bit about where you live.[38]

TERRI: I live in an apartment building. Actually, I occupy one of the three penthouses on the thirty-second floor of an apartment building in the city. It is spacious, has a beautiful view of the river valley, it's very central in terms of its accessibility to theater, the art gallery, those types of places.[39]

NORMAN: It requires its own life-support system.

30. The spat is ended with an information-gathering question to Norman.
31. Norman responds with another attack on Terri, . . .
32. . . . but mixes it with data.
33. A softening of Norman's position, indicating a willingness to compromise. This is directional information, indicating where he might move to.
34. A gentle redirection, because I do not want to offset Norman's softening. I repeat the question, to get Norman back on track.
35. Up to this point, neither parent has indicated anything regarding their time and their relationships with Susan.
36. This confirms my hypothesis: that it is not which school that is important, but who should decide on the school. I accept this as my working hypothesis for the rest of the session.
37. Neither spouse has given any independent data, and so I turn to collect other data, alerting the couple to my need to scan.
38. I turn to the issue of locale.
39. They respond entirely in adult terms. Neither party mentions their daughter's needs or her interest in the locale.

MEDIATOR: Okay. Great. Norman, what about your living situation?[40]

NORMAN: I am on an acreage, as I indicated. There is all of the kinds of amenities that children would otherwise have to look for in the city. There is a swimming pool there where my child, the children, the neighbors can come over and play in the pool. We have lots of room for any of the athletic, pet kind of activities that Susie[41] wants to get involved in. So it's got everything for her. It's got the mix of accessibility to the city, but the rural experience as well, and not necessarily having to be condemned to the lemming-like hysteria of the city.

MEDIATOR: I get the view that you both enjoy where you're living now.[42]

NORMAN: Absolutely.

TERRI: Oh, definitely.

MEDIATOR: And you both enjoy the time that Susan spends with you.

NORMAN: Susie—yes.[43]

TERRI: Oh, yes.

MEDIATOR: And I get an idea that Susie enjoys the time she spends with each of you.

NORMAN: Absolutely.

MEDIATOR: And so, in a sense, then, she's getting the best of two worlds. In the sense of your rural living and expansiveness, and your urbane living . . .

NORMAN: Oh, John, I've got to stop there. I'm not sure she gets the best of both worlds in Terri's environment.[44] I think she gets the best of both worlds in the environment I find myself in. There is a proximity to the downtown, proximity to all of the arts and all that sort of stuff, on, you know, a peripheral-menu basis.

MEDIATOR: I would assume that's another disagreement that you have between you, as to whether or not that occurs. I'm just hearing from you, Terri, that she gets the best from your setting, in terms of its urbanity and its availability to the art and theater, etcetera.[45]

TERRI: I believe so.

MEDIATOR: And I hear from you, Norman, that she's getting the best in terms of the space and heterogeneity of the area.[46]

Okay, you've both now given me some important material and background. It's clear that you have some differences between you as to the kind of education that would be best for Susan, that you have a different life-style, and you've some different philosophies about life in general, but clearly you have both been very successful in your own way.[47] You're very successful in advertising, Terri, and you're very successful in aviation, Norman. So you've both got success behind you, and I'm sure that you'd like to pass that success on to Susan.[48] So I suppose the issue is, how can you get Susan what she wants and needs, what you each want and need, in a way that [to Norman] meets your needs and her needs [to Terri] and meets your needs and her needs? So let me ask you now: If Susan wasn't in the picture, would you still be living just where you're living now?[49, 50]

40. I ignore Norman's dig at Terri and direct an information-gathering question to him.
41. Note that Norman calls their daughter *Susie;* Terri calls her *Susan.*
42. I limit Norman's sniping by weaving a shared-interest theme, while also testing my hypothesis. This and the following questions are designed to create doubt for each of them about the certainty of their original positions.
43. Norman sends a message regarding the name of the child. From this point on, I try to use *Susie* when talking to Norman and *Susan* when talking to Terri.
44. Norman interrupts, to prevent further development of the shared-interest theme by arguing with me and turning it to his advantage.
45. I give a nondefensive response, opting out of the fight with Norman. I identify Norman's issue as a marital one and turn to Terri to confirm her position.
46. This monologue develops a mutual and balanced concept of their parenting. It is designed to weave a cooperative environment. Note how I carefully balance my comments with Norman.
47. Their differences are identified and legitimated. I attempt to reweave the shared-interest theme by identifying their

individual commitment to success and the shared assumption that they want their daughter to succeed. This brings us back to the parenting.

48. BL: I use my hands to create a circle representing the daughter, to bring Susan into the picture. The mediator can bring in third parties through imagery.
49. Here, I partialize through the use of fantasy (taking Susan out of the picture), to see whether their respective locations are for themselves or for Susan.
50. This acts on my hypothesis, by testing the ability of either or both to move, and provides space for softening of either position.

TERRI: Most probably, from my point of view—where I live is very close to where I work. I work long hours. It's important for me to remain fairly central, so that I don't spend a great deal of time commuting to and from, as I would were I living where Norman lives. That's very important to me. Therefore, I think I would still be living in the same place.

MEDIATOR: Okay. All right. Norman?

NORMAN: I enjoy the rural flavor, the rural experience. It goes back to my childhood, and so on.[51] If I didn't have the responsibility associated with my job and, you know, responsibility financially and otherwise for my child, I suppose you dream about opting out of the system and really doing the rural experience. But, realistically, where I am now serves both my needs.[52] My need to be mobile, where I can fly out of town to where I am needed in relation to my consultation and consulting business. Yet I have the rural experience. So, I guess—yes, of necessity, where I am is a compromise. I need to be near to the city, but it allows me the rural experience.

MEDIATOR: All right. [to Norman] What do you do on the week when Susie is not with you?[53]

NORMAN: Really little different than what I do when she is with me, except perhaps I try to schedule more of my out-of-the-city kind of activities. My job is such that I can, with a pretty fair amount of accuracy, plan my trips to San Francisco, Montreal, wherever I have to go in relation to my contracts. It's convenient for me—when I have Susie I am on site, in town, working out of the home, working out of the small office I maintain. When she's not with me, that's when I plan my transit.

MEDIATOR: Okay. How about you, Terri? What do you do when Susan is not with you?

TERRI: My life is pretty well the same as it is when Susan is living with me.[54] Of course, the activities may change, in a sense that when Susan is with me I spend more of my free time involved in activities that she is interested in.[55] But, apart from that, my day-to-day schedule or routine remains pretty well the same.[56]

MEDIATOR: Okay. All right.

NORMAN: Shopping alone, shopping with Susie, it's all the same.

TERRI: I really wish—I really resent that.

MEDIATOR: Let me ask you: Do you travel out of town at all, Terri?[57]

TERRI: Occasionally. The occasional convention elsewhere.

MEDIATOR: All right. [to Norman] Does it ever happen that you have to travel out of town during the week that Susie is with you?

NORMAN: Very rarely. That has occurred on occasion, where I am delayed. Generally, I can usually get ahold of Terri or have the mall page her, or something, and get ahold of her.

TERRI: Listen. I earn my own money, and I really resent you telling me how I should spend it.

MEDIATOR: I was sort of interested—so that if Norman gets hung up out of town, then Susan stays with you, and there is no problem around that.[58]

TERRI: No. We've managed to work that out.

MEDIATOR: Okay. All right.

51. Each parents' response indicates that the choice of their locations is for themselves and not necessarily for their daughter, which completely confirms my hypothesis. Norman's response reinforces his commitment to his family history.
52. Norman begins with his family-history tie and cleverly expands his negotiating position by adding a covert threat of moving into an even more rural location.
53. I maintain control by asking another parenting question. It also helps the couple keep in mind the free time they each enjoy. Given their careers, I assume that the free week has many benefits. The responses confirm this hypothesis. Note my use of the daughter's name with each parent during this exchange.
54. Each parent reveals the value of the free week, confirming my assumption.
55. The responses also confirm the original hypothesis.
56. Since it is clear that they both enjoy their free time and therefore that sole custody is not the key issue, I will now concentrate on a third alternative.
57. The snipes are cut off with another fact question. The answer will inform me about the amount of cooperation the parents need as they juggle their careers and their parenting.
58. This identifies an example of parenting cooperation.

NORMAN: The child doesn't go without, certainly.

MEDIATOR: So there's a lot of cooperation between you, and there's a lot of digging back and forth, but also there's a lot of cooperation that goes between you around Sus . . . [59]

NORMAN: Of course, Susie is the focus of our lives.

TERRI: You can rest assured that if it weren't for Susie, we wouldn't be seeing one another.

NORMAN: That's for sure.

MEDIATOR: Yes, that's for true. Yeah, yeah. You fight a lot as ex-wife and ex-husband . . .

TERRI: Well, if he'd stop digging me.[60]

NORMAN: Ex-wife, yes.

MEDIATOR: . . . but you seem to cooperate as parents of Susie, it seems to me.[61]

TERRI: Well, we like to think we have her best interests at heart.

MEDIATOR: All right. I have got to ask you each to do something a little odd.[62] Assume for a moment that—Norman, first you, then I'm going to ask you, Terri—[63] assume for a moment that you decided that Susie was going to go to school in Terri's school district. How would you like to organize the time? And then I'm going to ask you, Terri, to think about if Susan lives with Norman, to go to school in Norman's school district, how you would like to organize the time. Okay?[64]

NORMAN: Well, I suppose what you're asking presumes that, for the sake of convenience, the child would be living with Terri while going to school.

MEDIATOR: During the school week, yes.

NORMAN: That's every week?[65]

MEDIATOR: She is obviously going to have to live with one of you during the school week, right? You've got really two options, as I see it. You can both live in the same school district, and then you could maintain the current arrangements, if you could live within relative proximity. Or . . .

NORMAN: Would you move?[66]

TERRI: Would you?

NORMAN: You're renting; I'm owning.[67]

TERRI: What's that got to do with it? I'm settled.[68]

MEDIATOR: It's a fair question to ask, but it's an answer that you should each give or both give, possibly: Would you be willing to move to the same district in which Susan lives?[69]

TERRI: Well, a move for me is completely out of the question.

I have very, very bad allergies to pollen and animals and that kind of thing. So moving out of the city and living on an acreage is completely out of the question for me.[70]

59. The spousal fighting is separated from parental cooperation.
60. This legitimate complaint, that Norman starts all the fights, provides me with a signal to exert more control over Norman's behavior.
61. A return to parenting.
62. Alerting them to the unusual nature of the next task, I make it more difficult for them to refuse.
63. I tell them that they will both be asked the same question. This allows Terri to listen to Norman and deal with her response, rather than plan a counterattack.
64. Use of dissonance theory.
65. In clarifying the question, I help Norman understand his WATNA.
66. Norman opens serious negotiations but . . .
67. . . . can't resist a dig, so . . .
68. . . . Terri responds with a block that ends the round of negotiations on a win-lose basis.
69. This makes the obvious alternative explicit and offers the possibility of a win-win or a lose-lose outcome.
70. Terri responds only to the idea of moving to Norman's district.

MEDIATOR: Oh, I'm sorry. I misasked the question.[71] It wasn't necessarily that you would move to where Norman lives—or, Norman, that you would move to where Terri lives.

NORMAN: I understood what you're saying.

MEDIATOR: You might both move to somewhere that's sort of in the middle. That's an option. You really do have options here.[72]

NORMAN: Or I suppose the child could go to the school in the middle. If not, there's possibilities.[73]

TERRI: That doesn't really solve the problem, though. What it means . . . [74]

NORMAN: Well, it does from the standpoint that the child goes to school in between the two of us. We can maintain the schedule we have already established.

TERRI: Maybe so, but we both end up being shuttle buses, is what it boils down to.

NORMAN: It's no skin off my nose. I shuttle now.

TERRI: Besides, we don't know anything about this abstract school district somewhere in the middle. You know, I've investigated the school district that I would like to see Susan go to.[75]

NORMAN: Look, you forget your humble beginnings.[76] When your family moved off the farm, your parents were damn glad there was a school within a four- or five-block radius of your home, so you could walk to school. They weren't too concerned whether or not all of the teachers had Ph.D.'s or whether the children were being videotaped during play therapy, and all that sort of stuff, when they make building blocks. They were glad there was a school where there were humans going—you know: reading, writing, arithmetic . . .

TERRI: Times have changed, Norman!

NORMAN: Now you have to have something where the children are rendered into a laboratory slide and examined every day.

TERRI: Norman, you don't know what you're talking about.

NORMAN: So there's a school in between the two of us. It's got teachers, it's got kids. I don't think there's any downside to it. It has possibilities.[77]

TERRI: Norman, apart from the basics, which I am assured that Susan will get at the school that I have looked at, there is also the enriched program that will foster her musical talents.[78] And you're very well aware of those musical talents. And, as well, this particular school is experimental, and I am particularly caught up in the idea . . .

NORMAN: You certainly are.

TERRI: . . . that the school promotes critical thinking in children. They don't accept everything carte blanche, as you do.

NORMAN: Well, the difference is that they may know how to think critically, but, unhappily, when they have to read, they have to hire someone, which is consistent with your life-style and your theorem . . .

MEDIATOR: I'm assuming that really you both want what's best for Susan, right?[79]

NORMAN: . . . but mine teaches self-sufficiency.

MEDIATOR: You both want what's best for Susie, right?

TERRI: Yes.

NORMAN: That's right.[80]

71. I accept responsibility for the misunderstanding and restate the alternatives, while alerting the couple to the possibility of more options.
72. This identifies some other possibilities.
73. Norman adds a variation on the obvious alternative.
74. This exchange is an example of the way the marital dynamics interfere with the negotiations.
75. This is an indication that if the third school district is checked, it may provide some space for movement by Terri.
76. The old marital fight reopens, and I sit back and observe, to see if, within bounds, some new ideas or possibilities emerge.
77. Norman takes ownership of the obvious alternative, . . .
78. . . . which evokes a negative reaction from Terri.
79. When no new information or ideas emerge, I redirect with a parenting statement designed to neutralize ownership of the obvious alternative.
80. Both parents respond very affirmatively.

MEDIATOR: You may think that "best" is a little different. You may define it differently one way, Norman; you may define it differently another way, Terri.[81] But you both want what's best for Susan, right? [goes to chart][82] So, let's see what we've got here. In essence, we've got a situation where, Terri, you live in one school district, right? And along with that school district is a whole living situation—in the apartment, and downtown, and all of the things that you want. Norman, you have another school district that you live in, and with that is a living situation in terms of the acreage and the . . . okay. Now, within the school system, then, [to Terri] you have here essentially an open-class philosophy, which you believe will foster her intellectual development and critical thinking. [to Norman] In your system, you have a basic and heterogeneous population that will foster her basic ABC's and also give her an exposure to a wide range.

NORMAN: That's right.

MEDIATOR: Okay. Now, if Susan lives in this school district, then she has to live with Terri during the course of the week, to go to school conveniently. Right? If she goes to this school district, then she has to live with Norman during the week, in order to be able to go to that school system. A third posssibility has now emerged: that perhaps there is another school district within reasonable proximity that, perhaps, you might each be able to travel to.[83] Or it may be possible for each of you to move to that same school district and live within some proximity.[84] So it might be that you could live on the east side, where there would still be essentially easy access to the urban aspect, and you would live on the west side, where there would be easy access to the rural aspect, and . . .

NORMAN: I'm not sure moving our residences is functional or realistic. I would be more inclined to explore whether or not the child could be enrolled in that third school district and we rotate; we accommodate that.[85] I would be open to that. I would compromise to that situation, because my notion is, it's not going to be this goofy, you know, prepubescent Wild Kingdom that happens in this experimental situation. I think it's a bit more of a compromise towards your basic three R's.

MEDIATOR: [to Norman] And you would be willing to give up Susan going to school in your school system, if you could both agree to a mutually acceptable third school system?[86]

NORMAN: I would have to look at it very hard. Thinking ahead here, as you've been going through the flow chart, I simply am not prepared to relent to Susie going to Terri's environment. Apart from the philosophical problem I have with the teaching, I feel cheated. Why have we gone through this joint custody for the last three years, which has been tantamount to time sharing, when suddenly the child's gone all week, and I'm going to be put back in the role of accessory parent? Maybe weekends, but not every weekend, because I'm sure Terri won't . . .

MEDIATOR: Don't worry about your being cheated. Make sure that Susan doesn't get cheated. Okay. That's the critical point here.[87]

NORMAN: Well, let's look at it reflexively.

MEDIATOR: Hold it there for just a second, Norman. Terri, what's your view on this?[88]

81. The couple's attention is maintained through a focus on parenting cooperation.
82. Having gained their attention, I summarize on the flip chart.
83. I claim no ownership of the obvious alternative. Rather, I allow it to reemerge organically.
84. Note that my proposal is made conditional, with the use of *perhaps.*
85. Norman suggests a willingness to compromise, but then he kills it with a marital dig.
86. Norman has control of the proposal, and so I restate it, in terms of what Norman is willing to concede, so that Terri can hear more clearly the movement Norman has made.
87. I chastise Norman at the point where he is about to open another spousal attack on Terri.
88. Norman has held center stage long enough, and so I put

him on hold, to give Terri some attention and maintain balance.

TERRI: Well, I agree with Norman in that I think it's unrealistic for us to relocate our residences to this hypothetical third school district. I would be prepared to continue with the same residential arrangement, one week with me, one week with Norman. However, I would want to look at this other school and satisfy myself that Susan was not merely going to get the basics, the three R's. I want to get her in some kind of an enriched program. I think she's an intelligent and creative child, and those areas ought be fostered at a young age.[89]

MEDIATOR: So you'd like her to have a good basic education plus the additional enrichment that would meet her particular needs.[90]

TERRI: Oh, definitely! I think she'd be bored in a school system . . .

NORMAN: Oh, how ridiculous.

TERRI: . . . in which she would receive only the basics.

MEDIATOR: And from your perspective, Terri, if that could be obtained, you would be willing to think about the third district and give up the idea that Susan would have to go to your school district?[91]

TERRI: Yes.

MEDIATOR: Okay. So now you've both agreed, right, that you would like to look at the possibility . . .

NORMAN: It's not going to happen. Unless the kids learn math in a tutu, she's not going to be happy.[92]

TERRI: Norman, how can you say it's not going to happen? You don't know. You're always jumping to conclusions.

MEDIATOR: Norman, you've been . . .

NORMAN: Well, my problem is—there's a built-in problem here. She says, "I have to look at the school, satisfy myself . . ."

MEDIATOR: Let me interrupt here, because it doesn't help me.[93] It helps me to understand and be most helpful to you if you each speak a lot for yourself. And so it doesn't help me for you to say to me whether or not you think it will work from Terri's perspective. It does help me if I understand whether it will work from your perspective.

NORMAN: I am prepared to say, carte blanche, that that third school district—to the extent that it is not the experimental school that Terri's university laboratory class is—I will go for it. I'll accept it.

MEDIATOR: Don't tell me what it's not, tell me what you want.[94] [goes back to the chart] You want a school system, and let's just list—that it has the basic three R's, right?[95]

NORMAN: Scholastic emphasis and extracurricular—the basics.

MEDIATOR: Okay. Athletics?

NORMAN: The things that made Terri and I both . . .

MEDIATOR: And extracurricular activities. Okay. Okay. Terri, what do you think you would need in that school system?[96]

TERRI: As I indicated, what really caught my attention about the school in my own district was the open-classroom setting that fostered the critical-thinking skills. It wasn't rote learning.

89. Terri indicates a willingness to match Norman's movement, if face-saving is provided by "some kind of an enriched program." This is directional information, indicating where she might move in the negotiations.
90. Restatement of the issues, to combine their goals.
91. Using the same "give up" language as at 86, I check Terri's willingness to move in the same way as Norman, provided that her needs, as defined at 89, are met.
92. Norman sabotages with a marital dig.
93. I use an increasingly powerful voice tone as I take control of the emerging spat and remind the couple of their need to talk only for themselves and not for the other.

94. This refocuses Norman on the positive, as I return to the chart for emphasis.
95. The chart shows a list of wants, and I focus on how Susan can get them.
96. Here, I talk about what the parents need, rather than what Susan needs, in the belief that parents should make the decisions. This also recognizes the adult view of the situation. Matching both sets of needs to the same obvious alternative on the chart visually emphasizes my verbal work.

NORMAN: May I ask you something? You didn't know a Chablis from a Bordeaux until we started making bucks. Okay. You never appreciated the opera till we started making bucks. We have to give our child the ability to make the bucks, so that she can . . .

TERRI: Norman, shut up!

MEDIATOR: Terri, you're telling me you want a system that teaches critical thinking. What else?[97]

TERRI: I want it to foster an appreciation for the arts, music, dance—those kinds of things.

MEDIATOR: Okay. All right.

NORMAN: BMW's.

TERRI: Norman, really.

MEDIATOR: Now, it seems to me that the list you have here, in terms of having a good basic education—with a scholastic emphasis, athletics, extracurricular programs, and an ability to foster critical thinking and have available arts and artistic programs—is all possible within one school district, right?[98]

TERRI: I don't know. The public school system here—I'm not so sure.

MEDIATOR: Okay. But my assumption is that she's going to the public school system in either case, right?[99]

TERRI: Yes.

MEDIATOR: You're both going to keep her in the public school system.

NORMAN: You bet!

MEDIATOR: Okay. So that, really, we have to look at what's available in the public school system. Now, I wonder if you'd now like to spend between now and next week looking at those systems around you that are within reasonable geographic proximity of each of you. We have to set a maximum mileage that you would have to travel, but you would look at those, to see whether or not they meet your criteria, Norman, and they meet your criteria, Terri.[100]

TERRI: Well . . .

NORMAN: Do we have to go together?

TERRI: I was about to suggest that we do. After all, this is our child, and this seems to be about the only thing we have in common.

MEDIATOR: Okay. It's also the only thing you have left to fight about, too. So, how would you like to do that? Would you like to go together?[101]

TERRI: I was going to suggest that we could arrange a mutually convenient time to meet with the principal of the school or someone else who could explain the facilities and the programs to us.

MEDIATOR: Let me suggest this, then—that you both do that. If you both feel that the school meets with your approval, then you really just need to call me and tell me.[102] I can then draft you a quick memorandum and send it back. If you disagree, then you can come back, and we can look at it again from that perspective.

TERRI: That's agreeable to me.

97. When Norman tries to start another fight about the fam-

ily history, I simply ignore him and stay on task with Terri.

98. Indicates the possibility that both can have their needs met.
99. Eliminates Terri's attempt to enlarge the complaint by clarifying that Susan will attend public school.
100. Assigns the task and identifies the parameters of the issue, in terms of geographical limits.
101. This sends an underlying message to them about how they use Susan to further their spousal battles.
102. Indicates the simplicity of the task and the next step they must take, if the needs of both are to be met.

NORMAN: Can we bring some of the materials back to you if we can't agree?[103]

MEDIATOR: Oh, absolutely.

NORMAN: Because, again—forgive me, but I just think that this . . . that we're going to break down, and I think we need an objective . . .

MEDIATOR: Don't knock it before it begins.[104] It will break down if you let it break down. But if you don't, and if you don't, it won't break down. It's up to you—not up to each other, it's up to you. You can't control anything that Terri does. You're in control of what you do, and therefore you can control that part. And you can't control anything that Norman does; you can control you, and you can control that part. If you focus on that piece that you can control, you don't have to worry about it falling apart, because you'll make it work. You're both very powerful people. You'll make it work, if you want to make it work. If you don't want to make it work, then you won't, but if you don't want to make it work, be responsible for yourself for it. Don't look to the other one for it. So, in the course of the next week, go look at the school. See if it meets your criteria, and your criteria. If it does, then we can simply continue the current situation, and Susan can go to that school. If it doesn't, we come back and look at it afresh, with all of that new information. Okay?

NORMAN: All right.

TERRI: Okay.

MEDIATOR: Good. So you'll call me—say, a week from today—and let me know?

TERRI: Yes. I think we should be able to investigate the school within that time.

NORMAN: Yes, that's fine.

MEDIATOR: Terrific. Okay. Thank you very much. Goodbye.

103. Norman lays the groundwork for another attack on Terri. This is probably an indication of his discomfort with my withdrawal, since he believes that agreement is not possible without the aid of a third party.
104. I cut him off and lay the responsibility for any failure at their feet. This emphasizes the control issue for the couple.

Analysis

The Mediator's Assumptions

It is, of course, impossible to mediate a dispute without some ventilation on the part of one or both parties. Mediation is a tense experience over major issues for every couple. Moreover, couples entering mediation do not have any experience in behaving in this context—that is, they are not sure whether mediation is going to be like therapy, where an expression of feelings and hurts is appropriate, or whether it is like being at the lawyer's, where adversarial behavior is expected. Little in their life experience has prepared them for the problem-solving, task-centered approach of mediation. Consequently, during the early part of each session, the mediator is role modeling appropriate behavior and encouraging mediation behavior from the parties.

The assumption (see Chapter One) that conflict over issues is resolvable in mediation while conflict over dynamic behavior is resolvable in therapy leaves a gray area for the mediator. A large part of any couple's behavior is conflictual, but not enough to require the parties' referral to therapy. Therefore, the mediator must decide how to handle behavior that impedes but does not prevent negotiations. In Chapter Four, I handled Michael and Debbie by allowing a low level of ventilation. In this session, I allowed a greater amount of behavioral conflict. I permitted it for as long as I believed both parties could deal with it and for as long as it did not prevent progress in the negotiations.

In working with Norman and Terri, I did not deal directly with most of the fighting, particularly the husband's sniping. First, when one party is more vocal than the other—or, in this case, more vociferous—the mediator can get caught in a battle with that party if he tries to deal directly with the sniping. Since the husband was the more vociferous, I avoided being drawn into a fight with him, essentially by ignoring his sniping behavior and focusing on the mediation tasks. Second, the wife appeared capable of holding her own in the fight and was not overpowered by his sniping. Thus, the marital fight did not seriously impede the process. As long as dysfunctional behavior does not interfere with mediation tasks, it is advisable for the mediator not to attempt to control it but to ignore it and stay on task. I did control Norman's sniping more closely, however, after Terri complained about it. (60)

Norman and Terri exhibited the behavior of many parents involved in custody disputes: They were confused between their parental and spousal roles. Whenever they fought as ex-spouses, they sniped at each other and effectively blocked an agreement. Neither was willing to make any concession to the other—as an ex-spouse. They were more cooperative, however, when the issue was sharply focused on their parenting.

I dealt with their dynamics by returning the focus of the discussion to parenting, whenever the dialogue got off track. I continually brought them back to their parental roles, where the solution lay, and away from their spousal roles, where the conflict lay. This is a classic example of the major difference between therapy and mediation. It also illustrates the difference between conflict resolution and conflict management.

Norman and Terri did not come to mediation to resolve

the conflict about their past marriage (dynamic behavior); they came to resolve the conflict about the future living arrangements for their daughter, Susan (issue). Thus, I managed the conflict between them as ex-spouses, confining the conflict as much as possible, ignoring it, and focusing on resolving the parental conflict. Not all conflict needs to be resolved. The art of mediation is to be able to identify those areas of conflict that need managing and those that need resolving and to act appropriately in each situation.

The way the mediator permits, encourages, cuts, or discourages various kinds of behavior determines clients' behavior. In this session, there are some good examples of my permitting and cutting ventilation of the marital fight. At the beginning, I realized that Norman's response to the first question directed at him had been carefully rehearsed (7), and as soon as I realized that Norman was not going to respond to the question, I asked a process-interruption question, which cut the ventilation. (8) This question was also task-focused and future-oriented. Nevertheless, I did not cut off Norman's next ventilation, since he began his response productively and on task, and as the ventilation developed I learned an important indicator of the invisible "loyalty" issue. Thus, I did not cut the ventilation, because it was providing me with some new, useful information. (9, 10)

Later (17), when Norman began with a response to my question and then quickly moved the dialogue back to the marital fight, I immediately refocused with a fact question. (18) Another example of a mixed ventilation-information response was Norman's attack on Terri. (31, 32) The attack was well mixed with data that were useful to the mediation; therefore, I permitted it to continue until Norman began to wander again and stopped providing any new data. I cut him off by going one-down and posing a refocusing question. (34)

Norman often ventilated about the invisible "loyalty" issue, and I permitted it when the discussion was mixed with comments about the third school district. (76) I wanted to see whether he would respond to the idea of the third school district. Norman not only agreed to it but took ownership of the alternative. (77)

I dealt with Norman and Terri very much the same way I dealt with Michael and Debbie. I ignored much of the spousal bickering, unless it interfered with the negotiations concerning their parenting. I permitted ventilation, provided that it was about the speaker's feelings or fears and not an attack on the other party. I also permitted the ventilation whenever it revealed some new data useful to me in my management of the process.

Many couples use a child's behavior as a weapon in the spousal fight, even though the behavior may be a normal developmental response to a situation. One parent may deliberately use the child or may honestly feel that the child's behavior is a product of the divorce or of the other parent's behavior. In either case, I attempt to disarm the parent who is using the child by normalizing the child's developmental response to the situation. This prevents the behavior from becoming a divorce issue and a spousal issue. For example, Susan experienced a different life-style in each parent's home. I normalized this and pointed out that she got the best of both worlds. Each parent would have preferred that I approve of his or her life-style versus the other's. Their marital fight was about life-styles. They used the adult life-style issue to cover the real conflict: who would get to make the decision about where Susan lived during the school week. Whoever won would be able to incorporate Susan into his or her particular life-style.

The Mediator's Strategies

Dealing with an Underlying Issue: Family History. I believe that the task of every couple in the early stages of a marriage is to negotiate whose family of origin will survive in the new family. Successful marriages manage to blend elements from each family of origin, keeping the most important aspects of each one. A common denominator in divorcing families is an unsuccessful resolution of these negotiations, and the defense of the different values is often a key marital fight. In this session, the husband's loyalty to his family is clearly stated. The wife's upwardly mobile position is equally firm.

An underlying issue in this session was the husband's

loyalty to his family of origin and particularly to his father's values. This was probably a cause of the divorce, and I identified it as such. (15) I did not challenge the husband's allegiance but, in acknowledging it, I pointed out to Norman that now that he was divorced, he could bring more of his family's influence to bear when Susan was with him.

When one spouse has a strong identification with his or her family of origin, the mediator cannot challenge it and, within the time allotted for the mediation, cannot deal with it. Therefore, the mediator honors it and keeps the situation moving. If the allegiance interferes with the mediation process, or if it is seriously dysfunctional to the spouse, the mediator gives a referral for therapy. Norman's loyalty came up early in the session. His saying, "I am a self-made man and brought up in a small town. My father was a miner . . . " was the first indication. (10) He reinforced his point with the display of money in one hand and a credit card in the other—clearly a prepared stratagem. (12)

Terri confirmed the family-ties issues and pointed out that she wanted the opposite of what her upbringing had been. (14) Thus, the marital fight was clearly drawn. Norman defined his living on the edge of town as going "back to my childhood." (51)

Developing the Hypothesis. In every situation, the mediator makes a hypothesis about the couple's behavior and/or strategies, any underlying issues shaping the negotiations, and the real goals of both parties. The hypothesis becomes the working guide for the mediator, helping him determine how to proceed and what questions to ask. To be useful, the hypothesis does not have to be totally correct; rather, it is a useful guide even if it is only more or less true. Once a hypothesis forms in the mediator's mind, it must be tested through questioning or observation of the couple's interaction. If responses or behavior prove the hypothesis incorrect, the mediator discards or modifies it. Once the hypothesis is shown to have some validity, however, the mediator uses it to guide his activities.

The hypothesis should be thought of as a tool that, used purposefully, increases the mediator's efficiency and helps him stay in control of the process. The hypothesis provides the purpose of the questions. The answer will tend to confirm or deny the hypothesis. The next question is selected or modified according to the previous answer, so that the mediator's work is guided by the hypothesis.

In this case, although the presenting issue was the school for the daughter and the corollary residency arrangements, the parents did not talk about the amount of time they spent with Susan or the depth of their relationships with her. This led me to the hypothesis that the struggle was not about what was best for Susan but about who would make the decision. Therefore, I attempted to create an environment for developing a solution that would not be seen as a loss to either parent.

My initial hypothesis—that Norman and Terri had different value systems, particularly around childrearing and schooling—emerged from the couple's initial responses. (5–7) The question of family loyalty emerged, causing me to amend my first hypothesis, since the family-loyalty matter was a marital-fight issue. (9–10) With this modification in mind, I needed to understand the extent to which family loyalty was key to this conflict. Therefore, I tested my original hypothesis with a summary. When Terri confirmed that it was a key marital issue, I acknowledged it and moved back to future parenting, with that in mind.

I was now operating under a new hypothesis: that the question of the school district might not be so much a question of what was best for Susan as a continuation of the marital fight. (18) As the session continued, I developed a private insight: that the couple had not thought of options, but only of winning. (24) This idea was prompted by my earlier use of the hypothesis and is an example of how the purposeful use of a hypothesis can increase efficiency.

When Norman provided some directional information, indicating that he was "soft" on the choice of educational system, provided that he could win the right to make the decision now, I took this as a confirmation of my working hypothesis. (33) The hypothesis also helped me recognize that the couple had not talked about their time and relationships with their daughter. (35) This insight tended to confirm the hypothesis that the loyalty of the husband to his family was a major part of the marital fight and was being continued in the divorce discussions over Susan. This led to the confirmation of the hypothesis and determined my next line of questioning. (36)

If the marital fight was about Norman's insistence on doing things the way his dad had done them, and about Terri's insistence that they move upscale to match their success, then asking about their current living arrangements and their commitment to these arrangements would show the kinds of options that were available to this couple. Would either or both of them move? Was Susan or each parent's location more important? Could Susan get what each parent wanted for her somewhere other than her parents' existing residences? (38)

The responses confirmed the residency hypothesis, and a further modification emerged: that neither parent would move for the sake of the other; but perhaps they might both move for Susan. I tested my amended hypothesis. (50) The parents' responses confirmed that choice of location was determined by each parent's need and not necessarily by the needs of their child. (51) The original hypothesis, which had been steadily modified, was totally confirmed in its modified form, and this suggested an obvious alternative strategy to the mediator. Thus, I was able to move toward what would become a productive strategy, in less than fifteen minutes of work with the couple. (54–55)

I continued to modify my hypothesis, which was now about specific strategies to solve the problem, as defined by the previously confirmed hypothesis. (57–69) Looking again at the various aspects of hypothesis development, one sees that I developed my hypotheses on the three important components as follows: on the couple's behavior at 4, 7, and 24; on the underlying issue at 18, 46, 50, 51, 54, and 56; and on the real goals at 6, 36, 39, and 42.

Using an Embedded Suggestion: The Obvious Alternative. Norman and Terri were involved in a spousal battle. They had relatively equal power. Thus, neither side could accept a solution that involved losing, because both had defined the issue in a win-lose way. I reframed it into a neither win, and therefore, a neither lose, proposal.

Despite having had three years in which to prepare for this decision, neither parent had considered an alternative other than winning (and, therefore, having the other lose). In many disputes, there exists an obvious alternative (Schelling, 1960), or third option, that neither party has considered. Since this couple had not thought of options, I directed their attention to an obvious alternative, which was very clear to me but had not been considered by the parties to the dispute.

The options for this couple were as follows:

- Susan could live with her father and go to a school in his district, and Terri could stay where she lived.
- Susan could go to a school in Norman's district, and Terri could move to a location in the same district, and they could maintain joint custody.
- Susan could live with her mother and go to a school in her district, and Norman could stay where he lived.
- Susan could go to a school in Terri's district, and Norman could move to a location in the same district, and they could maintain joint custody.
- The parents could both move to a third school district and maintain joint custody.

The current shared-parenting arrangement could be maintained only in the second, fourth, and fifth options. The second and fourth options meant a loss of face. The first and third options meant a loss of access for one of the parents. Since neither Norman nor Terri would accept losing anything to the other, I chose to point their attention to the fifth option.

In this case, the obvious alternative had existed all along but had been ignored by the couple. I suggested a possible alternative through an embedded-suggestion question about what lay between the school districts each now lived in. I raised it early in the session but did not pursue it; rather, I let it sit with the couple for a while and did not raise the issue again until much later in the session, when I thought they were more receptive to the idea. During the discussions, the couple created a sixth alternative, which was not to move but to place Susan in the school district that was between their two residences.

The embedded-suggestion question (19) was designed to provide ideas to the couple and information to me. The follow-up question, specifying school systems, elicited a clear and obvious alternative from Terri. (20) At this point, however, the obvious alternative got lost in the battle. I felt comfortable not dealing with it, because I knew that I could raise it later, when the couple would be more receptive to the idea.

I returned to the obvious alternative when I perceived that the timing was right. (69) The couple now paid attention to the idea, and Norman offered a variation on it. (73) Terri indicated an area for movement on her part. (75) Norman, as part of his negotiating strategy, took ownership of the obvious alternative. (77) Having taken ownership, Norman opened negotiations on the alternative. (85) Terri matched Norman's movement (89), and so I tried to assist the negotiations with a reciprocity question to Terri. (91)

Timing. The emergence of an alternative should not be forced too early in a session. If the mediator suggests options or ideas too early in the process, they are almost certain to be ignored. This is true even though the suggestion may be logical for the couple to consider.

I raised the obvious alternative through an embedded-suggestion question early in the session, and it was ignored. I left it for a while and raised it again later, when I thought they would be more receptive to it. Indeed, when I raised it the second time, the husband took ownership of it, and it formed the basis of the negotiations from that point on.

Language. I gained and kept the couple's respect by noticing and using the language they used. In summarizing, I used the same language as the spouse for whom I was summarizing. This showed them that I had heard what they said and was in tune with them. In this session, I took this skill one step farther: Norman referred to *Susie,* and Terri referred to *Susan.* I picked this up after the husband corrected me on the daughter's name. From then on, I used *Susie* when talking to the husband and

Susan when talking to the wife. When I was not directing comments to only one party, I used my personal preference, *Susan.*

Process Management. In working with this type of couple, the mediator controls the agenda, determining who speaks when and about what. There is no danger of losing clients as a result of being in control, since clients whose interaction is highly conflictual, and who engage in an ongoing power struggle, also experience chaos. By providing structure, the mediator circumvents marriage fights and keeps control, to the benefit of both parties. Most disputants in this type of situation believe that the other party makes all the decisions and usually wins. When the mediator controls the agenda and keeps the process neutral, the parties stay in mediation, because each sees the mediator's neutrality and control as beneficial: It does not leave the other party in control.

Clients' Negotiating Behavior

Directional Information. Norman provided some directional information when he told me that after children have completed elementary school "their individual likes and preferences and all that sort of stuff can be accommodated." (33) This told me that Norman was not blindly opposed to what Terri wanted for Susan; rather, he was opposed to Terri's making the decision now. He softened his position, to provide that Susan would get the kind of education Terri wanted later if they cooperated now. Once someone indicates willingness to move in the future, it is safe to assume that, given some reciprocity, the person may move now, rather than later.

Conflict Expansion. When Norman and Terri were negotiating over which school Susan would attend, the possibility emerged that each of them could move to some equi-distant location. Norman sensed that the talks were leading in that direction, and he expanded the conflict to defend against his having to move. Responding to my question about whether, if they did not have Susan, they would live where they lived now, Norman expanded the conflict, to give him more negotiating space. He said, "If I didn't have the responsibility associated with my job

. . . I suppose you dream about opting out of the system and really doing the rural experience . . . . So, I guessed—yes, of necessity, where I am is a compromise." (52) Obviously, if where he currently lived was a compromise, then moving closer to the city, although it would be a move matched by Terri's moving farther from the city, would be an additional compromise. Thus, he did not have to match Terri's move, because he had already compromised. He enlarged the conflict by suggesting that he would really like to move farther from the city.

At the close of this session, when agreement appeared close, Terri, apparently nervous about the agreement, tried to expand the conflict by raising the issue of whether the child should be in private rather than public school. When that issue was put to bed, Norman engaged in the same negotiating behavior by claiming that Terri would never be satisfied with the proposed settlement. He did this in a typical marital-fight manner, which normally would have produced a response from Terri that would have blown the agreement. I prevented this, and the agreement survived.

Triangulation. At one point, Terri misunderstood a question I had asked. When I apologized for the misunderstanding and asked the question more clearly, Norman quickly commented, "I understood what you were saying." Such a comment is fraught with danger to the mediator's neutrality. It could easily be mistaken by Terri as a "We guys understand this kind of thing" comment, which would alienate her, or it could be taken as a straight attempt by Norman to win the mediator over to his side. Triangulation seems more likely to occur between the mediator and the spouse of the same sex because of the "shorthand" way that same-sex people have of communicating with each other. "We guys together" and "We women together" statements inevitably make the opposite-sex spouse uncomfortably aware of the sexual politics of the situation.

Belittling. Norman was fond of this tactic. In his early comments, he noted that the joint custody arrangement had "allowed both of us an opportunity to preserve our relationship with Susie, and that's fluffy and all the nice things that really stroke Terri. But it is time to get down to basics." (17) He frequently characterized the school Terri proposed in negative terms: it was "experimental" (33); "the children were being videotaped during play therapy, and all that sort of stuff, when they makc building blocks" (76); and it represented a "goofy . . . prepubescent Wild Kingdom that happens in this experimental situation." (85)

Conclusion

It might have been productive to hold separate sessions with this couple. Indeed, if Terri had not held her own in the face of Norman's sniping, individual sessions would have been useful. Individual sessions might have been used to help each party shape a new position that would take account of the other's needs and Susan's needs. This couple began to negotiate after Norman's initial overture. If this had not happened, I could have used separate sessions, to share the obvious alternative with both parties and explore their receptivity to it.

10

MANAGING DIVORCE MEDIATION: APPLYING SKILLS TO PRACTICE AND A LOOK AHEAD

In this final chapter, we will explore ways in which the ideas and styles discussed in the preceding nine chapters can be applied to the reader's daily practice. To do this, we have classified the major categories of mediation practice that we believe had the most impact on the sessions reported in this book. Of course, numerous specific ideas and strategies were identified in the annotations of the cases and in the subsequent discussions.

We have chosen three areas for further discussion: the use of language to change clients' perceptions (moving from the past to the future, moving from spousal to parental roles, and moving from ambivalence to action); the use of thinking styles; and identifying when mediation does not work and three possible causes (becoming a participant, being caught in sexual politics, and doing therapy rather than mediation). Finally, we will discuss some thoughts about the development of a theory of mediation.

Language Changes

The hurt and the unresolved and often unresolvable emotions that people carry into mediation are from the past; solutions and hope lie in the future. Therefore, the central task of the mediator is to move the couple from the past to the future. The case studies in this book demonstrate that as long as discussion is focused on recriminations over the past, no movement is possible. Once the focus of the discussion is on the future, however, movement begins, options emerge, and agreement can be hammered out. The mediator is the key to this change, and changes frequently follow a semantic shift by the mediator. The questions she asks determine whether the discussion is about the past or the future. The way she addresses the couple determines whether they respond as spouses or parents. The verbs she uses determine whether they are ambivalent or active.

Moving from the Past to the Future. The couple most often prefer to stay in the past. That is where they are most comfortable, because it is known to them. If the mediator uses a past tense, then she also stays in the past and "in the soup" with the couple. As soon as the mediator's language and focus move the couple into the future, however, a shift takes place in their behavior. There are numerous examples of this type of mediator-levered shift in these cases. One of the clearest is in Chapter Four, when Michael asks me to "tell her where I'm coming from" and I respond that I am more interested in where he wants to go.

Each time clients are required to think about the future, two things happen. First, they begin to visualize a situation different from the one they are now in, and the different situation often has new possibilities. Second, while they are thinking about the future, they have to let go of the past. Letting go of the past and visualizing a different future often present a better alternative to the couple than the rut they are in. The tasks of the mediation process continually impel the parties into the future. You cannot talk about future parenting plans, for example, without conceptualizing a future. The mediator facilitates the continual focus on the future through the process and through language. Thus, the future tense is the correct tense for mediation.

Another way of moving people toward the future is to ask them to think about where they will be and what they want to be doing two years from now. For example, I often use this question to help a wife who has not worked outside the home think about ways she can become economically independent of her husband. The choice of two years is deliberate: Less than two years often evokes a reply like "I only hope I can get through each day," and more than two years seems longer than most people can visualize. A two-year period often elicits a reply that helps the wife set a goal for herself. Once she has a goal, the couple can solve the problem of achieving it. The mediator identifies for the husband how the wife's goal matches his goal. If the wife's goal is in the couple's mutual interests, and if the husband understands his self-interest in helping his wife meet her goal, then the couple can proceed to negotiate an agreement that will meet their individual needs.

Mediators often try to get people to talk for themselves—that is, when a husband tells the mediator what his wife wants, the mediator interjects and says, "I'm interested in what *you* want." This sentence is future-oriented and can be made specifically so: "I'm interested in what *you* want in the future." If the question and the husband's response are in the past, he will be telling the mediator what he does not want—that is, he does not want more of the past. The positive request—"Tell me what you *do* want"—projects the husband into the future.

Moving from Spousal to Parental Roles. Each couple engages in a number of different relationships during mediation (husband-wife, mother-father, daughter-in-law–son-in-law, breadwinner–home manager, and so on). Each relationship has a different dynamic, and people view their problems from different perspectives, according to which relationships they are acting from.

When spouses negotiate about support and parents negotiate about parenting arrangements, their relationships and issues are consonant. When spouses negotiate about parenting, however, particularly when an initiating husband negotiates with a rejected wife about how they will parent in the future, relationship confusion complicates discussion and leads to deadlock.

The mediator helps keep relationships consonant with tasks by the way she addresses the couple at different stages of the negotiations. When they are talking about support, the mediator uses their first names. When they are talking about parenting, she uses *Mom* and *Dad* to describe them; this helps the parties respond as Mom and Dad. As the mediator helps them separate their various relationships (and as the couple accept, for example, the Mom and Dad designations), they work on the problem as parents, rather than as disaffected spouses.

When negotiating support issues, the mediator may move the parties toward their new roles as spouses with independent careers by the tenses she uses. Thus, in asking a rejected wife and mother who has not worked outside the home what she would like to be doing two years from now, the mediator moves her from being a homemaker to being an ex-spouse and a career woman. The next task is to move the husband in tandem. Obviously, the new relationship holds good possibilities for both parties. The husband can discard his guilt at leaving the marriage and can view a future in which his ex-wife is economically independent from him; the wife can forget her rejection and view a future that she controls. Obviously, in each of those new relationships, problem solving and joint negotiating are much more likely and more likely to be productive.

Moving from Ambivalence to Action. The third area of movement that can be prompted by the mediator's intervention is the move from ambivalence to action. I try to redefine problems from *whether* (ambivalent) something will happen to *when* (action) something will happen. The way the mediator frames her contributions to the discussion helps the couple move from ambivalence to action. Language changes in this area include using *when* rather than *if, how* rather than *maybe*, and *how often* rather than *perhaps*. The mediator uses these levers individually and in combination. Thus, she may move a couple from recriminations over how much money the wife spent last Christmas by asking how the parents will structure their children's time next Christmas. At times, asking a future-oriented question raises new fears and doubts for one or both parties; this is almost inevitable. By uncovering the concerns and legitimating and normalizing them, the mediator gives the couple a chance to deal with them before moving on to more productive responses.

Thinking Styles

When the spouses have different thinking styles, the mediator can become unbalanced, since his thinking style will match one spouse's but not the other's. Thus, if the wife is a deductive thinker and the husband is an inductive thinker, then a deductive-thinking mediator will align with the wife; they will communicate in a kind of shorthand, each one comfortable with ignoring the details while shaping the big picture. The husband, however, thinking inductively, will be concentrating on the details and will be unwilling to consider the big picture until he sees how the various parts fit together. When the wife and the mediator continue to discuss the issue in terms of the big picture, the husband will become increasingly frustrated at not having his point of view considered. He will feel shut out by the alliance between the mediator and his wife.

The husband's frustration can increase, and if the mediator is unaware of the husband's discomfort, the talks can break down. By continually monitoring each client's response to each situation, the mediator can determine when there is a lack of harmony in the room. Since it is unreasonable for the mediator to expect the husband to change his style of thinking, the mediator must change her own style to attain consonance with the husband. The responsibility for this change rests with the mediator, not with the clients.

In one case, a wife did not want her husband to come into the house when he picked up the children, because she saw that as an invasion of her privacy. I focused on the privacy issue—the big picture—and was thinking deductively with the wife: If we could agree on a basic understanding of the need for privacy, then all the details could be filled in. The husband, however, was focusing on the details. If he could not come into the house, where would he meet the children? At the mailbox? On the street corner? What if it rained? What if the children were not ready when he arrived? As he pursued these questions, the wife and I were still trying to get agreement on the basic issue of privacy.

The husband became increasingly disturbed and frustrated. Finally, a combination of his body language, his vocal tone, and his pursuit of questions not on my immediate agenda caused me to stop and see what was going wrong. As I recognized that we were approaching the problem with two different thinking styles, I was able to shift to the inductive mode and consider the details the husband was raising. As they were settled, we achieved agreement on the basic question of the wife's right to privacy.

An example of this type of shift is seen in the case of Ron and Mary. Mary was an inductive thinker, and I shifted my approach on a number of occasions to deal with details, even though I was trying to achieve a broad understanding first. As I dealt with Mary's need to understand the components of the big picture, she became more amenable to the direction I was taking.

When the Process Does Not Work: Three Possible Causes

The mediator monitors the clients' responses to everything that happens in a session. Whenever the mediator senses that they do not understand a question, do not follow the process, appear resistant, are uncomfortable, are stuck in the past, hold untenable positions, cannot move into the bargaining phase, or in any way impede the process, the mediator looks to see what she is doing wrong.

One of the great problems with much mental health practice is that failure is attributed to the clients; they are seen as resistant; they "don't want to change." In mediation, I believe, all failures are the mediator's, not the client's. I cannot expect clients to change or move unilaterally; they change because I establish a climate for change. If change does not take place in a session, then I have not established the climate for change.

If a client is resistant, then the mediator must look to see what she is doing to cause the resistance. If the parties do not want to change, then the mediator looks to see how she can create a different and more conducive environment for change. This means that whenever something goes wrong in a mediation session, I stop and look at my behavior, to see how I can change it. Once I change my behavior, the clients' behavior changes to match mine. In the new climate, more productive outcomes are possible. If, after I change my behavior, the clients do not change, I consider other ways of changing my behavior, and then I keep changing it until I find the behavior that is conducive to change in the clients.

When the Mediator Becomes a Participant. By continually monitoring my impact on the session and changing and varying my behavior to keep the session in its most productive possible mode, I increase my efficiency and achieve productive change on the part of the couple. With Neville and Cheryl (see Chapter Eight), I became more involved in the dynamics of the couple and did not monitor my behavior as frequently or as effectively as in the other cases. There are times when the particular dynamics of a couple do not allow the mediator to remain an observer. In those cases, when I realize I have become a participant as well, I use the time between sessions to think about how my behavior has been helping or hindering the mediation process.

Sexual Politics. Careful monitoring of his or her behavior also helps the mediator deal with sexual politics. Since there are two of one sex and one of the other in every mediated divorce case, the mediator inevitably faces the problem of either forming an alliance with the spouse of the same sex or being seduced by the client of the opposite sex.

Men use a certain shorthand to communicate men's issues to each other; women do likewise. The husband may say to a male mediator, "You know what I mean," and the mediator nods knowingly. The wife, watching this, has a sense of what is going on but feels excluded. If this feeling of exclusion continues, then she may see the mediator as being aligned with the husband. A similar situation arises when one of the spouses does not work outside the home, and the mediator and the other spouse talk about how businesses run. Likewise, a reference to a women's-movement issue by the wife to a female mediator will raise equal problems for the husband.

The other side of the sexual-politics issue is the ease with which the mediator can be seduced into helping the spouse of the opposite sex. Men can call on female mediators' nurturing aspects to get attention, sympathy, or support that they would not get from male mediators. Women can call on male mediators' paternalism to gain support and assistance that they would not get from female mediators.

The mediator can avoid being caught in sexual politics by carefully ignoring all "shorthand" references or messages and requiring the same-sex spouse to be as explicit about each situation as the opposite-sex spouse has to be. The mediator must also respond from a neutral, adult position and be aware of when she is hooked into a maternal role.

Therapy Versus Mediation. Numerous distinctions have been made in this book between productive and unproductive conflict, mediatable issues and nonmediatable issues, and manifest and underlying conflict. Another distinction that runs throughout the five cases is the difference between mediation and therapy. Too often, mediators with a therapeutic background engage in therapy with clients, rather than mediation. When this happens, mediation comes to a halt and often ends with issues still unresolved. Mediation can be defined as working with parties to find a mutually acceptable solution to an agreed-upon problem. Therapy intervenes when the mediator stops working on a mutually acceptable solution and works to change the behavior of one of the parties or the dynamics of the parties' relationship.

Obviously, the demarcation between therapy and mediation is sometimes fuzzy. Working with Neville and Cheryl and with Ron and Mary, I did some therapeutic interventions, which were designed to enhance my mediation work. A therapeutic intervention is designed to cause a shift in the dynamics of the couple, which enables them to reach an agreement on the issues. Generally, I am aware of when I move into the therapeutic mode, and I keep a clear idea in my mind of the direction that I want the *mediation* to take. Thus, at the end of each therapeutic monologue, I return to the issue. I maintain a task focus by remembering what the mediation goal is—even though I may be wandering, for the moment, to achieve a therapeutic goal. Therefore, before embarking on a therapeutic intervention, I ask myself whether I am clear about the purpose of the intervention. I must understand precisely how and why the therapeutic intervention will assist the mediation, and I must be able to determine the measurable movement that will result if the intervention is successful.

It is easier to be focused on a task if the task is clear. Thus, I find that I do fewer therapeutic interventions and am more aware of the purpose of each intervention when the tasks are clear. When the tasks are not clear, then I am more liable to drop into the therapeutic mode. This is clearly seen in the cases of Neville and Cheryl and Ron and Mary. I engaged in specific therapeutic interventions concerning Ron and Mary's rescuing dynamics, because I believed that such work was necessary to protect the mediated agreements. Each time I engaged in a therapeutic intervention, the task of getting Ron to pay child support was uppermost in my mind. As soon as I had completed the intervention, I returned to the task. When I was working with Neville and Cheryl, the tasks were not so clearly defined. In the early part of the session, I did not clearly understand the mediation task. As the session proceeded, the task also appeared to change, but it did not become clearer. Without a clear idea of the task, I lost my focus and therefore engaged in many more therapeutic interventions, and I could not clearly identify the purpose of each intervention as it related to the mediation task.

It appears that three questions can guide the use of therapeutic interventions in mediation: Does the mediator clearly understand the task or the issue to be mediated, and does the couple share this definition? Does the mediator clearly understand how the therapeutic intervention will enhance the mediation task? Can the mediator return to the task upon completion of the intervention?

Toward a Theory of Mediation

The process of mediation involves gathering data, sharing and verifying the data with both parties, defining a problem statement from the data, developing options to solve the problem, and negotiating over the precise option that best suits the parties' needs. This process has little to do with the legal or therapeutic processes. It contains elements of law and therapy but is different from both.

Divorce mediation became a field for lawyers and therapists because we had a strong foothold in the field of divorce. What we have seen is the appending of mediation skills onto our basic divorce skills. Prior ownership of a large piece of turf has given us first claim on the emerging field of divorce mediation; this is both the strength and the weakness of our field. The basic knowledge of our original professions has provided us with a solid base from which to operate. At the same time, it has hindered our search for a theory by limiting our sights to these two professions and the theories that guide them.

We have not dealt at length with the systems theory that underpins the therapeutic work described in these cases, because we have tried to search for emerging theoretical trends outside our disciplines. We imposed this constraint on our work in this book because at least a third of necessary mediation skills are not accounted for by theories of the legal and therapeutic disciplines (Haynes, 1982). Thus, we have begun to look elsewhere to explain a theory of mediation.

Any discipline is based on a theory held in common by the practitioners of that discipline. A discipline evolves over time. Some disciplines emerge purely from theory and then seek practice; sociology is a good example of a theory-based discipline. Other disciplines emerge from practice, upon which theory is then imposed; medicine is a good example of a practice-based discipline.

Mediation is also a practice-based discipline. It was established on the basis of the phenomena of the field. Disputes had to be settled; nonlegal disputes had to be settled outside the legal system. Thus, the discipline of mediation arose.

Labor-management mediation was the first area of specialization to emerge, and it drew its practitioners from among ex–labor-management officials. They in turn drew from their experience as negotiators to develop an approach to the management of others' negotiations. Community mediation emerged from society's need to reclassify minor disputes as social rather than legal. In this way, the specialization of community mediation emerged, and community problem solvers became mediators. Divorce mediation arose as a function of the rapid rise in the number of divorces after the enactment of no-fault divorce laws. The first divorce mediation practitioners were attorneys. They were quickly joined by therapists who had experience in handling divorce situations.

The field of divorce mediation was created in fewer than twenty years. Our colleague Harvey A. Farberman, a leader in the field of symbolic interaction, has pointed out that the first task of any new field is to describe and classify its phenomena (personal communication). The books published to date about mediation have done that well. We have a clear sense of what the field is and how it operates. We can classify its components and, in some measure, identify their various sources. In making this classification, Farberman notes, we "clear out the brush of other theories," enabling the development of a discrete theory of mediation. (It is clear, for example, that the theories of bargaining that were developed in social psychology are very relevant to mediation; that field appears to provide social psychologists with a practice. Indeed, many theorists of social psychology will find this book's case transcripts very useful for testing their ideas, because most bargaining theory has been developed from laboratory experiments with undergraduate students.)

An understanding of bargaining behavior and theories of negotiation is essential to the development of a theory of mediation. We have tried to explain clients' negotiating behavior, and the mediator's role as manager of the negotiations, as a step in this direction. We should recognize that the introduction of a professional third party in the negotiations changes the character of the negotiations because of the mediator's dynamics and her skill at negotiating, which is transferred to the parties. While it is unlikely that disputants would be as successful in handling negotiations without a mediator, their behavior with the mediator is universal, and our understanding of the mediator as manager of the negotiations helps us understand and define the impact of the mediator on the negotiations themselves.

Another discipline that seems to hold significant possibilities for understanding a theory of mediation is sociology, particularly the field of symbolic interaction (see Farberman and Perinbanayogan, 1985; Stone and Farberman, 1981). Symbolic interaction helps us understand the identities and roles that people assume in everyday life. It also explains the way in which roles flow from each identity, as well as the need for identities to be validated by others before roles can be played. It is clear from the cases in this book that the mediator helps validate appropriate identities and roles for all the participants in every mediation. Some of those identities involve a problem-solving role. For example, the identity of parent tends to involve a positive problem-solving role, while the identity of divorcing spouse tends to involve a conflictual role. The mediator helps to construct alternative identities for the parties, identities that have problem-solving roles rather than conflict continuing roles.

We like to think that this book has made a useful contribution to "clearing out the brush." The task now is to theorize about the field through our understanding of it. The groundwork has been laid. Now we must understand and articulate the theory that is unique to mediation, recognizing which parts are imported and which are idiosyncratic to our field. From that understanding a discipline will take shape; from that discipline, a profession can emerge. We suspect that the profession will be considerably different from the image we have of it today. The cases in this book provide us with rich material for analysis, and analysis provides us with the opportunity to test some theoretical approaches to mediation.

This book has taken the first step toward a workable theory of mediation, by examining how people behave in mediation. The greatest contribution this book makes to an understanding of negotiating behavior is to describe and analyze how ten people behaved in specific negotiating situations. No coherent single theory of mediation now exists, but we hope that this book is the first step toward developing one. We hope our readers will share our search.

REFERENCES

Deutsch, M. *The Resolution of Conflict: Constructive and Destructive Processes.* New Haven, Conn.: Yale University Press, 1973.

Farberman, H. A., and Perinbanayogan, R. S. (eds.). *Foundations of Interpretive Sociology: Original Analysis in Symbolic Interaction.* Greenwich, Conn.: JAI Press, 1985.

Fisher, R., and Ury, W. *Getting to Yes: Negotiating Agreement Without Giving In.* Boston: Houghton Mifflin, 1981.

Folberg, J., and Taylor, A. *Mediation: A Comprehensive Guide to Resolving Conflicts Without Litigation.* San Francisco: Jossey-Bass, 1984.

Gulliver, P. H. *Disputes and Negotiations: A Cross-Cultural Perspective.* Orlando, Fla.: Academic Press, 1979.

Haynes, J. M. *Divorce Mediation: A Practical Guide for Therapists and Counselors.* New York: Springer, 1981.

Haynes, J. M. "A Conceptual Model of Family Mediation: Implications for Training." *American Journal of Family Therapy,* 1982, *10* (4), 5–16.

Haynes, J. M. "The Process of Negotiations." *Mediation Quarterly,* 1983, *1,* 75–92.

Haynes, J. M. "Mediated Negotiations: The Function of the Intake." *Mediation Quarterly,* 1984, *6,* 3–15.

Haynes, J. M. "Matching Readiness and Willingness to the Mediator's Strategies." *Negotiation Journal,* 1985, *1* (1), 79–92.

Haynes, J. M. "Power Balancing." In J. Folberg and A. Milne (eds.), *Divorce Mediation: Theory and Practice.* New York: Guilford Press, 1988.

Minuchin, S. *Families and Family Therapy.* Cambridge, Mass.: Harvard University Press, 1974.

Mnookin, R., and Kornhauser, L. "Bargaining in the Shadow of the Law: The Case of Divorce." *Yale Law Journal,* 1979, *88,* 950–997.

Pearson, J. "An Evaluation of Alternatives to Court Adjudication." *Justice System Journal,* 1982, *7,* 420–444.

Pruitt, D. *Negotiating Behavior.* Orlando, Fla.: Academic Press, 1981.

Raven, B., and Kruglanski, A. "Conflict and Power." In P. Swingle (ed.), *The Structure of Conflict.* Orlando, Fla.: Academic Press, 1970.

Schelling, T. *The Strategy of Conflict.* New York: Oxford University Press, 1960.

Selvini-Palazzoli, M., Boscolo, L., Cecchin, G., and Prata, G. "Hypothesizing, Circularity, Neutrality: Three Guidelines for the Conductor of the Session." *Family Process,* 1980, *19,* 3–12.

Sheppard, B. H. "The Art and Science of Mediation." *Negotiations Journal,* 1988, *4* (2), 161–169.

Stone, G. R., and Farberman, H. A. (eds.). *Social Psychology Through Symbolic Interaction.* (Rev. ed.) New York: Wiley, 1981.

Strachen, J. G. *Alcoholism: Treatable Illness.* Vancouver: Mitchell Press, 1967.

Swingle, P. (ed.). *The Structure of Conflict.* Orlando, Fla.: Academic Press, 1970.

Tomm, K. "Interventive Interviewing: Intending to Ask Lineal, Circular, Strategic, or Reflexive Questions?" *Family Process,* 1988, *27* (1), 1–15.

Wilmot, J. H., and Wilmot, W. W. *Interpersonal Conflict.* Dubuque, Iowa: Brown, 1978.

INDEX

U

V

W